Nick Seneca Jankel is a Cambridge-educated psychological coach, wisdom teacher, social-change champion and world-renowned innovation, creativity, and leadership expert.

Nick has starred as a psychological coach in four-part BBC TV series; coached a major celebrity on an MTV show; and helped design and host a three-year mental wellbeing experience for the BBC (that featured Kelly Osbourne). Nick has advised government bodies (including No. 10 Downing St, BIS, and the NHS), Fortune 500 and FTSE 100 companies (including Nike, Microsoft, Kraft, Fujitsu, Smirnoff, Unilever, and Disney), written for newspapers (including the *Guardian* and the *Financial Times*) and is a popular keynote speaker all over the world.

He has a triple First from the University of Cambridge and is a lifelong raver and serial (ethical) entrepreneur, starting his first company, a creative agency, aged 25. Nick teaches social entrepreneurs and change-makers on four continents. He lives with his wife and kids in the UK.

SWITCH ON

UNLEASH YOUR CREATIVITY
AND THRIVE WITH THE NEW SCIENCE
& SPIRIT OF BREAKTHROUGH

NICK SENECA JANKEL

WATKINS
Sharing Wisdom Since
1893

This edition published in the UK and USA 2015 by
Watkins, an imprint of Watkins Media Limited
19 Cecil Court
London WC2N 4HE

enquiries@watkinspublishing.co.uk

Design and typography © Watkins Media Limited, 2015
Switch On and Ripe & Ready branding © Ripe & Ready, 2015
Text © Nick Seneca Jankel, 2015
Original Illustration Concepts © Nick Seneca Jankel, 2015
Published Illustrations © Watkins Media Limited, 2015

1 3 5 7 9 10 8 6 4 2

Designed by Gail Jones
Illustrations by Richard Horne

Printed and bound in Europe

A CIP record for this book is available from the British Library

ISBN: 978-1-78028-833-8

www.watkinspublishing.com

PUBLISHER'S NOTE: The information in this book is not intended as a substitute
for professional medical advice and treatment. If you are pregnant or are suffering
from any medical conditions or health problems, it is recommended that you consult
a medical professional before following any of the advice or practice suggested
in this book. Watkins Media Limited, or any other persons who have been involved in
working on this publication, cannot accept responsibility for any
injuries or damage incurred as a result of following the information, exercises
or therapeutic techniques contained in this book.

For Jai Milo and Noah Tao. May this book guide you whether you are looking for real answers, or simply better questions.

In memory of the forgotten millions who have struggled with adversity and come back able to heal their corner of the world.

Contents

Acknowledgments viii

Personal Note from the Author ix

The Switch On Experience xvii

Prelude: Born for Breakthrough 1

Session 01: Problems 23
Switch On to Problems 48

Session 02: Patterns 51
Switch On to Patterns 76

Session 03: Pain 79
Switch On to Pain 100

Session 04: Presence 103
Switch On to Presence 126

Session 05: Peace 129
Switch On to Peace 150

Session 06: Purpose 153
Switch On to Purpose 168

Session 07: Possibility 171
Switch On to Possibility 192

Session 08: Power 195
Switch On to Power 212

Session 09: Play 215
Switch On to Play 232

Session 10: Proactivity 235
Switch On to Proactivity 252

Coda: Riffing on the Breakthrough Curve 254

Endnotes 256

Glossary 265

Acknowledgments

THIS BOOK WAS HELPED along its way by the unflinching support of my best friend, craniosacral genius, business partner, fellow dancer, and wife, Alison. I am love with you. It would also have been far less elegant if it were not for the various friends, family members, agents, and editors who have read drafts, sparred with my thoughts, and provided advice and nourishment. Kate E, Simon H, Scott V, Tom F-M, Rohan G, and Will P, special shouts out to you. I also have an unending gratitude to the many living and dead giants of insight, wisdom, and compassion on whose shoulders I stand (and groove). I would also like to thank all the current (and former) friends, lovers, business partners, employees, random ravers, clients, collaborators, and connections who have helped me formulate the life philosophy in this book whether through collaboration or conflict, and often both.

Personal Note from the Author

THE LASERS ARE FIRING and the sweat is dripping at an underground club in London. It's the early 1990s. A tingle of excitement ripples through the crowd as the pounding bass-lines begin to build. The ravers are preparing to go off, in a scene that is both scandalizing and revitalizing Thatcher's Britain. A very fat, geeky 18-year-old, with lame glasses and even lamer clothes, wanders onto the empty dance floor. It's his first time at a club like this; and he's certainly no dancer (witness the embarrassing moment in a school production of *West Side Story*). Oh, and this kid has never had a girlfriend. In fact, he has never so much as kissed anyone.

Something peculiar starts to happen. As beat after beat pierces his mind and body, the music demands that he let go of his anxieties and awkwardness. All his beliefs about himself that have held him back, shredding his confidence for years, fade to black. Soon he's jumping about in breakbeat heaven. The faces, popping in and out of the laser lights, smile at him without judgment. None of his neuroses seem important now, as a crowd starts to form around him, inspired by his unfettered self-expression to dance too. For a few hours, he's at one with himself and the crowd: Lost in joy, free from worry, and dancing surprisingly well. Dance and dancer, breakbeat and brain wave, become one. He is feeling the love. He is expressing his truth. He is pulling shapes, busting moves. He is switched on.

The problem comes the following Monday (and all the rest of that week). Far from enjoying the fruits of his breakthrough, he finds he is still the shy, lonely, messed-up kid he was before. All the old habits and negative beliefs are still there. In fact, with him being so exhausted from a night of raving, they even get a bit worse.

WTF??!!!

Where did all the love go? Why is he feeling so jaded? What happened to that oceanic feeling of oneness, of communion, of creativity? Even though he will continue raving many times a week for the next decade, in a few years' time he will be diagnosed with clinical depression, suffer a spate of panic attacks, and be wracked with daily agony by a strange condition called fibromyalgia, or chronic pain syndrome. It will take him a few years to get to kiss the girl(s), and many more for the self-loathing to fade. Nevertheless, something awoke in him that night. He realized that if he could feel so loved-up, connected, and innovative on a dance floor, he must also be able to feel that way at any given moment in everyday life. The question was, naturally, how? How could he thrive not just on the good days and in the happy moments, but on the bad days and in the difficult moments too?

That teenager was, of course, me, and this book sets out to answer that question. Those teenage experiences, and many more like them, inspired in me an irrepressible thirst for true and lasting freedom. Night after night, for years upon years, I reveled in the creative spirit of the rave, where people from every social class and walk of life expressed themselves as equals in a sea of unity. I still do, from time to time. Yet it was actually that Monday morning, when I felt so down and depleted, that really galvanized my life's work. Every time I have felt the juiciness of life fade after an amazing moment, it has sparked me onward to find a way to recapture that switched on feeling—where everything is possible and everyone is my ally—24/7 without using anything other than my own heart and mind.

Inspired to understand and heal our human minds and bodies, I went up to Cambridge University to study medicine. There, I got a fine grounding in anatomy, physiology, pharmacology, psychology, psychoanalysis, sociology, and more. However, I soon realized that most of the everyday emotional problems I, and many others, face are not really 'medical' in nature. Although they may involve hormones and neurotransmitters and the like, they are not so much issues with our cells as with our thoughts. So I switched to study philosophy, particularly the philosophy of the human sciences, in an attempt to understand more about how we each construct our thoughts, and so our experience. I ended up graduating with a (triple) First class degree (roughly the equivalent of summa cum laude) . . . but I still found myself stuck in a rut, and neither years of psychotherapy, nor a course of anti-depressants, seemed to be able to do much about it.

After a stint applying psychology and philosophy to the world of big-name brands (like PlayStation and Nivea) at a global ad agency, I decided to start my own business in the late 1990s, lured by the excitement of the dotcom boom. I realized that the vast array of insights from the human sciences had the potential to transform entire teams, whole companies, and even societies, not just to make great commercials. All the while, I was having breakthroughs in my own life, as an entrepreneur, lover, friend, and leader, but I never quite managed to land on a way of living that could help me *sustain* the breakthroughs through thick and thin, and so be the best version of me possible. I was getting there, but something was missing. Something huge. But it took another meltdown to help me find it.

In 2004, I had what I believe to be my last painful breakdown experience. After five years in the fast lane of high-tech entrepreneurship, I was emotionally frazzled and physically burned out. However, that breakdown was less about the stress of running a fast-growing business and managing scores of people, and more about the realization that I was running a company that was not aligned with my deepest aspirations. My heart was broken by my career. Working with my coach at the time, I grokked—in a moment of inconvenient truth—that I was using the majesty of psychology, neurobiology, philosophy, and anthropology to help rich companies get richer by inventing stuff that most of us don't need; and then persuading us to buy it with marketing that suggests that we're not sexy/smart/rich/good enough without it. In the middle of this breakdown experience I had a massive breakthrough. I knew, without a shadow of a doubt, that I had to focus on using my skills and talents to remind us all that we are already enough; and with that sense of abundance, harness our collective creativity to make a difference.

Every single one of us runs every moment of our existence using a life philosophy. Naturally, many of the beliefs and ideas within it are passed down from our parents, acquired from the media, or invented by a younger version of us. Many of these assumptions and habits get us into trouble and lock us into suffering. The great poet William Blake wrote in *Jerusalem*: 'I must create a system, or be enslav'd by another man's; I will not reason and compare: My business is to create.' We can only become free to create a life, and a world, that fits our deepest aspirations when we invent (or discover) a life philosophy that helps us thrive. I knew back then that I wanted a life free from breakdowns of any kind, relationships full of love and excitement, *and* a career of real purpose. So I set out to discover a life philosophy that could offer me all three; one that would help me to thrive, all of the time, because it was designed to work in the world we find ourselves in today, which is full of creative possibility and everyday tragedy in equal measure.

When I was growing up, my father was (and still is) a hardcore atheist and I became one too, once I was struck by the lunacy of the idea of a wrathful, hierarchical and separate God (I had the hubris to give a sermon to that end in my mother's synagogue, aged 15). I studied science at a university famous for being a temple to the godless pursuit of hard facts. But radical atheism was only able to take me so far. Science is very good at predicting and controlling physical things. Yet it finds it much harder to provide answers to some of the big questions, like 'What am I doing here?' and 'What is my life's purpose?'

Even something as seemingly simple as backache (which costs Western nations 1% of their GDP each year and is the single greatest burden on global health) isn't that easy to solve with science alone. Over 80 percent of cases have no known scientifically identifiable cause.[1] Yet I was so blinkered by my own scientific view of the world that it took me years of lost potential to see what had been staring me in the face since I was an early teen: We cannot be fully creative (or feel totally free) when fears abide in our hearts; and only love can free us from them for good. The massively innovative Russian composer Igor Stravinsky said, 'In order to create there must be a dynamic force, and what force is more potent than love?'[2] Science has little to tell us about what love is, and how to fall head over heals in love with ourselves, our work, and our world so we can enjoy the sense of peace, purpose, and possibility most of us desire. To understand love, we need to look beyond reason.

So I went long and deep into the world's great wisdom traditions and transformational techniques, which focus on how to master love, compassion, gratitude, collaboration, connection, relationships, mindfulness, and more. I engaged in all manner of weird and wild experiences, from Advaita Vedanta and Ayurveda in India to the medicine plant ayahuasca in Peru; from indigenous wisdom in the deserts of the USA to Taoism in China. I also explored theories of social change that are centered on love and connectivity, from Gandhi's philosophy of non-violence to spiritual anarchists such as Leo Tolstoy.

I began to weave together the wisdom with the science to achieve a working model of how to thrive that worked for my secular, not religious, sensibilities. As many eminent scientists and wisdom teachers testify, there is no reason on Earth why we should have to choose science *or* spirituality, as long as we don't need either a scary God or a (perhaps scarier) scientific fundamentalist in the mix. Carl Sagan, one of the most famous scientists of our times, came to realize: 'Science is not only compatible with spirituality; it is a profound source of spirituality.'[3]

The synthesis that has emerged from these multiple strands of inquiry—into scientific insight, spiritual intuition, and social change—is centered on the marvel that is *breakthrough*: Amazing, unpredictable, transformational creative solutions to any problems that matter. My discovery of the *Breakthrough Curve* (described more fully in Prelude, see page 16) brought it all home. This framework, which I believe may hold the secrets of all creativity and transformation in our universe, comes complete with a series of tools and techniques for mastering our capacity to thrive. It provides us with a life philosophy that is geared to what Aristotle called *phronesis* or 'practical wisdom'. In other words, it helps us to deal with real-life problems, in real-time. I have called this field of exploration *Breakthrough Biodynamics*.

Breakthrough Biodynamics is a science-inspired yet heart-wired life philosophy, process, and toolset for the rapid transformation of *any* problem at all, whether utterly individual or totally global. It is as inspired by the future-creating impulses of social change, innovation, and coaching as it is by the compassionate spirit of meditation, therapy, and healing. Above all it is *biodynamic*, which means it is responsive to what is emerging *now*—in mind, body, relationship, system, and environment—rather than being locked into what worked in the past (or what the facilitator or coach assumes is the 'right' way to do things). As a life philosophy, it is itself alive and growing through lived experience and constantly emerging scientific evidence. Anything at all in it can be discarded, if a more compelling and empowering insight or technique surfaces as time goes by.

Never one to pontificate from the sidelines, I've put all my ideas into practice at the forefront of the business, creative, and civic worlds. I have spent years helping individuals, teams, and organizations find solutions to their most pressing challenges using the toolkit that Breakthrough Biodynamics provides. I've had enormous amounts of fun, and honed and crafted the tools, helping some of the most interesting and innovative leaders and organizations on the planet come up with big, breakthrough ideas that can help them and the world flourish. I've tested out processes and thinking while supporting kickass starts-ups and amazing social entrepreneurs grow furiously to fulfill their potential. I've had the honor of using Breakthrough Biodynamics coaching and training social workers, teachers, probation officers, doctors, unemployed youths, top MBAs, aid workers, and more. I have also used it as a psychological coach on TV, on radio, in lifestyle magazines, high-end newspapers, at festivals, and for celebs.

However, the *ultimate* test of any life philosophy has to be whether it can help us deal with the worst things our world has to offer. Can it help us get through the tragic loss of a child? Being confined to a brutal prison? A concentration camp? If it can provide us with peace and hope in the darkest of moments, it should be able to help us choose the right career track and deal with a relationship worry. So I continuously push Breakthrough Biodynamics to the limits, to ensure it can engage fully with, and help heal, the tragedies that are everywhere in the world around us.

Put simply, Breakthrough Biodynamics seems to *work* to solve massively varied problems, across radically different types of people, and in a broad array of cultures and environments.

However, *my* version of Breakthrough Biodynamics is just a map, a blueprint: One of many. No map is the territory itself, so don't take my, or anybody else's, word for it. Every individual has to develop and fine-tune *their own* map for how to find peace, purpose, and possibility. No one has ever lived your life before; and nobody else will. So I invite you to try everything out, test it for yourself, and decide what works (or not) for you.

Be aware. I am not, have never been, and never want to be a shrink, doctor, neuroscientist, or academic philosopher. I am simply a human being who has been driven to build a life philosophy (and innovation, leadership, and social-change process) that helps us break through to something better, *much* better. Although professional help can be valuable at times (and I urge you to seek it if you think it might help), remember that all the professions are a very recent invention; they've been around for a few hundred years at most. But for *tens of thousands of years*, our ancestors have been healing themselves, finding a route to happiness, and creating new solutions to their problem without any qualifications except being members of the human race. My experiences with indigenous tribes, including the Maasai in Kenya and Shona in Zimbabwe, have shown me that people can thrive very well without college degrees. That means every single one of us on the planet has the potential to thrive—it is our shared human inheritance. I hope this book becomes a handbook for how to have, sustain, and enjoy breakthroughs over your lifetime as you thrive more and more each single day.

Albert Einstein said, 'There are only two ways to live your life. One is as though nothing is a miracle. The other is as though everything is a miracle.' Every single person alive today has access to endless possibilities for creativity that can improve their lives and their world right now. Every creative act, even just typing on a keyboard, has taken millions of years of evolution to perfect, and relies upon billions of synapses, cells, and molecules working together in symphonic harmony to create the masterpiece called human being. Any one of us can harness this orchestra of biology to invent and design anything we want: A juicier love life, a liberating career shift, a cultural sensation, or a world-changing invention (and even all of these at the same time).

Now *that*, my friends, is a freakin' miracle to me.

I'll see you on the dance floor.

Nick Seneca Jankel, 2014

P.S. If you feel called to connect with me to share your comments, challenges, or contemplations, you can reach out to me online.
You are most welcome to contribute to the emerging thinking (and feeling) around Breakthrough Biodynamics. You can find me through Ripe & Ready, the wisdom and wellbeing company and community I am part of at www.ripeandready.com or, alternatively, at my website www.nickjankel.com.

The Switch On Experience

SWITCH ON PRESENTS A life philosophy for optimal creativity and maximum thriving. But it is also designed as an experiential journey of breakthrough to boost real-time feelings of happiness, wellbeing, and purpose as you read.

Each chapter, or session, begins with a picture that shows which stage of the Switch On experience you are at. Within each session, you will find the following icons:

 Switched On Science: The latest insights from neuroscience, psychology, biology, physics, anthropology, and more

Switched On Stories: Case studies and examples from real life

Switch On Now: Experiential exercises to help you engage fully in each stage of breakthrough (at the end of each session)

Breakthrough Questions: Smart questions that hack the way the brain works for instant breakthrough creativity

This means you can read the book without getting waylaid by science, stories and detailed definitions of terms. If you are intrigued by some of the ideas within, there are endnotes with key scientific papers that you can use as a jumping-off point (see page 256). Words in **bold** are key concepts from Breakthrough Biodynamics that you can refer to at any time in the glossary at the back of the book (see page 265).

The important thing is this: To be ready in every moment to sacrifice who we are for who we could become.

Charles Du Bos, Approximations, 1922

Prelude

Born for Breakthrough

Everything in the world that any human being has ever created, whether it is the glorious Golden Gate Bridge or pioneering polio vaccine, started off life in exactly the same way—as an idea. Every story, movie, sculpture, painting, invention, building, and business, as well as the whole of science, began with a possibility before it became a probability. Our creative spirit defines our species, and our success on this planet, as nothing else does. However, our amazing creativity can also get us into a mess too. Just as everything awesome has been created with ideas, so have all the not so cool things. Exploitative industries, homelessness, climate change, conflict, the credit crunch—not to mention depression, addiction, and obesity—all originate with ideas about ourselves and our world.

Many of the ideas we use to run our lives and our society are past their expiry date. This is to be expected. The world is *constantly* changing, so it can be challenging to keep up. Friends, colleagues, cities, brands, politics, and cultural customs are continuously evolving. Change is relentless, natural, and unstoppable. It is built into the building blocks of every atom and the processes in every cell. A few years ago, there were no tablets or social networks. A few years before that, there were no cellphones, Internet or email. Imagine what is possible now that simply was not possible then? So many of the ideas in life, business, and society that worked back then (or at least looked like they worked) won't cut it now. If we keep on holding on to them, our lives, businesses, and communities will soon start to suffer.

Evolution offers us this simple truth: If we don't change our ideas as the world changes, they will eventually become redundant. This is what happens when we experience **breakdown**. Everyday signs of breakdown might be persistent backache (without a clear cause), constant complaints, regular fights, a sexless love life, boredom, resignation, uninspiring work, chronic road rage, loneliness, and repetitive feelings of guilt and shame. Most tend to be exacerbated by stress. It seems likely that even the blues, anxiety, and panic attacks are all possible symptoms of breakdown too (although each might be also be a signal to seek professional medical or psychological help). Failing businesses and lackluster careers might also be breakdowns **triggered** by redundant ideas.

The all-pervading principle of evolution dictates that we have to *fit or fail*. We need to break through the past to stay fitted with our present. If we don't, we simply cannot thrive. **Fittedness** requires us to remain in constant, open-hearted, open-minded conversation with our inner world, our environment, and everyone around us. As we engage in these conversations, we must always be prepared to jettison the old ways, no matter how comfortable, if it means finding a new way that fits better. This is what it means to be truly creative and have a **breakthrough**. All the great joys of life—whether derived from intimacy, exploration, invention, or making a difference—come from the unpredictable but enlivening process of bringing forth breakthroughs instead of breakdowns.

Creativity is our species' lifeblood, from paper clips to rocket ships. Every time we get ourselves unstuck from a rut—romantic, professional, parental, financial—we are being creative. Every time we get ourselves out of a bad mood, find a new way to reach the soft spots of our lover, or invent a more imaginative response to the tantrums of a child, we are breaking through. If something is missing from our relationships, our career, or our wellbeing, creativity can supply it. Creativity is the 'Access All Areas' backstage pass for a life of meaning and richness (and possibly riches too). Change our hearts and minds—where our ideas live—and we can change anything in our world.

However it is not always that easy! Try to solve this anagram in the next 60 seconds (the solution is at the end of this chapter):

Bmusic

I have shown it to thousands of people and very few have been able to crack it, even though there aren't that many options to play with. The reason is that in order to have the breakthrough, our brain has to let go of 'Bmusic' first. But, because of how it is wired, it gets locked onto the word and finds it very hard to let go. The same is happening in every moment of our life. We get locked into ways of being and behaving that prevent us from enjoying a truly creative life. Our brain's wiring favors predictability slightly more than it does spontaneity. It does this because nature prioritizes safety and survival over the promise of **thriving** that creativity can bring.

Each time we react in a familiar way to a problem, we etch it deeper and deeper into our nervous system, like an engraving on metal. The nerves learn to fire together and we become hardwired to repeat the habit or thought fast and furiously. This is very helpful when we encounter danger: We can deal with it really quickly, which can save our life. However, if we keep on reacting with the same behaviors in our love life or work life while things change around us, we soon become stuck. Cue breakdown. We may have survived life but we are not thriving in it. And the point is to thrive! Walk in nature and you will instantly see that it is not interested in merely getting by; it wants its children to blossom!

Beyond surviving

OUR INSTINCTS ARE GEARED toward survival at all costs. Amid the soaring cliffs and lush bamboo forests of Wudang Shan (a mountain in China where Taoists monks have settled for centuries), I witnessed first-hand just how incredible our minds and bodies are at staying alive. I was walking along a tiny path out in the boonies, daydreaming of martial-art adventures, when my legs suddenly swerved off-course all on their own. Then, half a second later, my eyes glimpsed a long, dark shape slithering up the slope. Half a second after that, I realized that the shape was a huge snake. Newly conscious of this very real threat to my existence, I found my heart rate surging and my mind was flooded with terror. Once I calmed down, I burst into tears of joy. I was alive! How sweet that moment felt. My biological drive to survive, perfected over 13.7 billion years of evolution, was doing its thing with a perfectly orchestrated **stress response**.

The fact that you are here, reading this book, shows your drive to survive has been working well too. However, the stress response that keeps us alive is often cranked up to overdrive. For most of our time on this planet, we won't come face-to-face with deadly snakes. Yet we often engage with everyday problems— from parking tickets to fights with our friends—as if they are very real threats to our existence. When we react to problems, as opposed to create with them, we get hooked into stress. When we are under constant low-grade stress—and it's estimated that over 80 percent of us are all the time—this begins to hurt us.[1] When we are stressed, our nervous system tightens up and we lose our creativity. Stress stops us learning, and if we aren't learning, we aren't growing.[2] Stress, AKA fear, corrodes the curiosity and courage we need to experiment with the new. It is almost impossible to play big in life, if we are scared of looking like idiots, going bankrupt, or being rejected.

Stress kills creativity and kills us too. Whereas small amounts of stress help us focus, engage, and learn, chronic or elevated stress burns us out, literally as well as metaphorically. People who live near airports and deal with the stress of giant airplanes roaring above them have higher rates of cardiac arrest than those who don't.[3] People who deal with a controlling or uncommunicative boss have a 60 percent higher chance of developing coronary heart disease than those who don't.[4] Stress leads to tangible changes inside all the cells of the body. Specific genes start to express proteins, which leads to inflammation; and chronic inflammation is associated with killers such as heart disease and cancer. Over time, stress reduces our ability to prevent aging, heal wounds, fight infections, and even be successfully immunized.[5] Unmanaged stress, simply from having a sense of **disempowerment** at work, can be more dangerous than smoking or high cholesterol.[6]

Whether stress is due to worry, fear, confusion, over-work, or being overwhelmed, if we let our powerful biological protection mechanism dominate our everyday lives, we may survive to pass on our genes . . . but are unlikely to thrive as we do so.

If we move beyond surviving, we can thrive. *Thriving* is a very different concept to what most of us think of as happiness. Happiness is fleeting. It can last a second, a minute, or an hour, but usually not an entire day. Sure that bonus felt great this morning; but this afternoon that idiot just took my seat on the bus and now I'm upset. Few of us feel 'happy' when we are downsized, sacked, or dumped (and arguably nor should we). Emotions like sadness, grief, and confusion are very natural and helpful, and we can learn to thrive even when we experience them. We don't need to be happy all the time. A major study has shown that the pursuit of happiness, as opposed to thriving, can make us selfish citizens because we prioritize our happiness at the expense of others. In this study of over 400 adults, being happy was associated with being a 'taker.' Whereas having a meaningful life, thriving despite adversity, was associated with being a 'giver.'[7] When we thrive, we are more able and better-equipped to help those around us thrive too. The same cannot be said for happiness.

Happiness shifts like sand in the desert. It can appear and disappear in an instant. Thriving, on the other hand, sticks around for the long term. We can thrive and be happy. We can thrive and be sad. We can thrive and experience pleasure or pain. We thrive whenever we create *with*, not against, whatever is happening right now. Thriving is what the Ancient Greek philosophers called *eudaimonia*, translatable as 'having a good spirit (or demon) within.' They believed *eudaimonia* was the highest good. When we are thriving, and the shit hits the fan, we don't just 'deal' with it; we flourish *because of it*. What looked like shit becomes **sh!t**: Full of potential for creative breakthroughs that keep us in a state of optimal fittedness.

Fortunately, human beings are natural-born thrivers as well as survivors. Within the same biological circuitry that automatically *reacts* so impressively to danger lies the capacity to *respond* consciously to our problems in creative and original ways. Every bump and hump on our path can help us master our biological wiring, ensuring that we switch on to the moment and make the shift from surviving to thriving. Breakthrough Biodynamics can help us crack how to create, collaborate, and contribute consistently instead of getting frustrated, freaked, or stressed out.

Living in 3D

EACH ONE OF US can switch from surviving to thriving in an instant. The more we understand about how our mind and body works, the more we can discern what state they are in. The more we can decode our sense of state, the more we can choose if, and how, we want to change it. As we become aware of how vital parts of our biological wizardry work, such as the prefrontal cortex, insula, and vagus nerve, we have more conscious choice over what they do. Research has shown that understanding our biology empowers us. One study has found that people can learn how to activate and relax parts of their brain by choosing whether to focus on their more 'thinky' head or more 'vibey' gut![8]

Ideally we become familiar with the sensations and experiences associated with survival and stress versus thriving and creativity. Then we are more **empowered** to switch the circuits between the two at will. To help, the diagram opposite summarizes some of the key areas of brain and body that help us survive and thrive. (N.B. It is simplified for ease of use.

The Body.Mind

A massively simplified summary of
the biological wizardry behind the
experiences of surviving & thriving

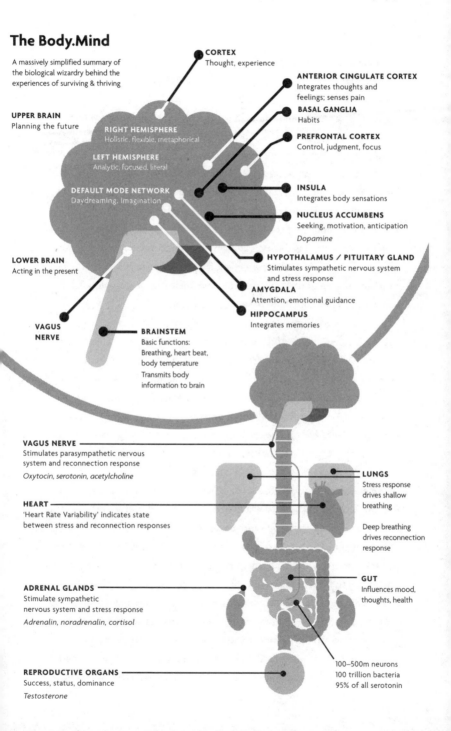

CORTEX
Thought, experience

ANTERIOR CINGULATE CORTEX
Integrates thoughts and
feelings; senses pain

BASAL GANGLIA
Habits

PREFRONTAL CORTEX
Control, judgment, focus

UPPER BRAIN
Planning the future

RIGHT HEMISPHERE
Holistic, flexible, metaphorical

LEFT HEMISPHERE
Analytic, focused, literal

DEFAULT MODE NETWORK
Daydreaming, Imagination

INSULA
Integrates body sensations

NUCLEUS ACCUMBENS
Seeking, motivation, anticipation
Dopamine

LOWER BRAIN
Acting in the present

HYPOTHALAMUS / PITUITARY GLAND
Stimulates sympathetic nervous system
and stress response

AMYGDALA
Attention, emotional guidance

HIPPOCAMPUS
Integrates memories

**VAGUS
NERVE**

BRAINSTEM
Basic functions:
Breathing, heart beat,
body temperature
Transmits body
information to brain

VAGUS NERVE
Stimulates parasympathetic nervous
system and reconnection response
Oxytocin, serotonin, acetylcholine

HEART
'Heart Rate Variability' indicates state
between stress and reconnection responses

LUNGS
Stress response
drives shallow
breathing

Deep breathing
drives reconnection
response

ADRENAL GLANDS
Stimulate sympathetic
nervous system and stress response
Adrenalin, noradrenalin, cortisol

GUT
Influences mood,
thoughts, health

REPRODUCTIVE ORGANS
Success, status, dominance
Testosterone

100–500m neurons
100 trillion bacteria
95% of all serotonin

Contemporary research indicates that no part of the brain or body only has one function.)

Most of us will have been educated to think that the mind and the body are different things. This is not because everyone believes this, just that it is embedded in most modern thought. We see a shrink for problems with our mind, a physician for problems with our body. The French philosopher René Descartes cemented this split in place way back in the 17th century when he stated that there was 'mind stuff' and 'material stuff' (i.e. 'body stuff'). He believed that mind stuff controls the body stuff; yet is also imprisoned by it when we are sick. This theory is still hardwired into the core of the world in which we live. Many doctors, scientists, lawyers, politicians, and economists all go merrily about their business unconsciously believing that the mind controls the body (and that they are separate things).

However, today's scientific journals are awash with studies showing the interconnectedness of the mind and body, and that each can influence the other in very profound ways. Both play a huge role in constructing our everyday experience. So believing that a hard and fast division exists between mind and body, and even brain and body, is not just misguided, it can be dangerous. We are **embodied** minds and thinking bodies. Our guts talk to our brains. Our hearts influence both. If we stubbornly insist on a mind that controls our body, we risk limiting what we can create and how much joy we can experience. Studies have shown that people who think in terms of a split between mind and body make less healthy choices. They are seduced into thinking that the body is just a container for the mind, and so feed it alcohol, stimulants, and fast food with careless abandon.[9]

We tend not to reinforce this split when we see the mind and body as one thing, which I call the **body.mind**. Of course, various parts of the brain do light up in fMRI scanners (machines that record changes in blood flow in areas of the brain, showing which are active and which are not) when we think certain things. Yet it is a mistake to think that one causes the other neatly. The body.mind cannot be categorized as a machine in the same way as, for example, an fMRI scanner can be. It is a massively complex, integrated, constantly adapting system that uses neurons and nerves, hormones and

MIND CONTROLS BODY CONTROLS MIND

Thinking things can change how the body works. In one experiment, people were encouraged to role-play being a jet pilot before having their eyes tested. They turned out to have better eyesight than those who didn't make-believe being a pilot.[10] In another study, one group of hotel maids were informed by scientists that the amount of effort they expended changing beds and cleaning rooms each day was equal to the daily level of exercise recommended for a healthy life. This group then started to lose weight (as well as reduce their body mass index and blood pressure) over a period of weeks. The other group, who were not told this fact, maintained the same weight.[11]

Mind power can even change the body's core temperature. Super-skilled meditators, draped in freezing cold wet sheets, are able to create so much inner heat that they can stay warm and even dry out the fabric.[12] The preliminary results of another study indicate that people can consciously change the way their immune system responds through a series of breathing, meditation, and experiential exercises (like plunging into freezing water and lying naked in the snow).[13]

People who believe in acupuncture experience a reduction in pain after a session; those that don't, do not. The pain relief even shows up in brain scans. What's more surprising is that believers feel as much relief after a fake acupuncture session as they do after the real deal.[14] This phenomenon is called the 'placebo effect' and has now been observed in thousands of drug trials. Believing that you're taking a medicine, even if you're not, can make the body heal. Placebos can mimic the benefits of many popular (yet still profitable) drugs. In one experiment, patients given fake pain-relief tablets showed increased levels of endorphins (the body's natural painkillers) in their cerebrospinal fluid.[15] Even when patients know that a treatment is fake, their health improves if they want it to.[16] Higher-priced placebos can make people get well quicker!

It's not all one-way traffic from the brain to the body though—far from it. What happens below the neckline can profoundly influence how you think, even if you consider yourself to be a totally 'rational' person. This phenomenon has been dubbed 'embodied cognition' by researchers and has taken the scientific world by storm. For example, holding a hot cup of coffee can make you perceive those around you to be 'warmer' people. Hold a rough object and you're more likely to experience social situations as a bit rough or 'tricky.'[17]

transmitters, genes and cells to create a human being who can feel, think, and act in the world. All of it interacts with every other bit in a two-way conversation.

To give us a handle on this complexity so we can learn to master it, I split the totally unified body.mind into three distinct dimensions: **HANDS**, **HEAD**, and **HEART**.

	Activities	Outcomes	Qualities
HANDS	Doing	Habits and actions	Creativity
HEAD	Thinking	Thoughts and stories	Truth
HEART	Feeling	Emotions	Love

A trinity like this can be found peppered throughout the various wisdom traditions around the world. In Ancient Greece, there were originally three creative muses: Aoide, the muse of song (**HANDS**), Melete, the muse of contemplation (**HEAD**), and Mneme, the muse of memories (**HEART**). In the Vedic philosophies of India, there are three paths to **enlightenment**: *karma* (actions of the **HANDS**); *jnana* (knowledge of the **HEAD**); and *bhakti* (love of the **HEART**). For millennia, Jews have put on *teffilin* every day—one on the left hand, nearest the heart, and the other around the head, so that all three centers are connected up in devotion.

In psychology and the other sciences of human experience, we also see the trio appear. First came behavioral psychology (**HANDS**). We worked out ways to use rewards and rules to change how people act. Then came a revolution in the field that brought us cognitive psychology (**HEAD**). This helped link thoughts to behaviors. This brought new tools for change like cognitive behavioral therapy (CBT) and neuro-linguistic programming (NLP). Finally, there has been an explosion of interest in how our emotions and social engagement drive the whole system (**HEART**).

It turns out that our emotions are vitally important in helping us succeed in life. Rather than try to suppress them, it pays to listen intently to them. They are our main GPS system for navigation. They signal to our body.mind to move toward or away from something. They provide us with a **charge** of attraction or repulsion. Fear pulls us away from threats. Love draws us toward people who can care for us. Eminent neuroscientist Antonio Damasio has shown that patients with damage to their emotional brain cannot make simple 'rational' judgments.[18] Decision-making may appear as if it relies on the HEAD; but it is ineffective without the HEART , and meaningless without HANDS. We need our HANDS, HEAD, and HEART integrated and aligned if we want to have and, crucially, sustain breakthroughs.

THINKING ISN'T ALL THAT IT'S CRACKED UP TO BE

Even though we tend to think that reason is the supreme attribute of humankind, our conscious, rational minds are actually quite limited and utterly prone to making mistakes. We can only hold seven or so discrete bits of information at any one time (this is why telephone numbers with more than seven digits are super hard to remember) whereas our unconscious minds can hold 10^{14} bits or more. This is a really big number. Pile that many pieces of copy paper on the floor and it would stretch to Venus and back . . . twice!

Even if we focus really hard on something, we often fail to see things that it would seem impossible to miss. In one classic experiment, people are shown a movie clip of a bunch of grad students passing a ball around. (Spoiler alert: Before you read on, you can watch it online. Search for 'selective attention test' by Daniel Simons.) Most people fail to notice the man in the gorilla suit wandering by. This phenomenon, known as 'change blindness,' shows that even when we think we are alert and on top form, we are often fooling ourselves.

Survival Trip vs. Thrive Drive

BEAUTIFULLY ORCHESTRATED WAVES OF biological activity occur throughout our **HANDS**, **HEAD**, and **HEART** whenever we are engaged in surviving or thriving (though it looks very different of course depending on which one is activated).

When stressed, the entire body.mind fires up quickly with one aim: To give us the edge we need to deal with danger. Some people tend to meet threats (both real and imagined) with raised fists (**HANDS**), angry thoughts (**HEAD**), and rage (**HEART**). This is the *fight* response. Others tend to go inward instead, with palms up toward danger (**HANDS**), scared thoughts (**HEAD**), and feelings of terror (**HEART**). This is the *flight* response. In reality, everyone uses both reactions but, over time, we tend to favor one over the other.

As well as fight or flight, we have a third option when dealing with threats. This is to *freeze*, known to kids everywhere as 'playing dead.' The theory is that predators are less likely to eat meat that has been rotting for a while, as it brings with it more risk of illness (as well as less nutrition). So we flip into the 'deer in the headlights' experience when we really get flummoxed. This may be wonderfully useful when being hunted; but when on a date or in a meeting, it can really get in the way of us thriving.

Whether we are in fight, flight, or freeze mode, our prefrontal cortex shuts down. In these moments, clear, calm thinking is no longer possible. We are emotionally activated. A massive cascade of neurotransmitters and hormones is triggered all over the body.mind. The hypothalamus, which links the nervous system to the hormonal system, releases a substance called corticotrophin-releasing hormone, which kicks the whole body.mind into fight or flight. Then the incredibly strong hormone cortisol moves through us, impacting everything in its path. Next, adrenalin (also known as epinephrine) gets pumped throughout the body, increasing our heart rate and making us breathe fast and shallow (a sure way to tell if we are stressed out). Just one deep breath will reset the system a little and shift you toward relaxation. Try it right now . . .

Breathe in . . . (pause) and out . . . relax . . .

Meanwhile, back to the action. When we are under stress, cortisol tells our cells to conserve as much energy as they can to feed those fighting fists and fleeing legs. The sympathetic nervous system is activated, tightening up our muscles (and giving us butterflies). Glucose is released from storage to power our limbs in case we need to fight or take flight. Cortisol also shuts down the immune system so that vital resources can be focused on the immediate threat instead of fighting off germs. Cortisol is so powerful that it can damage brain cells, particularly those that deal with memory and feeling. It is the most common cause of changes to the brain.[19] There's no room for subtlety. This is our basic survival mechanism and it overrides everything.

This is the **Survival Trip**, which many of us are familiar with because we live in a subtle version of it a lot of the time. Even after years of practicing self-mastery, I can frequently feel myself getting stressed out over things that are really not life-or-death situations. This can happen to all of us when we experience arguments at work, deal with missed deadlines, are criticized by a partner, or have a kid who decides to play up. Any of these, and a thousand more, can trigger us into reacting with stress. We can trip *out* for days, weeks, sometimes years, which then trips us *up*, sabotaging our ability to flourish. We survive the trials and tribulations of each day . . . but at the cost of thriving over the long term.

Whereas the drive to survive is governed by the stress response, the drive to thrive is governed by the **reconnection response** (Harvard medic Herbert Benson dubbed this the 'relaxation response' in the 1970s). Welcome to the original natural high. You can explore some of the practices that can help you activate it on page 122. When we feel safe and held, we relax. This is the equal and opposite version of the fight-or-flight response.[20] The reconnection response is characterized by curiosity, openness, and interest, instead of anger and fear. We engage with events and challenge with an open HEART, HEAD, and HANDS rather than slam them shut. We want to connect, communicate, and, above all, create! As we create, we feel more confident, in control of our lives, and engaged with the world. This is us at our best, enjoying the **Thrive Drive**.

KEEPING COOL UNDER PRESSURE

The prefrontal cortex is pivotal for attention and motivation. It was the most recent part of the brain to evolve and uses the most energy. It 'talks' to many parts of the brain, building up a framework for how to deal with a challenge as we experience it. With this wisdom it helps us control our impulses and dampens down the amygdala, so we aren't permanently fired up with fear. Information from our entire body, the hippocampus (which plays a crucial role in memory), and cerebral cortex all come into this area. It is the metaphorical center of the 'upper brain,' the part of the brain that helps us keep our emotional 'lower brain' from getting too worked up.

However, the prefrontal cortex doesn't work very well when under stress. We have to wait until we're calm before it provides us with its wisdom. When under stress, our body.mind relies on habit rather than engaging in the moment-by-moment act of pure creativity. The prefrontal cortex only develops fully when we are in our early twenties, which is why teens have such a tough time with impulse control and emotional reactivity. fMRI scans of people with low-impulse control, like addicts and those with ADHD (Attention deficit hyperactivity disorder), show reduced activity in this area. On the other hand, regular meditators who have built up their capacity to be both focused and calm show a marked thickening in the prefrontal cortex.

If we are very reactive, we can learn to switch on our upper brain and dampen down the lower, emotional part. This is not because we want to nullify our emotions; it is that we want to understand them fully. We can't do this when they are running amok in our body.mind triggering all sorts of reactions.

There has been a lot of interest in recent years in theories that propose that there are two different types of thought. In the current view, Type 1 thinking is characterized by a rapid assessment of the situation, pulling in information from our emotions, memories, and conditioned associations to make sense of events and prime us for action. It is more reliant on the lower brain than the upper and is pretty much automatic. Type 2 thinking takes longer to initiate, but gives us more chance to reflect on what we are doing and then choose an optimal response. It is associated more with the upper brain. One research study indicates that creativity demands we harmonize both types of thinking.[21]

When we relax and connect with the world, the hormones of openness and enjoyment are released (e.g. acetylcholine, serotonin and oxytocin). Working together, they slow everything down, including our breathing, blood pressure, heart rate, and metabolism. This seems to improve how well our mitochondria produce energy and how insulin works within. Relaxation alters how our genes are expressed, reducing cell death and inflammation.[22] Wounds begin to heal faster, stem cells become more active, and we start to think smarter.[23] Learning and memory are improved.[24]

The vagus nerve, which wanders from the brain to all the internal organs, is thought to be responsible for the feelings of warmth and expansiveness in our chests when we are relaxed and loving life.[25] It has long been known to transmit instructions from the brain to the heart, lungs, and stomach. However, it's only lately that medics have found that 90 percent of the fibers that run through the vagus nerve run *upward*, taking information from the core of the body to the brain and not vice versa.[26] The vagus controls the parasympathetic nervous system, which works to rein in our stressed-out sympathetic nervous system, and seems to drive the repair of brain tissue and neurons.[27]

When we reconnect with ourselves, we relax. As we do so, the length of the intervals between our heartbeats becomes more varied. This can be measured by something called HRV, or Heart Rate Variability. Long thought to be just irrelevant noise, HRV tells us where we are at between the stress response and the reconnection response. If we are stressed out, we have a low HRV (which is associated with depression). More relaxation gives us a high HRV, which is linked to 'thrivability'; the ability to bounce back quicker and stronger than ever after a curve ball.[28]

Whether we use our biology to spin out on the Survival Trip or engage in life with the Thrive Drive is down to us. No matter what has happened in our past, each moment gives us an opportunity to switch on and shift from surviving to thriving. The more we do, the more we open ourselves up for breakthroughs.

The Breakthrough Curve

NATURE HAS EVOLVED US into creatures that have the unique ability to switch on to problems, rather than switch off as we fight them or flee from them. As we do, we allow our **creative spirit** to shine, which has enabled us to become the most formidable problem-solving organism in the known **universe**. By innovating our way out of disaster time and time again, we have gone from having perhaps a hundred tools at our disposal (for example a piece of flint for an axe head and a loin cloth to cover our genitalia) to approximately 10^{10} tools in just 10,000 years. We all share in having a body.mind that can break through problems with stunning reliability.

Breakthroughs are our birthright. We each have the neurobiological capacity to be creative in any situation. However, our **HANDS**, **HEAD**, and **HEART** tend toward fear and reaction, as opposed to creativity and imagination. They will do this until we choose to switch on. If we can stay open, creative, and flexible when all we want to do is fight or freak out, we can enjoy breakthroughs at any time. By learning how to reconnect our **HEART**, feeling love not fear, we can overcome stress with curiosity and courage. By rewiring our **HEAD** so it stays open to ideas instead of shutting down, we can entertain new possibilities. Then, flowing with imagination, we get to remix anything in our world with our **HANDS**, which remain poised to craft something brilliant with finesse.

Every **HEART**, no matter how deeply wounded, can heal. Every **HEAD**, no matter how rigid and afraid, can find a way to imagine and hope. Every set of **HANDS** and feet, no matter how racked by addiction or bad habits, can find a way to flow.

You were born to switch on, break through, and thrive. As you read

This

everything you need to break through fully and permanently is inside you. Even depression, anxiety, panic attacks, nerves—which clearly have some genetic and biochemical components—can all be remixed so that you can fit more snugly, and peacefully, with the reality you live in today. Studies

VAGUS BABY, VAGUS

Studies show that people with a very active vagus nerve, even when at rest, are more compassionate, grateful, loving, and happy. They have high vagal tone. The higher our vagal tone, the more positive we are as people. Children who have high vagal tone are more helpful, co-operative, and generous.[29] You can train yourself to have a higher vagal tone, and therefore more positive and flexible responses to events. This process of amplifying our positive emotions enhances brain plasticity. Our prefrontal cortex, which dampens down fear and helps us focus, gets a boost, while our amygdala becomes noticeably more relaxed. Doctors have been experimenting with stimulating the vagal nerve within the chest. It has proved helpful in treating depression and can increase the speed of healing after paralysis from stroke.[30]

A part of the brain called the insula is key to the Thrive Drive. The insula is the interface between the brain and body. It helps us make sense of the world and attempts to keep everything in a state of integration and balance. It is abnormal in people suffering from a lot of trauma and stress. Advanced meditators, experienced warriors, and top athletes have a highly developed insula. They share a heightened ability to sense what's going on in their bodies. US Navy special forces personnel show increased activation in their insula when they anticipate a change in emotional state, which helps them stay in peak condition during moments of stress on the battlefield.[31] Elite troops and meditators who have increased insula activity also have enhanced vagal tone, which helps them perform better under stress.[32] The insula can even be directly stimulated to create feelings of ecstasy, bliss, and oneness with the universe!

show that who you become in life is at least 50 percent down to your choices not your genes.[33] Even superior physical performance is 50 percent down to mental and psychological factors, not how our bodies are built.[34] We can all come back from anything if we know how to reconnect, rewire, and remix.

There seems to be a fundamental blueprint for how breakthroughs burst forth, and then **break out** (becoming embedded and embodied for good). I have spotted this pattern in everything from how new chemicals are created to how democracies are formed (more on this in the companion title *Switch On: The Wonder of Breakthrough*, which you can find online). The journey of breakthrough seems to trace out the shape of the letter 'J.' I have called this J-shaped curve the **Breakthrough Curve** (see diagram below). It is around the Breakthrough Curve that this book is structured. Although the actual lived experience of breakthrough, from initial issue to Ah Ha! can happen within us in minutes, even seconds with practice, by splitting out the journey into its ten stages, we can learn how to master each one in detail. Each stage is covered in one session of this book.

By understanding the Breakthrough Curve, we can avoid years of wasted time by catalyzing the creative process within. We can reduce both the time it takes for us to get to a breakthrough and the amount of energy we need to put in from the start!

The Breakthrough Curve

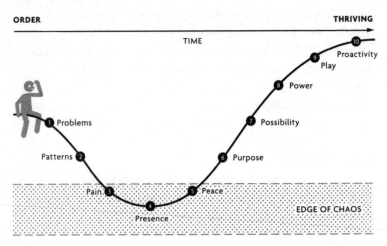

Reconnect. Rewire. Remix.

FEEL WHAT IT WOULD be like to experience a truly life-changing breakthrough in any area of your life where you feel stuck. Go on. Right

Now!

That breakthrough, and many like it, is waiting for you in every nook and cranny of your life. You can start with any problem, no matter how seemingly mundane, and open up possibilities for its resolution. No matter what is done to us, we always have the choice to be creative with the way things are. Even in some of the worst places the world has ever seen, people have chosen to switch on to life, rather than retreat from it, blaming, shaming, and complaining as they go. Psychiatrist Victor Frankl spent time in Auschwitz, where many of my great-grandparents, -aunts and -uncles died. In his profound book *Man's Search for Meaning* he declares:

> We who lived in the concentration camps can remember the men who
> walked through the huts comforting others, giving away their last piece
> of bread. They may have been few in number but they offer sufficient
> proof that everything can be taken from a man but one thing: The last
> of the human freedoms—to choose one's attitude in any given set of
> circumstances, to choose one's own way.

Even in the meanest of times, we can always switch on, create something meaningful, and contribute something precious. Just as cells in the body take in nutrients from outside and transform them into energy or proteins, we can **metabolize** problems into possibilities by engaging with them fully and fearlessly, bringing them inside us where the creative spirit flows freely. The emerging science of Breakthrough Biodynamics tells us that we *need* intense emotions to help us do this. Emotions will either sink us (rage, resentment, guilt, shame, etc.) or they will inspire us. Anger, fear, and bitterness are all destined to keep us locked in place and ensure history repeats itself. Emotions like passion, inspiration, and, dare I say, love are crucial if we want to transform things. We need to access something bigger and richer than our problems if we want to break through them.

DO BACTERIA DO THE BREAKING?

Ideas don't emerge in pristine packaging from a cool, clean, and ordered cerebral computer. Instead, they explode from a dizzying array of organic complexity, which includes neurons in our heart and intestines (not just our brains) and bacteria in our gut. It has recently been discovered that there are around 100 million nerves in the human gut, which is more than in the entire spinal column. This 'second brain' is about the same size as a cat's brain. It uses over 30 neurotransmitters and contains 95 percent of the body's serotonin (a substance which contributes significantly to our feelings of wellbeing and happiness).[35]

As well as millions of nerves, there are also trillions of bacteria inside the gut. In fact, there are 10 to 100 times more bacterial cells than human cells in the body. Their impact on us can be huge. The kind and behavior of bacteria in the gut can influence our moods, thoughts, and behaviors, and lead to stress, depression, and an increased waistline. In one study, medics put the bacteria found in fat mice into the intestines of thin mice, and the skinny rodents put on weight. Put bacteria from skinny mice into fat mice and the chubby ones lose weight.[36]

Bacteria in the gut may be able to influence the brain through the vagus nerve, especially the hypothalamus, which is a key player in our drive to survive. Parkinson's Disease, long considered a condition of the brain, may in fact be triggered by problems in the 'second brain' of the gut. The disease might travel to the brain along the vagus nerve.[37]

Feelings of love, connection, hope—all underpinned by the biology of oxytocin, serotonin, the insula, prefrontal cortex, vagus nerve, and more—melt away stress and release the creative spirit inside us. Love is the great synaptic solvent that liquefies old ideas (and the neuronal pathways that encode them), allowing new ones to burst free. When feeling romantic love, people think more expansively and less analytically, have a much longer-term outlook, and are more creative. When they are turned on but not in love, they think in a more short-term and less creative way.[38] Imagine what the results would be of a study that looked at the impact of feelings of love for ourselves and for life itself, on our creativity!

The more love we feel, the more we can bring forth bigger and bolder ideas. If we fall head over heals in love with the promise of a better world, we will do our part to bring that into reality. Ché Guevara, the iconic revolutionary, put it this way: 'At the risk of seeming ridiculous, let me say that the true revolutionary is guided by a great feeling of love.'[39] Mahatma Gandhi, Nelson Mandela, and Martin Luther King all knew this too, which is why they were able to lead such seismic breakthroughs that have impacted millions upon millions of lives (and continue to). There is a reason why we hark back to these three great leaders. They changed the world so profoundly because they encouraged and empowered us to switch on—**HANDS, HEAD**, and **HEART**—to what is possible when we come from love, truth, and creativity. And we love being reminded of it!

The more we connect with love, the more we can rewire our brains and bodies to thrive. The more we rewire our habits with new, more creative ones, the more we can remix our world so that it takes the shape we want it to. The more we remix, the more likely we, and the people we love, work with, and depend on, will all thrive too. When we know how to unleash our creative spirit, freeing it from fear and frustration, we can rapidly reach our collective potential to create together a brilliant world that works for us all. Moment by moment. Neuron by neuron. Line of code by line of code.

Problems are natural. Pain may be inevitable. But suffering is optional because a breakthrough is always available.

Breakthrough is not hypothetical. It cannot be gamed. It happens in real-time, with real problems. We need a bit of genuine grit to create a bright, shiny pearl. So I invite you to read the rest of this book with a tangible problem in mind, one that really affects your life. Shift from a dress rehearsal to going live and direct.

- What frustrating problem would you most like to be free of?
- What limitation, obstacle, or fear would you like to transform for good, so you can create something incredible?
- What pain or suffering is holding you back and stopping you from flying as high as you know you can go?

No matter what problem you pick, if it is causing you to feel at all down—stressed, negative, stuck, moody, or whatever—it has juice within it to power a breakthrough. Out of failure, triumph will fly. From constraint, freedom will arise. Within **chaos**, genius will be forged. So strap yourself in, choose a nice luscious problem and join me to switch on.

The solution to the anagram is cubism.

Session 01

Problems

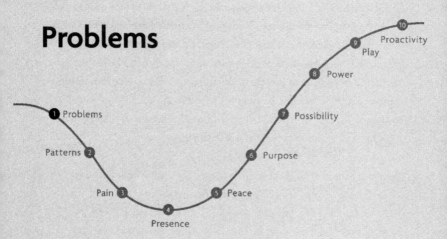

1 Problems

Patterns 2

Pain 3

4
Presence

5 Peace

6 Purpose

7 Possibility

8 Power

9 Play

Proactivity
10

PROBLEMS HAVE BEEN GIVEN a bad rap in human history. Conflict, aggression, failures, limitations, and disappointments are rarely welcomed as sources of joy. However, move beyond the initial intensity and we can start to appreciate them as enormously valuable sources of growth. Problems compel us to break through them. Humans have always used challenges to spark, fuel, and focus creativity, whether in science, business, or art. We can turn constraints into prisms of creativity by owning every problem we encounter, no matter how frustrating or frightening. As the blacksmith fashions iron into steel in a furnace, we can transform problems into possibilities in the cauldron inside us, as long as we bring them into our sphere of influence. Every crisis offers us a turning point, an opportunity to shift. After all, without problems, there would be nothing to break through.

THHHH ..... WONK

That's the sound of one of life's curve balls hitting us where it hurts, right when we least expect it. The bouncer finds our stash, kicks us out of the club, and calls the police. We panic the night before a big exam and freak out about a lifetime of failure. The person we are massively in love with turns out to be a two-timer who breaks our heart. Our child gets sick with a virus and we are powerless to do anything about it. Our folks announce they're getting a divorce, which turns the whole family inside out. The project we thought was going so well starts to falter, and we have no clue how to stop it crumbling. The funding that was due falls through and we can't take that next step. Our credit card bill, full of vacation expenses, arrives just as our boss announces another round of redundancies . . .

Let's face it, more often than not, life doesn't quite work out as planned. There tend to be many more curve balls than easy wins. Even if you don't feel as if you have any 'problem' as such, I bet you feel stuck, bored, unlucky, or exhausted from time to time. These mundane moments of everyday life—the frustrations with friends and irritations with partners—make the perfect training ground for breakthrough. Then, when it really matters, when perhaps our career, health, or marriage is on the line, we have confidence in our creativity and instantly find a way forward.

Problems are the doorways to possibility

PROBLEMS ARE SIMPLY ANY situation in your life where you are not thriving to your fullest potential. The more intense they are, the more you will notice them throughout your body.mind. Physically, in your HANDS, legs, and muscles, you might feel tense, anxious, or stressed out. In your HEAD, you might be blaming people, shaming them, or complaining about them (and that includes moaning about yourself). Emotionally, in your HEART, you might feel wound up, moody, or upset in some way. Have a quick scan through your three dimensions and see if there is anything in your field that is getting in the way of this moment being the best moment of your life so far . . .

Of course, not all problems are the same. Some we can crack as soon as we apply ourselves; others seem to hold us in their grip for years. Some everyone seems to share; others seem unique to us. Some, we tell ourselves, are just 'how the world works,' so we resign ourselves to living within their limitations. What *is* common to every problem is that it can always be broken through. I draw inspiration from the countless people who have come back from terrible illnesses, natural disasters, wars, and famines, and used their problems to open up possibilities for an extraordinary life. They reassure me that every one of my problems, even those where life and death hangs in the balance, can reveal new avenues through which I can become a wiser, brighter, more generous version of myself.

Problems don't just stop us from doing what we want, or getting what we desire, they also allow us to glimpse, in full Technicolor, who we have *become* as people. They reveal the shape of our character, the edges of our talents, and the vibrancy of our imaginations. They help us see where we're **switched off**, stuck, or being stubborn; and where we are vibing with life's endless possibilities for breakthrough. Problems point us in the direction of the parts of ourselves that require growth and expansion, if we want to stay fitted to our environment. Whether it's the car not starting or a project hitting a rocky patch, we can always learn and grow by engaging our entire body.mind in the problem. This is the way of breakthrough and it is essential to our thriving.

All creativity needs something to work on. A painter or musician has a medium to work in, be it bronze, spray paint, or dubstep. So artists at life need a substance to sculpt into brilliance: Problems. Our medium is made up of the challenging experiences, events, and encounters in our lives. When everything is awesome, we aren't given much to work with. When things are tricky, we are provided with the raw materials for breakthrough, which pushes us to invent and imagine. Challenges demand improvisation. Threats require adaptation. Limitation invites transformation. This is the 'source code' of the universe within which the entire process of evolution sits.

Each new problem brings with it an opportunity to explore, experiment with, and, eventually, master a new facet of our lives. This is the way that all life on this planet works, from an amoeba to Apple computers. All life is problem-solving—what doesn't break us, makes us.

Immediately you might think, 'Hang on a minute, things like poverty, child abuse, and disease are not gifts.' I agree, they are tragedies, and we'll be looking at the problems that face humanity later in the book (see Session 10, page 235). For the time being, hold that thought for a moment and consider: What defines a problem?

I'd suggest that a problem is only a problem if you're prevented from flourishing by it. That means a problem is something that stops *you* being at peace, prevents *you* from living your purpose, or limits *your* sense of power. We cannot control many things in life. But we can always control how peaceful we feel, how purposeful we are, and how much power we access. Which means *all* problems, from the terrifying to the mundane, can be transformed *within us* into a possibility to be more peaceful, more purposeful, and more powerful. If we were already maxed-out on those qualities, surely the issue wouldn't be a problem in the first place? Without problems, we are not called to step up our game and become more.

When we are given a low dose of a poison, it stimulates our body to become healthier. Yet too much poison and we die. A glass of red wine can make us healthier. Ten glasses will result in terrible hangover and possibly alcohol poisoning.[1] By the same token, a little stress stimulates us to dig within for new ways to grow. This has been termed eustress (*eu* as in *eudaimonia*: Happy, positive). Too many unresolved problems can often lead to *distress*.

It is not that eustress and distress are 'real' as such, because one person's eustress is another's distress. Our experience is intrinsically linked to how we *see* our problems. All problems change according to what perspective they're seen from. For example, I might see my death as a major bummer, but to the worms it's a real bonus. The same situation affects everyone very differently and we are all, at least partly, responsible for how we see it. Problems may affect everyone—like global warming, for example—but they don't cause everyone to react in the same way. How we react is always unique to us and ultimately depends on which perspective we are coming from. How we react is dependent on the **frame** we use to look out onto the world. For example, think of the difference between how a Nike-branded product is perceived and shoes that look similar but have no logo.

How might your problems look to other people? To your friends? To others who have gone through something similar before and cracked it? To Mother Theresa? To Steve Jobs? As long as you can imagine that there's one person who wouldn't find it a problem but the opening to a new possibility— whether Mandela, Gandhi, Jesus, the Buddha, Eddie Izzard, or whoever— then you know there must be a way of acting (**HANDS**), a way of thinking (**HEAD**), and way of being (**HEART**) that would help you break through the problem and grow.

We participate in some way with our problems because we see them from a certain angle. This may sound challenging but it is, in fact, awesome news. If we are involved in how problems look and feel to us, then we can change them. So . . .

BREA**THE**
&

.

All your problems, both now and in future, are changeable. Every problem you face can be seen differently. It can be a source of eustress or distress, and the choice is yours. Shit or sh!t? Take your pick. You get to switch one into the other simply by changing your frame.

The thing is, the sh!t *always* hits the fan sooner or later. Your future could bring illness, divorce, redundancy, bankruptcy, or worse. Don't shout at the messenger, but you will at some point have to deal with someone you love dying, the impact of climate change, and the curve ball of your own death. So the sooner you get practicing how to metabolize problems into possibilities for more peace, purpose, and power—*for you*—the sooner you get to thrive in the here and now. Today.

The question then becomes . . . How do we need to act, think, and feel about problems to break through them every time?

Every great breakthrough begins with a good crisis

MANY OF THE WORLD's greatest stories start with a character who has a sizable problem. The more interesting the problem, the more the story hooks us in. Harry Potter's problem is that his parents were killed and he must face the world and an evil wizard totally alone. Luke Skywalker's problem is that he has to come to terms with the loss of his dad while learning to avoid the dark side of 'the Force,' which can take down even the best Jedi. Katniss Everdeen's problem is that she (or her loved ones) might be selected to play in the Hunger Games while her hometown is on the verge of starvation. Each of these problems grabs our attention and gives us a stake in the story as the hero or heroine tries to resolve it. We want to read or watch to the end to learn how they cracked it. Stories are essentially vehicles for showing us *how* to deal with problems.

In the beginning, the protagonist (and that means us in our lives) is usually blissfully unaware that trouble is brewing. This is how we are in the moments before . . .

Pop!

Suddenly our boss drops us in it or our kid has a tantrum in a busy grocery store. The **crisis**, either mini or maxi, comes out of nowhere. Or does it? Most crises are simply the result of a hidden, but mounting problem being brought into the harsh light of day. Perhaps our boss has slowly been losing faith in us; or the organization has been getting into increasing difficulties. Maybe our kid is really unhappy at school and hasn't found a way to tell us; or they are upset that we haven't been around much lately. The crisis is the alarm bell sounding that something is amiss and it needs attention. We may have to search around a bit to find the true origins of the issue. The earlier we jump on it, the more likely that we'll be able to prevent the problem from swamping us. Ignore it, and it is likely to come back bigger and stronger, like the baddies do in the movies. We get to respond to a tickle or wait until it becomes a full-blown punch.

Crisis. What does that word mean to you? Does it trigger a happy feeling or a slightly stressful one? *Krisis*, the ancient Greek word from which the modern term is derived, doesn't mean something terrible. It means a 'turning point,' a moment for a major decision. Across the other side of the planet, the Chinese developed a word for 'crisis' that also brings with it a sense of change. Their word contains two characters: One means 'emergency' and the other 'opportunity.' Within every crisis there is something dangerous, which we can, and must, pay attention to. Yet, after we have dealt with the most pressing issues, we get access to an opportunity too.

We can use any crisis as a turning point to find more peace, purpose, and power inside us. Some wisdom traditions, such as the Eleusinian Mysteries in Ancient Greece, even *created* artificial crises for their adepts to ensure they got their money's worth. Few people want to engage in a transformational experience and not come out with a change in attitude or a shift in consciousness! A good crisis is the gateway to this. It serves as the incentive to switch on. The great psychologist Carl Jung believed that even psychotic crises could be deciphered as turning points for transformation and change.

So every crisis is asking you: **Which way will you turn? Toward the future or the past? Up onto the Breakthrough Curve or back into your comfort zone (even if it's getting rather hot and stuffy in there)?**

We can see every problem as confirmation that we're cursed, that life is shit or that God or our parents don't love us . . . which is essentially a description of **paranoia**. Or we can see them as confirmation that the universe is giving us (another) opportunity to grow and grow up . . . which we can call **pronoia**. Pronoia is the sneaky suspicion that the universe has somehow conspired to present us with problems that can help us expand and become more peaceful, purposeful, and powerful. The pronoid person sees an event, say missing the bus, as an opportunity to see how their actions led them to that experience. They might immediately set their morning alarm earlier. Or they might relax, believing it may have saved them from an accident. The paranoid person sees missing the bus as evidence that they are lazy, that the bus driver is selfish, or that the transport system is a mess.

No philosopher or scientist on Earth will ever be able to prove that either paranoia or pronoia is more valid or true. So, in the meantime, you get to choose which you find most helpful and inspiring.

At the breaking point

PROBLEMS ARE INEVITABLE. THIS is even more true if the way we are living does not fit with the way the world is becoming. Problems, and the crises heralding their arrival, are the result of us not keeping up. They are signals for us to adapt. If we are stuck or stressed-out, it's because we have not yet realized that something inside us is past its expiry date. We will keep on feeling more and more pressure from the world around us—whether in the form of a new job, a new lover or a new health challenge—until we reach a **breaking point**.

Here, the old ways of being start breaking apart, opening up space for the new. A child has to break apart their old LEGO model, no matter how awesome, in order to *experiment* with a new, possibly better (but possibly not!), construction. For breakthrough to burst forth we must be prepared to let go of the old, no matter how comfortable and certain it feels. If we are stuck in our ways and unwilling to do this, we cannot have breakthrough. That is true whether we want to have a breakthrough in romance, health, wealth, work, or society as a whole. End of story.

Problems shake up the system. Crises create unrest, forcing us out of our comfort zones. If you find yourself in tears, irritated, or obsessing over something, you could be reaching breaking point. It's worth paying attention to these moments, so you can learn how your body.mind signals to you that you are there. There are now three ways to turn:

1. React

Most of us react to problems many times a day. Shouting or silently cussing someone under our breath is a classic reaction to stress. As is clamming up totally or trying to leave a room if things get a bit tricky. The fight-or-flight reaction comes out in many ways. This is what happens when we 'act out' in some way, perhaps with a grown-up tantrum or a bit of the silent treatment. There's no value in feeling bad, guilty, or ashamed about it. Most of our reactions are mindless habits used over and over again to protect us. We are destined to repeat them until we switch on and notice the breaking point.

2. Repress

As well as (or instead of) reacting, we might try to burrow the problem as far away from our conscious mind as possible, telling ourselves it will go away or doesn't really exist. We suppress it, and then cover it up with ways to take our mind off it. Repression like this may work for a while but eventually we'll start to feel the problem holding us back in some way. Problems that have been repressed tend to pop up at the most inconvenient moments and stop us in our tracks.

Stress, the body.mind's natural response to change it is not comfortable with, will grow within even if we have locked our problems away. We will be in a state of tension, which we will need to release in some way. We might do this with drugs, chocolate, chicken nuggets, wine, whiskey, work, sex, extreme sports, running, or a bitchy comment—all of which can help to give us a boost and help us forget for a time what's troubling us. There's nothing wrong with any of these activities. In some way, most of us are addicted to something. Addiction is a way of not dealing with certain problems that we know, deep down, are there. Yet trying to smother the natural signals that we are at breaking point with some form of painkiller or tranquilizer only traps us further in the Survival Trip.

3. Remix

There is just one more option available: Engage with the problem fully and find creative ways to remix it. We meet life where it's at. Instead of reacting or repressing, we prepare to explore the lessons and learning that lie within, confident that there are always treasures to discover. There's never really a 'good' time to engage with a problem fully . . . apart from the moment we start noticing it's holding us back.

Problems serve us. They are useful. Valuable. Vital. Problems reveal to us what is fragmented within us. What is calling to us to become whole. There's no use getting too logical though. Logic alone cannot solve a problem that involves our emotions (and all real problems do). So if we want to have the deepest **insight** and the biggest breakthrough, we're going to have to involve our whole body.mind—**HANDS**, **HEAD**, and **HEART**—in the mix. The way to do that is to bring our problems inside us where we get to work on them properly using all our faculties. That is what we do when we **own** them.

Own it or it owns you

WE CANNOT PROGRESS ANY further down the Breakthrough Curve until we own our problems. Owning a problem means giving up complaining about it, blaming anyone, or shaming people. If we hear ourselves doing this, we haven't yet owned it. Owning a problem means giving up moaning and groaning, and instead getting busy with a breakthrough.

But doesn't it feel great to blame our parents for our sh!t? Or complain about a lover for driving us crazy? Or shame our kids for making a big mess? Or bitch about our friends for making us look bad? Or moan about a recession, the system, some politicians, or whoever for our money problems?

The downer with the blame, shame, and complain game is that if we insist that others *make* us angry (or happy for that matter), we immediately lose all our power. How can we change something that we claim is nothing to do with us? How can we break through a blockage that we say is due to somebody or something else?

The area where we all have control is how we see our problems, from our perspective, and what we do about them. When we own our perspective and reactions, we own the problem. If we deny them, we are powerless to do anything.

You can't remix something you don't or won't own.

The biological truth is that our reactions exist within us. When the pain centers of the brain light up, nobody has zapped them with a laser. When we enter the stress response, nobody has injected us with cortisol or adrenalin. Someone stealing from us, threatening us, even hitting us doesn't *cause* our body.mind to stress out. It *triggers* it. The anger or fear is already in there, waiting to be triggered. If we feel any tension, anger, or fear inside our body. mind, then only we are ultimately responsible for it.

Even when our body.mind is flooded with hormones—due to menstruation, orgasm, or rage—our reactions and frames don't enter from outside. They always exist within. Yes, hormones are very powerful and can massively *amplify* our feelings, but they don't *invent* them. Being an angry drunk means we have anger inside that wants to be expressed. Even psychedelics don't *cause* hallucinations. Our imagination does the creating; the drug simply triggers what's already possible.

It's time to reclaim our power by owning our sh!t!

No one on the planet can *make* you angry or afraid. But neither can they make you happy or creative either. Only *you* have the power to make yourself feel peaceful or spiteful, **mindful** or mindless. Other people's actions can trigger your reactions, but they don't cause them. The capacity to thrive, like the capacity to be stressed, is inside us. We create both within.

> **The difference between a cause and a trigger is the difference between a life of slavery and one of liberty.**

To be clear, taking ownership doesn't mean taking responsibility for the events or triggers. It isn't your 'fault,' for example, if your partner gets jealous or a colleague scuppers a project. Owning your problems doesn't mean you would choose to have them again or that you condone the actions of the other people involved. It just means you are responsible for the frame through which you see events and the reactions you have to them. If, on the other hand, you refuse to own your reactions and frames, then you risk being constantly stressed out by events outside your control, tossed around like a piece of driftwood on a stormy ocean. You either have to own your own problems or cede your power to them and let them own you.

Owning your problems is utterly life-changing. You are released from the curse of repeating mistakes over and over. You can escape your very own customized version of *Groundhog Day* and enter a new, more compelling experience. In these moments you have become totally **response-able**, able to respond in creative ways to the problems you face. This is nothing to do with morality or ethics. It is simply about seeking creative empowerment.

Any event that sparks a crisis, which we might usually love to hate or blame, is actually the beginning of the experience of transformation. It is the clarion call by which we know we have a new opportunity to radically boost our sense of peace, purpose, and power.

Small changes, big possibilities

ALTHOUGH WE MIGHT INITIALLY react to an intense crisis, once we've had a chance to chill out and reflect, we all have the choice to own it or not. This is the moment we get to switch on. We spot a problem or a crisis for what it is: The beginning of a breakthrough opportunity. If we repress or deny it, we risk entering the Way of Breakdown, where we are stuck merely surviving (see diagram on page 36).

Breakdown often happens when the effort it takes to repress or react to our problems takes too much out of us. We all show breakdowns in different ways. Most of us have weak spots in our body.mind that 'go' when overwhelmed. A bad back, a bad cold, burn out, an old condition, exhaustion, panic attacks, and the blues can all be symptoms of breakdown (which doesn't mean we shouldn't seek professional help for them). It does not have to be something spectacular. Many of us live in breakdown for years, putting up with it rather than using it as a stimulus to take ownership and ride the Breakthrough Curve.

We live in a complex world, where small differences—in our genes, early experiences, decisions, and environments—can all play a large part in how our lives turn out. We are subject to the rules of Chaos Theory. One different decision can radically alter the future. In the same way a butterfly's wings flapping in the Peruvian jungle can trigger a storm over Chicago, hitting on a hottie, rather than leaving the party having felt too shy as usual, can end up in marriage. Speaking up in one average meeting could lead, many years down the line, to you running the firm. This is what makes life so exciting. Breakthroughs are **non-linear**. A teeny-weeny break from our usual reactions can turn our lives around.

The Way of Breakdown

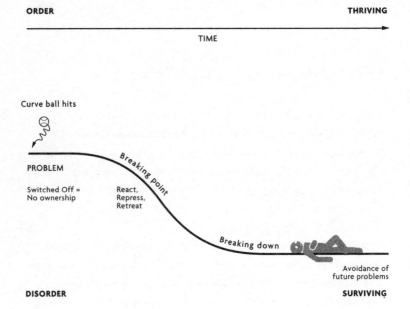

ORDER

THRIVING

TIME

Curve ball hits

PROBLEM

Switched Off =
No ownership

React,
Repress,
Retreat

Breaking Point

Breaking down

Avoidance of
future problems

DISORDER

SURVIVING

Each choice you make, at every turning point, opens up a unique **field of possibility** within which your future will play out. Some futures are simply not possible if you make certain choices. Push away your problems and you push away possibilities for a more meaningful, **thrivadelic**, and connected life. Own them, and you get to co-create a fulfilling future with whatever curve balls come flying your way. When you own your problems, you enter the Way of Breakthrough where you can thrive (see diagram opposite).

The Way of Breakthrough

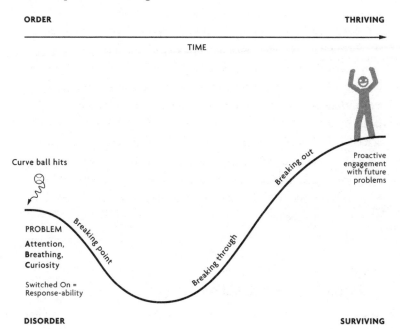

ORDER   THRIVING

TIME

Curve ball hits

Breaking out

Proactive
engagement
with future
problems

PROBLEM

Breaking point

Attention,
Breathing,
Curiosity

Switched On =
Response-ability

Breaking through

DISORDER   SURVIVING

Response-ability is the prerequisite of opening up positive fields of
possibility. To reiterate, ownership is absolutely not about blame. It is
impossible to blame any one person or situation anyway because every
problem has been created by a complex interplay between multiple
perspectives, actions, beliefs, stories, habits, and much else besides. In a
world of complexity, singling out one cause of any event is misguided,
inaccurate, and often quite unhelpful. This is **linear** thinking, looking at
the world as if it were a machine in which predictable outputs come
from known inputs. Put the foot on the gas pedal and the car goes faster.
Sell more products on your website, at a higher margin, and you make
more profit.

However, we human beings are anything but predictable. Some people
can undergo a traumatic event and come back stronger than ever. Others
crumple under the weight. Some develop AIDS with an HIV infection.

Others never even know they have it. Every situation is 'over-determined'; it has multiple causes, influences, and origins.

For example, if you've just had a massive fight with your partner, the fact that it's hot and humid could be playing a part. So could a rumbling belly and low blood sugar. You or your opposite number may have a genetic predisposition to a temper, or have been taught to respond defensively by a parent. Who can tell which of these is to blame? Instead of looking for a single cause to blame, you can opt for a small change in life philosophy by assuming 100 percent response-ability for every problem you are involved in. As you switch on, you open up multiple fields of possibility that would have remained shut. By making tiny shifts in how you respond each day to the many problems you face, you can enjoy a very different future in a few years' time (see diagram below).

Switch On for a Very Different Future

ORDER

THRIVING

TIME

Curve ball hits

PROBLEM
Small change in life philosophy

Breaking point

Breaking point

Breaking point

Breaking through

Breaking down

Breaking out

Field of possibility
Our future when switched on

Massive difference in life reality

Field of possibility
Our future when switched on

DISORDER

SURVIVING

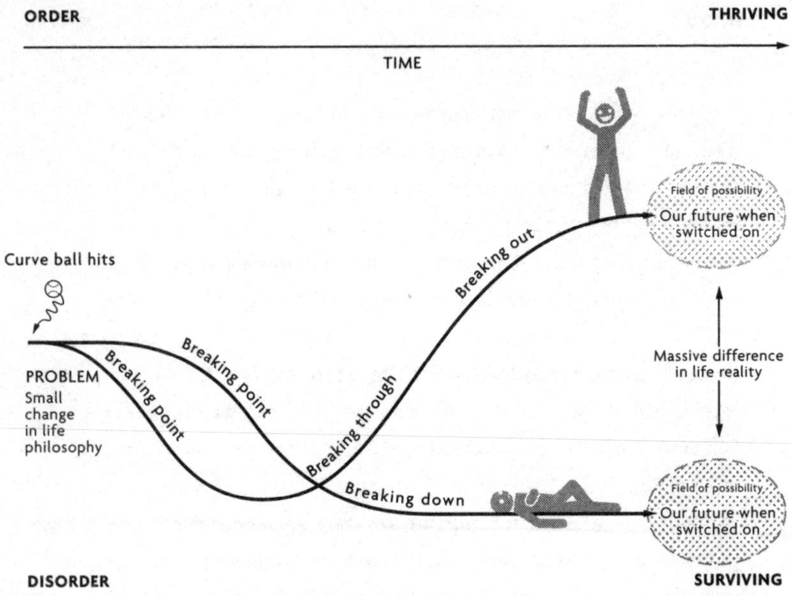

**When we give up knowing who is right and wrong,
we can focus on creating something different.**

The same is true of organizations. A leader of any organization can only
open up possibilities for non-linear breakthroughs once they take response-
ability for everything that happens in and around it. A leader cannot control
employees, competitors, or the stock market. But they can take ownership of
the problems the organization faces and find new ways to perceive and react
to them. If a boss tries to blame things 'outside their control' (which seems
to be the majority of the time if you listen to corporate trading updates), they
are simply stating that they don't have the power to make changes and they
cannot be relied upon to do better in future. If you've invested your entire
nest egg in a company with a string of bad results, do you want the boss to
blame the market? Or take response-ability and come up with a new strategy
to break through?

 ## REFUSING TO BLAME THE SYSTEM

A few years ago, I ran a workshop for doctors and nurses within a large mental
health facility in Britain's National Health Service (the largest employer in the
UK). They claimed that their biggest problems were due to politicians and the
system as a whole. They claimed this was all 'beyond their control.' Fast-forward
an hour into the workshop and together we had created a list of more than 100
ideas they hadn't yet tried that could help solve their problems. One of them
was writing to the Minister of Health every day until they got a meeting. The
bottom line is, until you've tried every avenue, whether your list of ideas is 10 or
10,000, there is absolutely no value in blaming anyone or anything else (including
yourself). It creates nothing but predictable outcomes. Breakthroughs come the
moment we switch on and open up to the unexpected.

If a leader is a true visionary, they don't just take response-ability for their
organization, they take it for the whole sector and world. This is how leaders
like Jeff Bezos at Amazon, Muhammad Yunus at Grameen Bank, Elon Musk
at Tesla, and Reed Hastings at Netflix have creatively transformed entire

sectors with breakthroughs. They took response-ability for what wasn't working for us—the citizen or consumer—and created revolutionary new ways of doing things that have changed the world forever. Leaders who complain they cannot do the same are lying to themselves. They can break through anything, but only if they are willing to take full response-ability. And that is a big step that many are not willing to take.

Small changes within the body.mind of one leader can lead to a radically different future for billions.

Lighting up the way ahead

THE BREAKTHROUGHS LYING DORMANT within our problems are like pearls in the murky shadows of a lagoon. We usually have to go in deep to get the rewards. This means getting stuck into parts of us that are likely to be confusing, unpleasant, and unappetizing. It is within our least shiny reactions and frames that the most learning lies. The parts of us that we are least happy to go public with—that shame or embarrass us—hold the greatest potential for breakthrough. This is what is called the **darkside**.

Every embarrassing habit—from rampant jealousy to being secretly vindictive—is part of our darkside. Every petty, dirty, or sordid thought we have (and I for one know that I have many) comes from our darkside. Every time we are mean-spirited or down-right nasty it comes from our darkside (Jung called it our 'shadow'). Even being inauthentically nice is the darkside.

The descent into our darkside is the first stage of the Breakthrough Curve. A powerful metaphor of this journey comes from St John of the Cross, a 16th-century Spanish priest and church reformer, who wrote a poem about his experiences trying to find the light at the end of the tunnel. It has since become an enduring image of the confusion and challenges inherent in wrestling a breakthrough from the jaws of a breakdown. Here is St John, from *The Dark Night of the Soul*:

In that night of secret lucky night
Unseen by others and where I could see nothing too
I was without light or guide
Except that which was in my burning heart
I was guided by it
With more certainty than the sun at noon
To the place where I had always waited
The place I always knew I could go.

Our darkside is where much creativity emerges. In complexity science, the space where most newness emerges in evolution is called the **edge of chaos**. For all of us involved in breakthrough, the edge of chaos is the zone of maximum creativity and also maximum confusion. Confusion is a sign that two versions of us (with different frames and reactions) are in conflict inside. We cannot hold on to them both. One has to go for the fields of possibility of the other to sprout. Sometimes the dark night, the bewilderment and consternation, can seem to last for ever. However, by following the Breakthrough Curve, we will always reach the sunshine (although folk wisdom has it that the dark before dawn is the gloomiest!).

As we know, our entire body.mind system has been set up, and repeatedly trained, to shut down when it feels unsafe and uncertain like this, well before we ever get to the light at the end of the tunnel. After millions of years of cultural and biological evolution, we have learned to avoid the darkside in any shape or form, preferring instead to pretend it isn't there. When we watch TV, grab a vodka, or bury ourselves in work instead of embracing our problems, this is what we are doing. But to crack open a problem and suck out the most opportunity from it, we must first open up and go hang out at the edge of chaos.

This is a real conundrum, for it does not always feel good as we begin.

St John of the Cross learned on his journey that it was only a switched on HEART that could provide the light he needed to get him through the dark night. But switching on your **HEART** opens you up to being vulnerable. If you've been hurt before, which most of us have at some point, few things can be harder than choosing to be vulnerable again. It can actually feel painful to be that open, that tender, after years of being shut down and switched off.

Take comfort though. Even if you have locked up your **HEART** with layers and layers of defensive barriers, each time you switch on and own a problem, you release one layer of defense. It can take years but what's the rush? As long as you treat each crisis as an opportunity to open up just that bit more, you'll thrive. That's what switching on is all about: The gradual release of the old to embrace the new. Every time we switch on to a problem, and are response-able for it, we open up unprecedented fields of possibility and plant seeds for the future within each of them.

However, the confusion can sometimes be really challenging to deal with. So, if your darkside is getting you down, a quick way out of the blues is to focus on what you're thankful for, because even in the darkest moments there is always *something* to be grateful for. It's like striking a match in the gloom. Gratitude, even for tiny things like the fact that strawberries exist, can short-circuit your stress response, stopping you reacting negatively and opening you up instead.

 ## THE GRATITUDE ATTITUDE

Studies show that gratitude boosts feelings of wellbeing and positivity.[2–7] Our mood becomes more positive, which is important if we want to stay creative.[8] Gratitude can also lessen our fear of death.[9] In one study, people who kept a gratitude journal, noting down three things that they appreciated each day, were almost 10 percent happier than those that didn't. They enjoyed the task so much that they kept on doing it after the study finished. Gratitude can harmonize our heart rate and accelerate giving to others. Sharing what we are grateful for with others leads to even more creativity and flexibility![10]

We no longer clench our fists at the life lessons we are being offered. Instead, with open **HANDS**, **HEAD**, and **HEART**, we accept them with gratitude.

For example, you might be grateful for your health; a child's eyes you saw on the street today; your own existence against all the odds of nature; the heart that pumps to keep you alive and the brain that works tirelessly to engage with the world; salted peanuts; your Converse shoes; the sound of deep house music; birdsong; air travel; the art of Banksy or Botticelli; or the smell of fresh bread.

What are you feeling grateful for right now? Can you get to 20 things in 60 seconds? Can you get to 30? 40?

Go!

Holding it down

NO MATTER HOW MUCH you fine-tune your 'attitude of gratitude,' problems are still likely to trigger your stress response from time to time. As long as your body.mind is cycling through the Survival Trip, switched off, you won't be able forge a new way forward and open up those crucial fields of possibility. So, in order to seize the possibilities in a problem fully, we need to be able to hold it down, without reacting or repressing. By holding it down, we avoid exploding or imploding with tricky situations, which gives us precious time to **process** a problem. If we react, we are likely to trigger those around us to react back and everyone gets stuck on the merry-go-round of melodrama.

Being able to hold it down, even in the middle of a sh!t storm, is called **equanimity**. The Buddha said it is one of the four most important virtues a human being can develop (the other three are loving-kindness, compassion, and being able to celebrate with and for others). Equanimity allows us to see problems through multiple frames, both pronoid and paranoid, before we decide how to react to them. We become able to dance around an issue, seeing it from all sides before making our move. We give ourselves time to create a more imaginative way out of a crisis before we yell at our gorgeous kids, say something stupid to the boss, or bitch about our most supportive friend. It is not about being flat, gray, or dull; it is about being alive to the possibilities within all human experience without reacting on autopilot and making things worse.

BEING CHEATED ON

In a training session on relationships, a former partner told me she had been unfaithful during a 'trial separation.' (I'm still not sure exactly what that means!) Cue a reaction: Dizziness, spinning lights, and indignant rage. A therapist, who was working with us at the time, urged me to hold down my reactions. So I did. I allowed my ex's actions to sink in, to swirl around my body.mind triggering all sorts of intense imagery and emotions; yet I didn't yell and rampage, as my instincts were screaming at me to do.

Instead, I gave myself time to find some possibility for insight within it. I worked hard (really hard!), to understand more about why she'd done it and what I could learn from that. As I owned the problem, the emotional Godzilla inside me settled down and allowed a wiser version of me to join the conversation. It doesn't mean that I thought what she did was 'right' or 'good.' But I did discover in my vulnerability that there was something for me in the experience. I found a way I could grow in intimate relationships, and this has been instrumental in ensuring that my (second) marriage has thrived. I am a wiser, calmer man because of it.

It is a natural desire to want to categorize an event as being 'good' or 'bad.' When we hold it down, we refuse to make such simplistic comparisons. We can even hold space for it to be both good *and* bad (or neither). I find that it helps to re-label a problem from bad, awful, messed-up, freaky, or whatever, to simply 'intense.' This acknowledges it is important and challenging but can stop us getting carried away with only one perspective. Then we get to stay unperturbed, a pond without too many ripples, as we work out what an event might mean for us and how we can handle it most creatively. Although we hold off making a firm judgment, we can maintain a

sense of optimism and hope, as opposed to being completely neutral. This keeps us connected, positive, and creative as we explore all the angles of our intense experiences.

I don't know anyone who finds this effortless but it does get easier with practice. The switched on version of me still finds itself observing the irresponsible, switched-off, version of me being a massive drama king rather than sucking it up and looking for the breakthrough. It can take me many minutes, sometimes hours (and occasionally days), to calm down and own my sh!t. Yet is it always possible. As you begin to master how to hold it down, the amount of time it takes to recover from your reactions gets smaller. Eventually you'll find that you can remain loving, even laughing, when a curve ball comes rushing toward you.

Here's the ABC of holding our sh!t down:

Attention

First, you want to bring the insane power of your attention to the problem you are facing. The more you bring it into your awareness, the less extreme your reactions are likely to be. Assuming you are physically safe (if you aren't, let your stress response do its thing), you can then observe, with as much distance as possible, what it feels like to react. Is there a squirrely feeling in your belly? Do you feel hot or cold? Do you feel nauseous or want to vent your rage? Do you want to hit something or run away and hide under a blanket?

In this moment, you are now boosting the capacity of the insula in your brain to spot changes in your body so you can alter things. This is how elite athletes outperform others. The more you practice becoming aware and attentive when you are triggered, the quicker you will sense the charge before it becomes a full-blown hurricane. Now, if you become aware that you are beginning to react, you can excuse yourself from the situation until you have allowed the wave of stress to recede.

Meanwhile, let go of any desire to blame yourself or anyone else. Instead . . .

Breathe (and Bounce)

Before responding to anything that feels at all difficult, particularly when your nervous system is over-excited, you have to calm down. A great way to do this is to take long, chilled-out breaths, deep into your abdomen. As you do this, breathe the blame, shame, and complain away. Studies show that this kind of breathing can prevent the obsessive whirring thoughts that often accompany a reaction.[11] This kind of breathing can also boost your Heart Rate Variability,[12] a key mark of shifting into the reconnection response and the thrivability it brings. Every human being can use their breath to put the brakes on their reactions and override the Survival Trip. You don't have to be an expert meditator to do it. Just breathe as calmly, deeply, and effortlessly as possible.

Another powerful way to release a build-up of tension in a healthy way is to move your body.mind. Stretch out, shake your limbs, jack your body, flick your hands out. It's all good. Movement and exercise not only helps to reduce stress but also the risk of both emotional and physical disease.[13-15] Singing can also help. By bouncing around like this, you release energetic tension from the system. As you breathe and bounce (**HANDS**), you'll start to feel more peaceful (**HEART**), and think more clearly (**HEAD**).

Curiosity

Time to explore the problem. What could this intense experience mean for you? What triggered it? Have you noticed being triggered like this before? What are the commonalities? What might open up because of these insights? How might the problem be a springboard to dive into the Thrive Drive?

Questions like these activate our upper brain, especially the prefrontal cortex, which stimulates our curiosity and coaxes out our creativity.[16] The more interested we get in finding the missing pieces to our own puzzle—the puzzle of how to live a thrivadelic life—the easier it is to bring the full force of our brilliance to bear on our problems. Studies show that the more inspired we are, the higher our attention is, *and* the longer it lasts. This leads to increased creativity. We can create the right conditions for ourselves to become inspired by staying open and curious.[17] In fact, staying curious is the single character trait most associated with creativity![18] When you cultivate a sense of curiosity, you can embark on the Breakthrough Curve willingly, rather than slide down it on your butt!

No matter what the provocation, you *can* keep it down long enough to switch on and move forward with curiosity and courage. Even if you're a little apprehensive, you can trust that no matter what the problem is—no matter how enormous or threatening it may feel—there is always a creative way forward. Every problem has within it the seeds of a breakthrough that can leave you feeling more empowered, more peaceful, and with a more expressed purpose.

A problem is an invitation to come fully alive and open up to what is possible in the space between you and the world.

SWITCH ON TO PROBLEMS

Switched Off: A problem is proof that the world sucks, that people are out to get us, or that something is wrong.

Switched On: A problem is an opportunity to grow by discovering ways to boost peace, purpose, and power within, which we can then use creatively to break through a blockage in the world.

 SWITCH ON NOW

Start by bringing to mind (and body) a current problem.

HANDS: Scan your entire body.mind slowly, from your feet to the top of your head.

Do you feel any tension at all? Any stress? How would you describe it? How do you want to react? Fight? Flight? Freeze?

If you're sensing a 'charge' to or from it, shake your limbs around.

Bring your awareness into the space around your solar plexus (the area between your ribs and belly button). Consciously breathe into it. As you do, allow any tension there to ease away.

How does it feel to hold it down like this? Log how it feels.

HEAD: What is your mind saying about this problem? Have you noticed it say this kind of thing before? Does your mind want it to be your fault? Someone else's fault?

Now, name five things that happened today that you're grateful for, no matter how small or ordinary. Can you say thank you for each one?

HEART: Can you feel any fear? Any anxiety? Worry?

As you shake, move, and breathe, can you transform any charge within into a sense of curiosity about what the future might bring?

With this curiosity in place, can you bring the problem fully into your whole body.mind as you own it, so you are ready to transform it and enjoy the breakthrough?

BREAKTHROUGH QUESTIONS

Your body.mind moves in the direction of the questions you ask it. Some questions inspire and motivate you, while others limit your creativity and sense of freedom. Ask **disempowering** questions, such as, 'Why does this always happen to me?' and you get disempowering answers like, 'Because I am a loser.' Breakthrough Questions flip this around. They help you to think constructively, switching on parts of your body.mind that flip out when you get stressed out.[19] This connects you to your upper brain and so enables more creative and considered responses to life.

 If I were the most pronoid person that has ever lived, optimistic, positive, and trusting, what could this cloud's silver lining be?

 What does everyone usually say about this kind of problem, and if I ignore those opinions, what opportunity could I see in it?

Session 02

Patterns

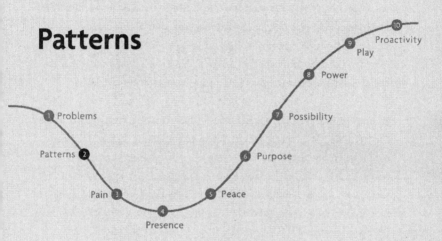

OUR PATTERNS ARE VERY much like those old-fashioned cards used in knitting machines. You stick in a 'pattern card' and the machine produces the sweater shown on the card. In the same way, our reactions to problems are designed to give a predictable result, even at the cost of creativity and happiness. Just as a building reveals something about the architect, each **pattern** we use tells us something about how we developed our personality. Each points us toward areas within us that are ready to be transformed. No matter how ugly they might seem to us (and others), our patterns are the breadcrumb trail we need to follow to find our way to breakthrough. As weeds are plants whose virtues have not yet been discovered (to paraphrase the philosopher Ralph Waldo Emerson), our patterns are possibilities for breakthrough waiting to be revealed.

The clematis, a climbing vine found in gardens from Shanghai to San Diego, usually flowers with four petals, which are shaped like little bells. This is true across perhaps 250 species of clematis worldwide. However, every now again, you might spot a plant that flowers with anything up to ten petals. This isn't because of a genetic mutation. Stress, the same kind that messes up our lives, triggers it. It can take years for a freaked-out clematis to return to form. Moving the plant, repotting it, or a bad frost can all trigger the plant to react in this way. Given that plants don't (as far as we know) have anything like the rich, creative consciousness of human beings, it's not surprising that we develop even more imaginative patterns when we have been stressed.

Patterns are . . . slamming phones, compulsively working, trying to get in the final word, thinking there is a right way to do something, being inauthentic, gossiping behind people's backs, playing the fool, avoiding conflict, continuously looking in the cookie jar, reaching for a cigarette, repeated procrastination, and a million more. If you find yourself being rigid, closed-minded, fearful, or lacking flexibility, then it's likely that you're stuck inside one of your patterns.

A simple way of defining a pattern is a predictable response to a specific type of situation. It will always be made up of a symphony of HANDS, HEAD, and HEART components. That means emotions and feelings; beliefs, stories, myths, **assumptions**; and habits, actions, movements. The most obvious patterns are those that pop out when we are tired, feel attacked, in the middle of a conflict, a little ill, or overwhelmed. This is because we have less energy and attention to keep them locked down.

Some patterns are designed to save our lives, such as driving safely. So let's keep them. Some are useful, like brushing our teeth automatically before we go to bed. Let's keep those ones too. But when we become ruled by our patterns, we cannot adapt to the changing nature of the world around us and so cannot thrive. Any time we *react* to a problem with a familiar habit, an established belief system, and a persistent emotion—rather than actively co-creating something fresh in the moment—we are running a limiting pattern.

Like the petals on the clematis, the patterns that limit our potential reveal to us that at some point, somewhere, we were stressed out. We created or copied the pattern because we thought it would protect us and/or get us what we want. No matter how we end up with them, patterns signal that we are stuck in a Survival Trip—even if we don't feel stressed out any more. In fact, the main function of each pattern has been to minimize stress and maximize **order** (although, as we will find out, they often end up generating both stress and disorder). What is lost with each pattern is creativity. Every time we become aware of a pattern that is limiting us, it is a juicy opportunity to have a breakthrough.

Trigger unhappy

IF WE LOOK AT ourselves honestly, we'll probably find that much of what we say or do follows a pattern to some degree, as opposed to being a specific-to-that-moment created thought or act. Patterns dominate our way of being. Although they will often share similar features with those of others, each pattern—with its specific mix of **HANDS**, **HEAD**, and **HEART** elements—is unique to us. We might think that reacting the way we do is totally 'normal' and 'what everyone does.' Yet, on closer inspection, we will usually discover that some elements of it are idiosyncratic. That helps us own them fully. These are our foibles (and breakthroughs) and nobody else's!

Here is a simple example of one of my patterns (which I am enjoying breaking through):

'Dad, can I have a snack?'

'We just had breakfast. Let's wait a while.'

'Dad, I want a snack.'

'Not yet, darling.'

'Dad, I'm hungry, please can I have a snack?'

'Son, I told you, you can have one later.'

(A few minutes of silence.)

'Hmm. I want a snack now!'

grrrrrrrrrr BAM!

My **HANDS** become tense. Maybe I hit the steering wheel or the kitchen table. My **HEAD** thinks and sometimes shouts: 'NO! Stop asking me. You always get lovely snacks at snack time so why are you being such a %^@er about it?' My **HEART**, if I have enough self-awareness to sense the state it's in, might feel powerless, not appreciated, and trapped.

My body.mind has been triggered into a powerful stress response. The emotion circuits have gone haywire. My upper brain, especially the prefrontal cortex, has stopped being able to hold my sh!t down. Tunnel vision makes me focus on the issue, stopping me being able to think openly, and fixing on one frame of perception. A **story**—that my son is trying to mess with my head on purpose—pops up, limits my compassion, and tanks all creativity. A potent cocktail of adrenalin and cortisol is coursing through my arteries, damaging my cells for no reason. I am no longer connected to him or myself. I am totally switched off.

In this moment, and hundreds more like it each week, I have become the pattern as opposed to being a switched on, creative human being. I can neither feel the sunshine nor smell the roses. What's more, when I react to my son with an anger pattern, he naturally feels threatened and so reacts back. An hour, sometimes a day, of shared happiness will be frittered away while we both run our offense/defense patterns. We'll never get that time back. It may seem like a small instance, no big deal, but put all these kinds of moments together across a year and they add up to a large chunk of life spent missing out on gorgeous times and brilliant fun.

Thankfully I'm aware of this pattern and many of the others that prevent me from being my fully loving, imaginative, and generous self. As each year of switched on living passes, I get better at holding down my reactions and using the moment to enjoy a breakthrough. I have discovered ways to rewire my patterns so that I can wake up *before* I act out and hurt the people I treasure (at least sometimes). By switching on in such mundane moments of life, I learn to how to flow with the challenges I face.

> **Every problem, every trigger, is a moment to break from the predictability of the past and invent a new possibility that brings more love into the present whilst also shaping the future.**

All patterns stop us being creative in this moment,

RIGHT HERE . . . RIGHT NOW

that has never existed before. They suck the creativity out of the system we are in—whether family, community, or at work—imploding fields of possibility and shutting down rich, alternative futures.

Patterns create more problems

THINK ABOUT THE VARIOUS ways you respond when you encounter
a problem. What happens to your HANDS, HEAD, and HEART when,
for example:

- A driver cuts you up dangerously?
- A trusted colleague or lover criticizes you harshly?
- You're passed over for a major promotion or miss out on funding
  for a project?
- You think about the state of the environment or child poverty?
- You want to get your own way and feel unheard?
- You want to get laid (or avoid it) in a bar or club?
- Your children's bickering has developed into a full-scale war?
- You walk into the gym?
- You read books like this?
- You look in a mirror?

Even if the patterns you run make you look or feel smart, cool, or in control,
can you see how they might be preventing you from being tender and
open-hearted? Can you imagine they might be stopping you from accessing
unique fields of possibility, which are ready to sprout when you respond in a
different way?

What is that costing you? What problems are your patterns creating?

Our patterns were designed to create predictable results. They are there to
guarantee an outcome: Either less of what we didn't like (neglect, criticism,
or powerlessness) or more of what we did (praise, attention, or control).
Like a train on a track, once we start to roll with our patterns, there can
only be one, pre-arranged destination. That might be . . . losing it, floods of
tears, avoiding people, shutting ourselves in a room, threats of ending it, or
pouring a glass of wine, rolling a joint, or reaching for porn. Whatever the
end point, the outcome can only change if we lay down new track as we go.

Established patterns often create more problems than they solve because the old ways of acting (**HANDS**), thinking (**HEAD**), and feeling (**HEART**) are no longer fit for purpose. What worked wonderfully on the savannah in Africa doesn't work so well in an office cubicle in Savannah, Georgia. What worked brilliantly when we started our career as an intern at a multinational may not work so well in a Silicon Valley start-up. What worked well as a five-year-old to keep our parents happy may not work so well as a lover or spouse.

Patterns tend to reduce our fittedness. Once a pattern is locked in place, whether it is to avoid pain or boost pleasure, it stops us adapting, inventing, and thriving in the now. This is why so many of our patterns sabotage our potential. They are rigid and not spontaneous; brittle, and not **biodynamic**.

It's easy to see the stuff in the outside world as the problem. Yet the real problem is really *how we react*. There are no problems if we respond in peaceful, purposeful, and powerful ways. Businesses don't go bankrupt for no reason. People don't divorce randomly. People don't just get depressed. When these things happen it is usually because the patterns being used to deal with life are no longer appropriate or useful. There is a fittedness gap. The result can be dramatic but the logic is plain (if we look with 100 percent response-ability). Our patterns temporarily remove fear and tension from our body.mind system when under stress. But, as we grow up and change, then they start to push people and possibility away, which ends up creating more stress, more problems.

Rely on old patterns that are no longer relevant and you'll always encounter problems. The great news is that as your patterns were *created* at some point, then they can also be uncreated, or broken through, just like LEGO. Adult brains can create new neurons as well as trim and change existing neural pathways.[1] So we can break through our patterns by rewiring our brains (and bodies). To do that, we have to understand how and why patterns form.

STOP BEING A JOKER

If we continue to use outdated patterns later in life, we risk failing. When I was being bullied at school for being overweight, I made up a whole load of patterns to help me get by. I became funny (well, comical at least). I became smart. I even tried my hand at being cool. Today, all of these patterns can be useful. However, being a joker, intellectual, or hipster can also stop me feeling connected to those around me and limit my scope.

It's not about rejecting any of these patterns. It's about being able to choose which is most appropriate, what fits best, and what is going to create the most thrivadelic outcome for all involved. Is it letting out that joke that has just bubbled up into my mouth? Or is it taking a sincere interest in the issue someone is sharing with me? There is always a win–win–win (win for you, win for me, and win for the world) available in every situation, no matter how many competing agendas there are. But if we play out old patterns without choice, without awareness, we are unlikely to find them.

Eight-lane superhighways of the mind

ALL MAMMALS USE MIMICRY to learn. It is one of the things that makes humans such a successful species. We spend our formative years copying the patterns of people who care for us. Our parents, teachers, friends, and enemies all leave an imprint, like a boot on snow. We also mimic the patterns we see in adverts or magazines, thinking they may help us to be cool, rich, or sexy. We might take on the patterns of the teachers or bosses that we respect (and those we fear) because we figure this might be the best way to succeed. After a while, we may no longer be sure whether our beliefs and behaviors are our own, inherited from our parents, or acquired from the world around us. Every now and again we might also invent a brand-new pattern if we need to.

With each pattern, a series of nerve pathways is active, connecting millions of neurons through synapses all the way through our body.mind, from toe to cerebral cortex. Every time we react with the pattern, the same sets of nerves fire. As they fire together, they wire, ever stronger, together. Over time, each pattern becomes coded into our body.mind as a tangible imprint in our nervous system. Each one of these unique **neural signatures** can be observed in brain scanners and is always ready to be activated whenever we are triggered. Some neural signatures are used so often that the neurons within them become myelinated (myelin is the white stuff that insulates neurons), which makes them transmit up to 50 times faster. This is like turning a small country road into a freeway; we become ever speedier to react.

There's a good reason for having such quick reactions. If we had to study a saber-toothed tiger for a few minutes before deciding whether to run away or reach out and stroke it, we wouldn't be around long enough to develop a pattern. So we use a rule-of-thumb to make a quick decision. This is what happens when we are using Type 1 thinking (see Prelude, page 14). Patterns are fast, reliable, and efficient ways to deal with the world.[2] We rely on them to help us negotiate our way through the dangers of living. If everything we did were always an act of pure creativity, invented in the moment, we would be overwhelmed by the simple act of making a cup of coffee.

Once a pattern has proven its use, it gets stored in the lower brain, especially in the basal ganglia. Here, it's ready to be used without any excess energy being needed. Nature loves efficiency! This process is known in behavioral science as **conditioning**. First brought to fame by Ivan Pavlov and his dogs, conditioning is what happens when you train animals to react in a certain way to specific triggers. Blow a whistle when you give a dog food and, after a few days of repetition, just blowing the whistle will trigger the dog to salivate. Repeatedly show arousing hot guys in Diet Coke commercials serving up cans of pop at 11 a.m., and some people will start to want some of the fizzy stuff when they take their morning break. We can even be conditioned to associate smells with sounds *while we sleep*! Even while in a coma, patients can be conditioned to blink when air is puffed into their eyes.[3]

Our body.mind can be conditioned to respond in a predictable way to pretty much anything, relatively quickly, just by repetition. We store up all the useful **conditioned responses** in the lower brain (and beyond). If, as an infant, we liked the feeling of getting our own way when we whined, then it can easily become a pattern. If we learned that being angry felt better than being scared, we will probably get angry now when we feel threatened. If having a tantrum helped to release stress and restore balance to our system as toddlers then it is highly likely that it will be conditioned into our nervous system and pop back out whenever we get overwhelmed as adults.

Before long, a reaction that may have begun life as a vague goat track in the nervous system—say a negative reaction to something our parents did when we were young—becomes an eight-lane superhighway. For example, let's say we used to get really upset when our parents left for work. It both scared us and saddened us. So we developed a pattern of anxiety around people leaving. Fast-forward ten or twenty years, and we will be super-sensitive to goodbyes with the people we love. Even the mere hint of a departure might trigger us to get anxious. We will probably have invented another pattern to cover up the anxiety (which is painful), like pretending we don't care. Then people around us think we don't care when they leave, so they make no effort, which is exactly the opposite of what we want. This is low fittedness and thriving is unlikely. We won't be aware that this is going on. We will just execute the conditioned response like one of Pavlov's dogs. Woof!

For thousands of years, generals have relied on the meaty power of conditioning to ensure predictable responses in their troops. Take soldiers away from their normal environment, put them in uniform, train them to duck when they hear a blast and attack when they hear a whistle, and they become formidable fighting machines. Conditioning can also, tragically, be at play when those same soldiers return home. While in the war zone, they will have been conditioned to respond to bomb explosions or machine-gun fire with quite natural fear or aggression (flight or fight). So, each time they experience something similar back home, like a car misfiring or train going by, they can react with that pattern. This can destroy any chance of a normal life until the conditioning is unpicked and resolved.

Just like a police or cab dispatcher who is tasked to get vehicles to their destination in the quickest time possible, our body.mind uses the path of

THE DOPAMINE RUSH

The multiple roles of dopamine in motivation are still being unpicked by scientists, but what we do know is that dopamine helps us focus on what we need, what we like, and what is new and thrilling. It urges us to forage for food and fornicate (to reproduce), the mainstays of survival. The nucleus accumbens is packed full of dopamine, and stimulates both the planning and emotion-processing regions, rewarding anticipation, prediction, and goal-achievement.[4] Our brains also provide us a little reward of dopamine when we see a pattern we recognize. This explains why we can get hooked on seeing the world as we want it to be, and disappointed when our expectations are not met. Dopamine also seems to be key for our capacity as human beings to hold a possibility in our body.mind for years while we strive to bring it to life.

Dopamine also 'tags' experiences and puts them into pigeonholes in our memory. Experiences that are intense or meaningful are highlighted, including both painful and pleasurable moments from our past. This gears us toward avoiding or craving certain experiences and so powering-up our patterns. Chocolate (and other more toxic drugs) flood the brain with dopamine, causing intense thrills. Addictive substances can also alter cell receptors and transmitters in the brain, which can be tough to reverse.[5] Doing sport, hanging out with friends, and even listening to music release rushes of dopamine, which might explain the powerful cocktail that is dance, dance floor, and drugs.

The dopamine pathways and the nucleus accumbens get out of kilter when we become addicted to something, whether tweeting, sex, food, or drugs. We keep on seeking out the chills and thrills, even when we know they aren't good for us. Unfortunately, the rush of dopamine is more intense when we anticipate something, as opposed to when we actually get it. We get a juicier rush for planning and buying a bag of chips than we do from actually eating them. So it's easy to get locked into a cycle of constant cravings (whether for cake or cocaine) that doesn't stop even when we get what we desire. If we want to rewire our brains away from addiction of any kind, we need to find a way to hack into this powerful system.

least resistance to react. The most used neural signatures fire over and over again, conditioning our responses still deeper. Over the years, entire areas of our body.mind get recruited into the neural signature of a pattern. It ends up containing words, memories, movements, sounds, and emotions in full panoramic richness. As soon as we spot something in our environment that has been associated with a conditioned response, dopamine fires and we will be triggered. This is why we spend so much time reacting. Our incredible pattern-spotting skills tell us that we are seeing dangers and disappointments everywhere, even if we are slightly mistaken. The system works on a 'better safe than sorry' principle: Better to run the pattern when it's not needed than not to run it when it is needed and not survive to tell the tale.

This is a double-edged sword. On the positive side, our ability to spot common themes in the world around us quickly enables a whole range of wonderfully human skills: A doctor spotting an abnormality on an X-ray in seconds; a DJ spotting a new vibe emerging and changing the track; or a parent spotting the telltale signs of toddler tiredness. The downer is that we often see patterns where there are none. We take a thin slice of information from our reality and our system guesses at what it might mean for us. Often we have jumped to a conclusion but it's too late because we're already triggered. What happens next is . . . predictable, of course.

Our patterns shape us. We not only have predictable responses to the world, but soon we start to see the world in a predictable way too. We develop frames that make an unruly and chaotic reality seem consistent and coherent. We look through the frame at everything, interpreting everything according to how we have been conditioned. We happily (but unconsciously) jettison information that might challenge our dominant world-view (see cognitive biases, page 67). This is how **projection** works. We see 'out there' what has been imprinted 'in here.' For example, if we have been conditioned to react aggressively, we will interpret situations to be confrontational, which will justify our aggression. We twist reality to fit our conditioned responses and the memories associated with them. We then make sense of these distortions by acquiring and/or making up a set of beliefs that cast our habits and reactions as totally normal and natural.

We excuse and justify our patterns with a personal mythology. This is the 'story' we enact each day as we walk around pattern-spotting and pattern-reacting our way through life.

Spinning stories

IMAGINE THIS. THE PHONE rings. You're tired. It's been one of those days. A load of angst comes streaming through the handset. Your boss/accountant/ partner/parent/child is worried but, to you, it feels like an attack when you just don't need it. You feel a charge within your body.mind, propelling you to run away or attack them back. You start to react. As you do, a story pops into your mind about why they are being this way, and why they deserve the response you're giving them. You are now the hero or heroine, who's always right; and they are the villain, who is clearly wrong. A little while later, once you have chilled out, you might feel guilty and enact another story that now puts you in the role of villain who should be blamed.

We spin stories like this from the moment we get up to the moment we go to bed, all in an attempt to make sense of what is happening to us and how we are reacting to it. Organizations and countries also spin stories that help them stay in control and minimize the discomfort of uncertainty and risk of failure. We tell ourselves bits of these stories through constant chatter in our mind, called **self-talk** (or backchat!). Our HANDS act, our HEAD explains it, and our HEART is locked into a specific emotional sensation to match. Some of this self-talk is useful and **empowering**. However, a lot is disempowering. The stories we tell change our life for good or ill, depending on the narrative. Is the story you are telling yourself right now one of freedom and creativity, or one of limitation and hopelessness?

If our self-talk is critical, it will always limit us. If we hear ourselves blaming someone, shaming them, or complaining about them, it is definitely a disempowering story. The same goes for blaming, shaming, or complaining about ourselves. On the other hand, positive self-talk can make all the difference. In one classic study, gymnasts in the US Olympic team in the 1970s were interviewed to discover what their self-talk was like. The highest performers were those who constantly encouraged themselves with positive and empowering stories. They spun stories about how brilliant they were. And then, in reality, they would fulfill that prophecy.[6]

> **Whether you tell yourself you can or can't do something —you are right. This may be worth remembering next time you hear yourself saying 'I can't do . . .'**

THE STORYTELLING BRAIN

Our brain doesn't just like to create reasons for things happening. It has to! There is a compulsive storyteller within us all, generating a rationale for everything. We are compelled to make sense out of things that may not make much sense so that we feel a bit more certain and settled. Just as nature abhors a vacuum, humans hate a vacuum of meaning. So, when faced with uncertainty and confusion, we fall back on familiar stories to provide us with some comfort about what is happening around us.

A few decades ago, a pair of neuroscientists began experimenting with people whose brains had been split into two during surgery to treat severe epilepsy (one was eventually awarded the Nobel Prize for the work). In studies, patients with such 'split brains' happily make up stories for why they choose an image in a matching task, even though the left side of the brain (responsible for much of the story-creation) has no way of knowing why the other side of the brain (which it is not connected to), chose a particular image.[7]

Likewise, patients with retrograde amnesia make up stories about the periods in their lives they can't remember. They tend to weave real and made-up things together into a coherent narrative. They don't think that they are inventing these stories. When it's suggested that their stories might be untrue, they get very upset (as all of us do if we are made out to be lying when we believe we are telling the truth).[8]

We tend to project our stories onto other people, labeling them as say 'stubborn' or 'sexy,' when really these are the themes of the self-talk inside us. What occupies our attention within will be projected onto others. This is how the darkside (see Session 01, page 40) gets darkest. We don't own our stories but push them onto other people, casting them as assholes and ourselves as awesome (or the other way around if we have low self-esteem). We become totally unresponse-able and uncreative as a result.

Now, to some extent we are all *always* projecting our beliefs and assumptions onto others. After all, we see the world through our eyes, not anybody else's. However, with a little effort, we can make like an anthropologist and travel into the world of others, which helps us understand more about both their stories and our own. The more fresh insight we collect on our travels, the more breakthroughs we can have.

Inside every story, whether about ourselves or others, is a set of implicit assumptions and beliefs. These act as the girders and support columns of the story. We assume things about human nature, science, God, the economy, our past, our future, the industry we work within—everything—so that we don't have to question our stories. Plato called them **'noble lies'** because they are there for a 'good' reason. These assumptions are packaged up into stories, and become hidden away so we no longer notice them. We don't see our stories as being fictional. We see them as truth. We then defend our assumptions vigorously, often arguing for our own **lack** of power when others believe in us!

While some assumptions are empowering, many limit us by dictating what can and can't be done in the world. If a computer manufacturer assumes all computers should be beige, they'll never invent an iMac. If a young man assumes all women are crazy, it will be tough to date one that isn't.

Limiting beliefs and out-of-date assumptions prevent breakthroughs and constrain creativity.

Every single personal choice, job role, business model, political ideology, or scientific theory is based on a set of assumptions. They are rarely questioned by anyone, which is why often they end up not fitting with the world as it changes. Every life philosophy, whether conscious or not, is based on a series of assumptions. That means that every one of the seven billion or so people alive who are making choices are doing so based on assumptions that are unlikely ever to be tested. If we want to change our story to open up new fields of possibility, we must **surface** our own assumptions.

Finish the following sentences with whatever first comes into your body. mind. Don't second-guess, edit your words, or try and look good. Just answer from the top of your head.

- **When it comes to creativity, I am . . .**
- **When it comes to relationships, I am . . .**
- **The way to get ahead in life is to . . .**
- **The ideal boss would . . .**
- **All men are . . .**

Take a moment to reflect on the words that came to you. This is just a quick way of beginning to surface your assumptions. It's not always accurate, but it can be surprising. A more rigorous way to bring them into awareness is to keep asking yourself, 'Why is this the case?' or 'Why do I believe this?' until you get to an answer that can go no further: An ultimate assumption. Imagine yourself going from the tip of the iceberg (the initial belief) down and down until you get to the ultimate assumption. This deepest driver of your story will usually be a belief about human nature and our place in the universe. In other words, our everyday stories about ourselves contain our ultimate assumptions about life itself. This is why we are all living by a life philosophy, all the time. Here are some examples of everyday assumptions and the ultimate assumptions they could be based on, as well as some common problems that might emerge if we hold onto them in everyday life.

♣ ASSUMPTIONS ARE THE MOTHER OF ALL $#&*-UPS

Most people believe they are better drivers than average. Do you? What about an above-average lover? Not everybody can be though—many of us need to be average or below average to make the spread work. The story that we are above average is characterized as the 'self-serving bias' or the Lake Wobegon Effect, one of the many 'cognitive biases' permeating our body.mind. They have us think in ways that may not be 100 percent rational but are useful because they impose some sense onto a seemingly senseless world.

One of the most important is the 'confirmation bias.' We seek evidence that supports our existing beliefs and ignore or reinterpret evidence that goes against them. We even attract people into our life who have similar stories to our own and can 'confirm' our belief systems. Hence moaners attract moaners and visionaries attract visionaries. They reinforce each other's guiding narratives.[9] When our stories become out-of-date and redundant, instead of changing them we usually dig our heels in and believe in them even more. People will happily change their opinion about a political initiative depending on which party they are told came up with the idea.[10]

Scientific research is riddled with these cognitive biases too (which is natural as the people who do science are human beings). What we are told are 'facts' are really data points that have been interpreted within a coherent story about how nature works. We call those kinds of stories 'theories.' The ruling story of the day is called the 'truth' (for a while). Scientists, under the spell of biases, tend to discount data points that don't fit the story by calling them 'anomalies.' When enough of these outliers start showing up, as they did before quantum mechanics was accepted, the story (or theory) has to change to accommodate them. This then gets described as a breakthrough.[11] Our personal story also has to change if we want to have a breakthrough in any area of our lives.

The 'Life is tough' story
Ultimate assumptions about human nature/the universe

Life is a battle against the odds to stay alive. We have to compete with others, tooth and nail, for scarce resources to get our share. It's a dog-eat-dog, survival-of-the-fittest reality. The weak die. The strong survive.

Problems that might emerge, driven by patterns

- High levels of stress, and near permanent exhaustion, reinforce the story that life is tough. This fuels complaints, such as, 'Why is it always so difficult?'
- A competitive, verging on combative, attitude in the workplace that limits collaboration and connection with colleagues.
- Trouble sharing with, and being supported by, colleagues, friends, and family. This leads to energy depletion, which further reinforces the story. Project onto others by calling them unsupportive.

The 'men are untrustworthy' story
Ultimate assumptions about human nature/the universe

Biologically, men are driven to have sex and move on. They can't help but be untrustworthy because they don't have the capacity to be romantically true.

Problems that might emerge, driven by patterns

- To defend against being let down, intimacy is avoided, which leads to unfulfilling relationships where trust cannot blossom.
- Protective patterns stop more vulnerable, open, and trustworthy men getting near. Instead, to confirm the story, there is a tendency to attract (and be attracted to) untrustworthy men, which reinforces the story and fuels complaints such as, 'Why do I always hook up with assholes?'

The 'eating/drinking/smoking helps me relax' story
Ultimate assumptions about human nature/the universe

The body is like a machine. It can be made to relax with certain substances. There is no need to learn how to manage our own stress when substances can do it for us.

Problems that might emerge, driven by patterns

- A tendency to believe that external substances work, which leads to over-reliance and possibly addiction.
- Cravings take up lots of energy to manage, which amplifies stress, so making it even harder to relax without more of the substance. If you become concerned about addiction, shift into an 'I'm stopping/binge' cycle.

- Addiction triggers shame and guilt, fueling more stress and complaints, which drives more reliance on substances.

Virtually all the assumptions we have, and the stories that form around them to explain them, are based on the ideas of the 4-, 7-, or 15-year-old we were when we invented them. Which means the life philosophies that run our lives were created by younger versions of ourselves. Kids and teens are not only missing some key insights about life; they also have very fertile imaginations!

Many of the assumptions and stories we have picked up are from parents, teachers, and other people in our lives who may never have stopped to question their own assumptions, stories, and habits. Even cartoon and movie characters transmit assumptions. The creators of kid's stories don't tend to spend much time examining their assumptions and checking their veracity! Every story we read or watched on TV as kids contained a bundled-up load of beliefs, which we may have taken on. Wile E. Coyote's life philosophy anyone?

The stories, assumptions, and life philosophies we acquire become a self-fulfilling prophecy. We strive to behave in ways that fit our story. The brain observes what we do and uses it to guide our future behavior. And then we spin a story that explains it away.[12] The only way to escape this cycle is to break through the pattern, change the story, let go of old assumptions, and invent a new behavior. If you want to change the world, your business, or your family life, first you have to change the story that dominates it. Stories don't change the world but they do change the people who change the world. Creating an empowering narrative for the future (and helping people find their place within it) is what leadership is all about, whether you are leading just yourself or others too.

We can lead first ourselves, and then others, into new possibilities by breaking through the old assumptions and weaving a fresh, future-focused story in their place.

Putting up a front

WHEN STEAM IS COOLED to below freezing, it becomes a series of snowflakes. This is one of the fascinating phenomena that complexity science studies. It turns out that no two snowflakes are the same, and have never been the same, although the natural 'laws' that create them are constant and relatively simple. Each snowflake is a logical consequence of all the variables that went into its formation and the way the laws of physics work. Temperature, humidity, altitude, and location all help shape the beautiful and utterly unique six-fold symmetry of each snowflake.

In the same way, your patterns are all unique yet logical consequences of the variables within your past. Genes, other cellular contents, environment, experience, and setting all go to shape your patterns. Put all your patterns together and you get your personality, which is really an über-story that attempts to pull together all the individual patterns to form a more-or-less-fixed idea of who you are, what you are like, and what you can do in life.

Within your personality will be a number of **personality traits**. Often, they don't integrate well and hold conflicting views, which makes life confusing for us and the people we engage with. The American poet Walt Whitman captures this tragicomic reality when he says in 'Song of Myself', 'Do I contradict myself? Very well then, I contradict myself. (I am large. I contain multitudes.)' Our contradicting and jostling personality traits are mostly make-believe, but we do whatever we can to keep believing them, in order to keep the illusion of a stable personality. To break it down:

Each pattern = Conditioned responses + Stories + Assumptions

All patterns = Personality = Set of personality traits

In Greek, the word *persona*, from which personality is derived, means 'mask.' The patterns we exhibit, the stories we tell about them, and the assumptions underpinning them are masks. We put each mask on to deal with the challenges we face. Each personality trait is a mask. They help us to hide our fears and vulnerabilities away. They are like walls that we erect to keep out danger and make ourselves strong, even if that strength is inauthentic or illusory. This is our **front**.

Sadly, many of us spend so long hiding behind our front that we become fooled into thinking it's who we really are. We believe our own hype. But our personality is *not* who we are. It is who we have *become*. It is not that we are jealous. It is that we've learned to be jealous to help us deal with certain situations. Deep down we aren't stingy or mean. We have just learned to respond in a stingy or mean way. We are not angry. We just get angry sometimes. We didn't decide to be an asshole. We just become that way in moments of stress. Front is an act. There is something way more authentic behind it.

Let go of the front and our true nature, our essence, comes shining through.

There is a major difference between *being* a certain way, and *feeling* or *acting* that way in stressful situations. Your prefrontal cortex and upper brain stop being able to dampen down your emotional, lower brain under stress. Patterns pop out in these moments. As soon as you realize that you are not limited to your patterns or your personality, you open up space for creativity. You are no longer condemned to be a control freak, coward, or convict. Everything becomes possible.

You are more than your patterns. You are more than the stories you tell about yourself. You are way more than your front. Your friends and enemies are not their patterns either; they are also more. When you forgive yourself your human nature to have patterns, you can never be so hard on yourself, or anyone else, again. Compassion for your own quirks and foibles (patterns) is a prerequisite for breaking through. It also means you will be more understanding of others. As the saying goes, only the condemned, condemn.

We are all a work-in-progress. We can train ourselves to see people as they really are, their essence, before stress and fear triggered them to become someone else.

The curious thing is that our patterns are brilliantly helpful at providing us with the insight we need to break through. We cannot transform what we are oblivious to. Spotting the pattern gives us the opening we need for breakthrough.

There is always a clear, sensible logic behind every personality type, even those that appear totally insane or obnoxious. Unpicking that logic is the key to being able consistently to break through our patterns. So let's look at three classic personality types, three flavors of front. Bear in mind that everyone might play at being these personality types (and many more besides) within even just one day.

Front 1: The Big Shot

Arrogance is a pattern that aims to protect people from feeling vulnerable. They puff up to ensure that they don't feel powerless or insignificant. You can see animals doing this when confronted by a predator: They try to appear bigger than they are. The Big Shot pattern attempts to stop anyone from getting close to their weak spots. It may well work for a while. Perhaps it helps charm a date or two in college. It might even help them bluff their way into a job where swagger and boast are valued. However, relying on this pattern when trying to engage in an intimate relationship or collaborative project is likely to end in problems.

Friends and colleagues of people putting up this front will typically say: 'I can't get near them!' or 'I don't feel they ever see me.' If they have any sense, after a while they'll get the hell away. Cue even bigger problems. But the Big Shot will be tempted to blame these problems on everyone around them, because it takes vulnerability to own their problems. Eventually, if they don't break through, they will enter breakdown, perhaps with burnout or loneliness.

Front 2: The Control Freak

The desire to control the unpredictability of our surroundings kicks in as an infant and is totally normal. Yet if our earlier years are particularly uncertain or stressful, we may start trying to control *everything*. The Control Freak will develop great beliefs to justify this pattern: 'Order makes the world work' or

'Messy people are failures.' The Control Freak might be a collector of things, or get a massive kick from to-do lists and tidying up manically. Even a touch of OCD (Obsessive Compulsive Disorder) might creep in. No matter how uncertain the world is, the Control Freak knows they can control at least one thing (whether its a project, the tidiness of house, or a collection of dolls). A controlling nature can be brilliant when nailing detailed work. However, it can really make life difficult with lovers, employees, or children. What started out as a smart pattern to manage a messy, chaotic world ends up preventing them from relishing the spontaneity of those around them. They sell out creativity for the illusion of control until breakdown approaches, in one form or another.

Front 3: The Cynic

Even cynicism, which is so celebrated in many intellectual circles, is a pattern designed to help people deal with the challenges of life. If we've been let down, particularly by our parents, it's often less painful to assume that we'll always be let down by everything in future, rather than hoping and then being disappointed. The Cynic then starts to assume everyone is a bullshitter (even themselves). They pre-empt disillusionment by calling everything crap. But really, there is a part of them that just wants to believe in the magic once more.

As an adult, the Cynic is really good at spotting other people's weaknesses. They critique every dream and ridicule any crazy vision, including their own. They then invent a brilliant story that explains away their disbelief, perhaps telling themselves that 'science is built on cynicism' (which it is not). Science is built on skepticism mixed with a heady brew of optimism and imagination. But the Cynic will keep tanking people and ideas until their creativity is so diminished that they feel stuck or so disenchanted it hurts. Which is another way of saying they are in breakdown.

Breaking through patterns

As WE KNOW, WE can't change things outside our control but we can always break through our patterns. Every addiction, every foible, and every obsession is a pattern that we created to protect us. What once mystified us as inexplicable—such as eating a pack of cookies when we want to look great on the beach in two weeks' time; or ending a relationship with someone we love—suddenly becomes clear. We are exhibiting a conditioned reaction that was designed to protect us but is now messing us up. *Every* problem can be used to wake up from the trance that your patterns hold you in and start creating a more empowered response to life. Almost everybody sabotages themselves in some way with their patterns. Break these patterns, break through the front, and your true potential will shine through.

> **Switching on is not about becoming someone new. It is really about becoming who you always could have been, behind the front.**

When we are having a breakthrough, we are breaking through the patterns that have held us in place for so long. We are disturbing the way it has always been to allow something new to emerge. This is the breaking point. To do this, we have to resist the magnetic attraction of our conditioned responses and most compelling stories, no matter how bewitched we are by them. Although our patterns may seem permanent, particularly if we've been trying to break through them for years, any one of them, given time and **commitment**, can be broken through. Our neural signatures can be rewired to help us respond more creatively and spontaneously to problems in our life and in the world.

What pattern did you run with the last person you had a fight or disagreement with? How did it help you? How did it limit you? What is the story you have told yourself about what happened?

A quick way to loosen things up is to rewrite and edit the story. You can design a new one that empowers you as opposed to limits you to your conditioned response. When you change the story, you change the frame through which you see things. Changing your story **reframes** everything, including the problem itself. You can choose to see your room-mate's messy habits as an exuberant expression of creativity. Or, that they are practicing the art of living on the edge of chaos. Or, they are teaching you how to be more spontaneous and free (this is a very pronoid interpretation). You get to invent the story, the frame that enables you to be the most creative, most loving, and most authentic version of you that you choose.

Simply the act of spotting a pattern, right now, and then consciously interrupting it, can break through it. However, many of our most ingrained patterns just don't seem to shift when we try to change them. There is good reason for this. They were designed to protect us and won't go anywhere until they are not needed to protect us anymore. If we try to change them with our *thoughts*, they won't budge because they are driven by our *emotions*. We have to get into the emotional layer, the **HEART**, to rewire them. This is not always 'pleasant,' because we must enter our darkside. That means being radically response-able for our own sh!t.

Rather than do that, we may be tempted to run away from the problem (by leaving a conversation, relationship, job, project, community, etc.) rather than go further inside ourselves. It might seem a lot easier and more enjoyable. The greener grass does seem like it would be fun. However, the problem with **escape fantasies** like these is that we bring our patterns with us. They will pop up in the next relationship or job. Our patterns were designed for predictability. So we can predict that they will reappear and lead us toward a similar problem with a similar breakdown. It will just be in a different setting and with different people. It will also be a few months or years down the line, time we could have spent fulfilling our potential. Studies show that the ability to create new neural pathways, to invent new ways to respond to life, weakens with age unless you keep in mental shape.[13] As we age, we rely more and more on old patterns to help us navigate.

So, the sooner you switch on, the more patterns you get to transform and the more life you get to live. We now need to progress one stage deeper on the Breakthrough Curve to suck the full juice out of our problems.

SWITCH ON TO PATTERNS

Switched Off: A pattern is part of our personality, which is just who we are. You, me, and the rest of the world have to deal with it because people can't change.

Switched On: A pattern is a totally logical response to some kind of stress, lack, or fear. Patterns are not who we are but who we become in certain situations, when triggered. This is nothing to do with who we are in our **essence**. Patterns usually limit us, and therefore act as signals that we are poised for a breakthrough.

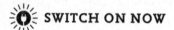 **SWITCH ON NOW**

Remind yourself of a problem you want to break through.

HANDS: How do you typically react to problems like this? What front do you put up to deal with them?

Can you remember your earliest memories of acting this way?

How do your reactions try to protect you? Are they successful? Do they have any downsides?

HEAD: What is the story you have made up about this reaction? Is anyone being shamed, blamed, or complained about?

What assumptions about people and the world are hidden away inside this story? Are they empowering or limiting?

Now edit the story and see what you come up with that is empowering. See if you can create five new stories. For each one, ensure the problem is a source of peace, purpose, possibility, power, and play for you.

HEART: When you tell yourself your usual stories, how does it feel? Where inside? Can you spot any feelings of shame or guilt?

Try on the different stories you have just invented until you find one that inspires really juicy, positive emotions inside. See if you can choose to have that story running from now on.

BREAKTHROUGH QUESTIONS

 If someone really wise had arranged this situation specifically to help me reframe things in an empowering way, how would I see the problem?

 If I was my favorite novelist or film-maker, what story could I make up about this problem that would inspire me and others to connect, create, and collaborate?

Session 03

Pain

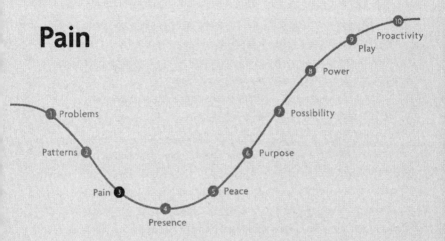

THE PATTERNS THAT REALLY limit our ability to create and thrive are hard to change through willpower alone. Disempowering stories will stick to our mind like honey to a finger if they connect with powerful emotions within. Habits will keep returning, no matter how much we want to be rid of them. This is because our most limiting patterns are there for a reason: To protect us from pain. We can manage these patterns by trying to control them, but we cannot fully break through them until the pain is dissolved. At this point, they no longer have a job to do. There are no 'quick fixes' for transformation, no matter how convenient it would be and no matter who tells you there are. Yet there is a tried and tested path available to every single human being who is prepared to follow their patterns to find the pain . . . and come out the other side again renewed.

Imagine a wide open space, a space so huge, so vast it has no horizons. It might be a limitless field of verdant green or the expansiveness of endless space. You choose what feels most *safe*, open, and free.

Take a minute to shut your eyes and feel this limitlessness.

This sense of pure possibility is everything that you could be, create, and express. It is the freedom to feel, think, and act as you choose. It is your potential to reinvent yourself continuously as your world changes, always being the incredible person you were born to be.

As far as we can tell, newborn babies don't think of themselves as individuals. They feel themselves to be fused with their mother and the world around them. Ahead of them is the potential for a thousand personality types, which will be determined by how their genes, environment, and experience interplay with each other. They (hopefully) feel oodles of love as they are held, cuddled, fed, and swaddled. Ideally, they feel an oceanic sense of safety around them. In theory, most very young babies can be left alone for quite a while and, if their basic needs are met, they will be content. However, all this is about to change. The shift can be challenging for everyone: The baby, its parents, siblings, and people in the checkout line. The baby is about to create some patterns so that it can continue to feel as safe and secure as possible.

By understanding what happens in this crucial period of development, we can learn how to 'hack' the system to rewire even the most fundamental of our patterns.

The big ouch

BEFORE A BABY REACHES their first birthday, they will start to become aware
that they are a 'thing,' an individual, not just an extension of their parents.
The baby becomes increasingly aware that there are boundaries between
what is their own body.mind and what is not. I assume (as no one can ever
really know) that they go from thinking they are at one with their parents
(and everything else) to realizing they are a totally separate being. This
can feel scary at first. Now, when they are left alone, they often cry. With
strangers, they are even more freaked out. This is called **separation anxiety**.

Separation anxiety is a totally healthy part of development and is experienced
by all babies to some extent. If you failed to separate from your parents, you
wouldn't have been able to become the unique, creative individual you are!
However, as infants, we experience this as the beginning of emotional pain.
Pain, whether emotional or physical, is felt in the same area of the brain, the
anterior cingulate cortex. Sticks, stones, and words all hurt us in the same
place. Every time we feel a *lack* of safety, security, or love we will feel an . . .

OUCH! That man who just came into our house looks scary!
OUCH! Not having my milk when I want it sucks!
OUCH! Having my toys taken from me is awful!

Quite sensibly, we protest.

OI! NO!

That NO! signifies that we want things to be different. We want more of
something (attention, cuddles, snacks) and less of other things (strangers, wet
diapers, neglect). The NO! comes out as a wail or cry, as we have few other
options. Plus, we've already discovered that doing this gets us what we want
most: Attention! Furthermore, when we cry or tantrum, our body.mind gets
a chance to release a build-up of tension, returning to a more balanced state.
When we discover language, typically between 12 and 36 months, we start

to enhance the emotional NO! using words, whining, and more. This is the time when we start to create our internal stories about the world too.

As we grow older, we experience new forms of pain, from being upset that we can't have the remote control to seeing our parents arguing. In these moments, we copy or create patterns as we respond to the emotions that are triggered. Remember, our emotions are vital evolutionary adaptations that guide us towards or away from things (see Prelude, page 11). Our new patterns are designed to defend us from scary emotions and increase the positive ones. Given our biology, we will always prioritize protecting ourselves from threats and danger (pain) over getting more pleasure. The less we feel connected to our carers, the more pain we feel. Psychologists estimate that 40 to 50 percent of us didn't enjoy a secure sense of connection, or **attachment**, to our parents as infants.[1] How we attach to our carers, as well as how they treat us in all sorts of everyday situations, begins to shape us. It leaves a big imprint. Many of our most stubborn patterns were designed to deal with pain felt around connection, attachment, and separation.

As we grow older still, we realize that we are not in control of much either. The resulting sense of impotence is a huge OUCH!—which is why so many of our patterns attempt to give us a semblance of control over a world where our parents, carers, and teachers were always the boss. Having a tantrum or sulk is better than feeling powerless because at least we feel in control when we're angry or moody. So this becomes another useful pattern, hardwired into the basal ganglia. Some kids discover that being 'good' and 'nice' usually gets them what they want, and so develop patterns like that to exert control over things. All these patterns try to stop us feeling a profound sense of powerlessness, which is often the origin of much of our grown-up rage (if we have any, of course!). Adult anger that explodes in the present moment often attempts to mask a sense of impotence.

These everyday experiences of separation, of OUCH!, don't need to be in any way 'abusive' or 'dark' to make their mark on us, and so stimulate the creation of our patterns. The act of growing up inevitably brings with it a whole host of experiences that feel threatening or disappointing (and occasionally downright terrifying). Parents do thousands of things unconsciously each week (often picked up from their own parents), many of which aren't exactly what their kids want in that moment. This is painful. Parenting is challenging and every parent loses it at some point. This is really painful. This doesn't mean our parents abused us (or we abuse our kids). It just means we are all human.

One thing we can't do in the first decade of life is leave where we live by choice as we depend on our folks for everything. So, faced with situations where we can't escape any pain (because we can't just get up and walk away for good), we are forced to develop patterns to survive it. Using the assumptions we explored in Session 02 (see page 66), we can now suggest the pain the patterns might be protecting us from.

The 'Life is tough' story
Ultimate assumptions about human nature/the universe
Life is tough and only the strong make it.

The pain
Mother is always working. When she's at home, instead of having fun with us, she is always stressed, hassled, and complaining about how life is difficult. She is very tough and makes it work . . . but is so defensive, that she never fully connects with us with an open HEART and an open mind.

Patterns developed for protection
To avoid the pain, we unconsciously decide to be hard too, to prevent any disappointment. As an adult, we are rarely vulnerable with the people around us.

The 'men are untrustworthy' story
Ultimate assumptions about human nature/the universe
All men are untrustworthy.

The pain
Father is flaky. He announces that he is going to take us somewhere, but rarely follows through. Something always comes up.

Patterns developed for protection

To avoid a repeat of the letdown after being excited to be with father, we unconsciously decide never to get too intimate in relationships, just in case we are let down. As adults, we dump people before we are dumped, because then we are in control. We unconsciously choose partners who are distant and closed off, because at least then they won't be disappointed.

The 'eating/drinking/smoking helps me relax' story

Ultimate assumptions about human nature/the universe

The body is like a machine. It can be made to relax by using certain substances.

The pain

As kids, we are shy, awkward, and lacking in self-esteem. Our parents don't have the wisdom to see this and help us. Every time we go out, it is painful, embarrassing, and shaming.

Patterns developed for protection

By copying people around us, we discover that food/alcohol/cigarettes help us feel better inside (for a few minutes or hours). They also distract us from our worries and help us look cooler and more confident to others. When we are adults, they become a social crutch for moments when we feel upset, frustrated, or lacking in confidence.

Surviving the pain

THE MIND OF A five-year-old can't reflect on a situation and think, 'Ah, Mom is exhausted and sleep-deprived from looking after me and holding down a job. She feels unsupported by Dad who is busy working to make the cash we need during this awful recession. Never mind, I'll chill out and wait until she gets back to get the cuddles I really want.' Instead, the emotions of disappointment or frustration overwhelm us, we react with some kind of behavior that lets out some tension and we wrap it all up in a series of stories that explain it.

> **The stories we spin are designed so that we get to believe something fundamental: 'I am safe with these people.' This is the number one priority for every child.**

It seems that we cannot feel safe if we think our primary carers are wrong or bad. So we have to cast our parents in a positive light no matter what they do. For example, if your father was busy and didn't play with you much, you will make that mean something about *you*, not him. If your mother had a harsh tongue, you will make that mean something about *you*, not her. Even if our carers were heroin-shooting, fist-punching wrecks who were utterly unfit to parent, that wouldn't stop us from seeing their behavior as normal. If we didn't, it would mean that we were unsafe and in bad hands. This thought is utterly intolerable to a child. Even love comes secondary to safety at this age.

So, rather than think our parents are in any way wrong or bad, we appear to invent a story that *we* are selfish/stupid/mean/angry/unlucky. We blame ourselves. We take the bad or naughty role (often playing into it quite successfully) and our darkside is born. But when we create this front, we leave behind the part of us that is most open, vulnerable, and creative. We sacrifice our spontaneity and flexibility for the promise of safety and protection from more pain. Rather than growing up and maturing, parts of us get frozen in time, acting out the same patterns over and over, instead of adapting as the times change. We do not allow our 'inner child' to thrive.[2] As soon as we leave an inner child behind, acting out to defend ourselves, we also lose access to some of our creative potential.

> **Every time we find ourselves stuck, upset, or worried, it is an opportunity to reclaim our long-lost inner child and bring them back from exile in the past.**

We have to explain away the behavior of the inner child, which is why we invent our stories and the assumptions that justify them. These stories can stick with us for a very long time and, sadly, can lead to ill health, crime, and much else besides.[3] Studies show that people with more optimistic stories tend to have had deeper attachment to their parents. Those with less optimistic stories, less so.[4] One of the longest studies of human thriving ever, the Grant Study at Harvard, followed men for 75 years, tracing their experiences over the course of their lives. They found that the men who had a warm, close connection to their mothers earned $87,000 a year more than those who didn't; were more effective; and were *far* less likely to get dementia.[5] People who have a warm, close connection to their fathers, tend to have lower anxiety, greater enjoyment of life, higher achievement, more curiosity, and are much less likely to become depressed, addicted, or turn to crime.[6]

The parental bond seems to inspire many of the stories we use to frame our entire lives. We also copy our parents' stories, just as we mimic their behaviors. If they have a pronoid story, we will tend to use it to guide our life too. If they have a paranoid one, so do we. Our story, there to cover up our pain in bubble wrap, tells us what we can do and what we can't do. Who we can date and who we can't date. How healthy we can be and how messed up we should be. Our stories are unlikely to change until we find a way to help our inner child feel safe enough to stop acting out. This is why so many of our patterns—including shame, self-esteem issues, and addictions— are so hard to shift. They are there because the inner child thinks it still needs them. Changes are unlikely to be embodied until the wiring within has been rejigged. If there is still pain in the system, in our body.mind, it seems to resist any rewiring until it is released. This is how the system has evolved: To defend, at all costs. Patterns remain locked in, needing constant management, until the pain within has been transformed for good.

Managing our problems is not the same as flourishing with them. No one is condemned merely to 'deal' with life. We can choose to switch on any time and release the pain into peace.

Pain on the brain

EVERY TIME WE FEEL some kind of lack or loss, we feel pain. We store memories of it, **pain memories**, in and around the amygdala, where our emotional activations and guidance system are located. This means our most intense memories are very close to where all the action is, able to influence our behavior quickly. Less intense memories seem to get stored in the hippocampus, which is a bit further away (see page 17). The more emotionally charged the experience—the bigger the OUCH!—the stronger the memory. The tricky thing about the body.mind is that in moments of intense experience, it develops 'tunnel memory.' We don't remember the original event as it was. We remember it through a haze, with the bits that made the biggest impression becoming outsized in our memory.

The first time we react with an OUCH! to something or someone, a small bunch of neurons fires, linking up the memory to reactions, including habits, assumptions, and physical sensations. Over time, these become 'consolidated' into a deep and profuse cluster of nerves. This neural signature, a lattice of pain memories and patterns, becomes a **pain.pattern crystal**. When we scan our environment, constantly looking for danger (and opportunity), the pain.pattern crystal will be triggered as soon as we spot anything around us that remotely resembles that initial intense experience. Then the Survival Trip is immediately activated. As we know, we seldom face a life-threatening situation as adults, just an echo of something that happened long ago. This doesn't matter to our body.mind: The whole hormonal and neurological cascade is unleashed upon our system. Our body.mind focuses on the perceived threat and nothing else. This is 'tunnel vision.' You know when you have it because you will obsess over an event or issue, ruminating, upset, irritated. Our system is treating it as danger.

Every time someone, or something, triggers a pain memory, we strengthen the neural signature and consolidate the memory still further. Our wiring is created in and through our relationships with others. Pioneering neuropsychiatrist Professor Dan Siegel suggests that the whole emotional system is wired to connect us to others.[7]

Our neurons are all interconnected in a relational field with the people we grow up, work, and live with. How they act changes our brain. How we act changes theirs.

Experiments with people suffering from Post-traumatic Stress Disorder (PTSD) suggest that if we recall a pain memory *without* attempting to transform it, we simply strengthen the memory and further embed the pain.pattern crystal. Over many years of **consolidation** and conditioning, the entire structure of our brain changes, in particular the prefrontal cortex, which is the seat of impulse control and attention. Repeated pain will diminish the prefrontal cortex.[8] In extreme cases, whole areas of the cerebral cortex become thinned.[9] Constant pain, whether physical or emotional, can shrink the size of the brain by 10 percent. This makes it even harder for us to regulate our own moods, fears, and upsets.[10] The brains of kids from disadvantaged socio-economic backgrounds (who have experienced a lot of pain) tend to be wired up differently, and this shows up on scans by the age of two.[11]

The good news is that all these changes are temporary and can be rewired as soon as we no longer experience pain and/or experience more love and connection in our relationships. The brain is remarkably resilient![12] Life's many painful experiences leave us with an array of sensitive spots in our emotional field, which can be triggered at any moment by an unsuspecting boyfriend, buddy, or boss. This is why others can be surprised when we react in extreme ways to things that might not seem very intense to them (and vice versa!). The original wound, the initial OUCH!, becomes a kind of splinter deep in the body.mind. Protective patterns crystallize around each wound, just as scabs form on the skin.

Losing creativity, gaining pain

NATURE HAS PROVIDED THE perfect solution to the difficulties of childhood by giving us the means and smarts to create patterns that protect us from difficulties and dangers. Over time, these patterns form our front: A brick wall that keeps out the bits of the world we don't like. Each brick is a reaction to OUCH! NO! As we grow up, we erect more and more of these walls in the wide-open space of our childlike minds. The walls are very successful at their job. The unpredictable and painful world is kept at bay.

Putting up Front

As kids, we erect walls to keep an uncertain, unsafe and even scary, world at bay

At the same time, it is common to project the frustrations and letdowns we experienced with our carers onto the universe itself. We start to distrust the world we live in, human nature as a whole, and even the cosmos itself. This experience of loss is the origin of our ultimate assumptions about human nature and how the world works. So the walls keep both people and life out.

What is your relationship to the universe? Do you trust it? Do you believe it is supporting you or hindering you? Is this painful? What do you believe about human nature? What about the way the world works? Is this painful?

As we expand through adolescence and into adulthood, we start to push up against the self-created walls. What was designed to keep pain away now starts to hurt us by keeping us in. We are trapped inside our comfort zone. If we stay within the walls, we lose our capacity to create, grow, and thrive. Our creative spirit is ready to get to work but the walls block it. From a pronoid view, the universe may even be offering us a hand up, but we keep pushing the palm away.

Hemmed in by Front

As adults, the walls we built to protect us from pain start to hem us in, limiting our potential and causing us more pain

For a time, many of us manage to deal with the pain of being held back and constrained. Better deal with the new pain than risk the old pain that made such an impression on our childlike minds. So we become comfortable with the discomfort of a cramped inner life. We make the best of our comfort zone. But, for many, our potential—our drive to thrive—eventually pushes us to expand until the pain of being constricted starts to get too much. We are pushed up against the walls, hemmed in by our own front. Anyone who has experienced a bout of depression, failed relationships, a tad of anxiety, a touch of OCD, or a spot of addiction knows this. It can hurt like hell. Most of us sense that there is a way past the walls; we just don't know how to break through.

Hot off the press: Most of the letdowns and threats that you experienced as a child really don't exist anymore! If they do, you are unlikely to be the same essentially helpless being you were then. Can anybody emotionally hurt you any more unless you allow them to? No! You are free to heal the original wounds and liberate yourself from your pain memories. However, as you've probably found out, you can't achieve this by force. You can't will yourself to feel good and you can't simply tell yourself to move beyond the pain. Instead, you (and perhaps a professional) have to engage with the part of you that erected the walls and work with it to bring them tumbling down.

INHERITING PAIN

Intense emotions, such as those accompanying pain memories, can alter the synapses, DNA, and chromosomes in nerve cells. Changes around the genes are called 'epigenetic' changes and are setting the scientific community alight. For centuries, scientific dogma held that we could inherit genes but not behaviors from our parents. Now that is being reconsidered. Recent studies have shown that stress-driven changes, and the resulting pain.pattern crystals, can be passed down to descendants. We don't just mimic patterns of our parents; we inherit them directly in our cells.[13]

The early work in this field has been done on rats, because their nervous system is similar to ours. Baby rats that get licked a lot by their mothers (the equivalent of a loving family environment) have a different setup of anti-stress cell receptors in their brains when compared to those that don't get a lot of love. The unlicked rats end up with blocked anti-stress receptors and soon become permanently stressed out. Stress-driven changes have been passed all the way down to their grandchildren.[14]

Early research on humans has shown that growing up in a stressful environment frays the ends of our chromosomes. These protective 'caps' are 20 percent shorter in children from poor and unstable families compared to those from more nurturing homes. It is not certain whether these caps can be healed and whether they can be passed down to offspring.[15]

Meet the Protector

BEHIND ALL THE PATTERNS that make up your personality is a fundamental force for survival that I call 'The Protector.' It's the energy that keeps up the walls and sustains the front. Every human being has one. It's the power behind our drive to survive. This hard-working (and usually unappreciated) part of us has defended us against actual and perceived threats since we were tiny; and is helped along by stress hormones like cortisol, adrenalin, and testosterone. It continues to protect us from threats at *all* costs, even if it means living within our comfort zone. Better safe and predictable than spontaneous and sorry, it believes. Although we may be frustrated with our patterns, they were designed by **the Protector** to help us. It will keep activating them until it feels that the danger has gone and the pain memories are no longer locked in.

Over the years, the Protector learns important rules for preventing the world, and the people in it, from hurting us. For example:

- Don't touch a hot stove.
- Don't walk into traffic.
- Avoid poisonous snakes. (Yeah!)
- Never talk to crazy people and definitely don't fall in love with them. (Oops!)

These are all useful strategies to avoid physical and emotional pain. However, as we have seen, many of these rules persist well beyond their expiry date into adulthood, where they become personality traits:

- Avoid disappointment by never risking anything = the Slacker.
- Commitment feels terrifying. Don't ever do it = the Playboy or Playgirl.
- Avoid being vulnerable at all costs = the Ice King or Queen.
- Scream at people and they will listen to you = the Terrifying Boss.
- Work as hard as you can and they will respect you = the Workaholic.
- Make everything perfect and then you will be safe = the Perfectionist.

The Protector's job is to stop us having to experience pain by triggering patterns. The Protector blocks out the world and then hypnotizes and soothes us with stories of our own creation. The patterns are not wrong. They are not evidence we are bad. They are not stupid. They are not disgusting. They are simply well-designed solutions that the Protector created to save us from pain. They are the Protector saying:

NO, NOT AGAIN, **EVER!**

No more fear of looking stupid, of being nothing, of having nothing, of failure, of not succeeding, of being wrong, of being found out, of life itself. Above all, *no more lack*! Instead, a pattern is created. So our patterns are actually evidence of how good we all are at protecting ourselves from pain. The problem is that the Protector's work can deplete our energy. Every time it thinks someone has disrespected, ignored, abandoned, or rejected us, the Protector uses up precious energy defending us. So when you're feeling down or exhausted, it's often a sign that the Protector is on high alert, keeping your pain on lock-down and your protective walls up.

Imagine how much more energy you would have if the Protector wasn't defending you so much of the time? More importantly, imagine what creative things you could do with all that energy!

By design, the Protector can only *deflect* things it does not want for you. It can make a valiant effort never to let the pain of a letdown hurt that much again, but it cannot help you *attract* the love, peace, and possibility you want instead. It hits away potentially hurtful curve balls but cannot knock them out of the park. It's job is survival. It says OI, NO! It knows nothing about thriving, which needs a YES! So we need to find a way to help the Protector take some time off.

Resistance is futile

THE PROTECTOR IN US all will never give up pain-preventing patterns until it feels safe. This can only happen when we learn how to provide for ourselves the kind of secure connection and unconditionally-loving environment that every infant craves.

> **As adults, no one else can provide us with the safety, security, and love we need to thrive. Only we can create it for ourselves.**

The first step in this fundamental transformation at your core is to accept your patterns for what they are. The more you try to fight your self-sabotaging patterns—by hating yourself for being grumpy/fat/thin/unlucky—the deeper you lock them in. The Protector is triggered by pain. So, every time it feels you attack yourself for not being what you want to be, it will hunker down and defend with more patterns. The Protector needs to be loved, hugged, and tickled to change its ways. Blaming, shaming, or complaining about it just exacerbates the pain and so reinforces its activity.

The Protector will attempt to defend us by any means necessary, as it is designed to do, even if that means more addiction, more anger, or more depression. If we try to force change on ourselves, just with our willpower, our patterns will often come back even stronger. Anyone who has binged after a period of abstinence will testify to that. Trying to destroy patterns, without first reassuring the Protector that it is safe, can never work. It is contrary to the design of the system.

Whatever you resist, you ensure persists.

The more harshly you talk to yourself, the more you criticize yourself with negative self-talk, the more likely you are to trigger more patterns. Then you might well feel more pain—anxious or ashamed about your patterns. Then more patterns will play out. This is how cycles of pain within us spiral around and around until they bring us to breakdown, as we trip out on stress in an effort to survive . . . it goes on and on and on. The Protector within us makes us loop around the Survival Trip of Problem—Pain—Pattern like a scratched record, in a cycle of surviving and suffering (see diagram opposite).

Unlike on the TV show *The Apprentice*, the Protector can never be fired. Ever. If you can't fire the Protector, and you can't force it to change either, then the only other option is to work with it. Rather than flog it . . . give it a break. Rather than attack it . . . be grateful for it helping you. The more it feels the love then the more it will be up for a breakthrough. The Protector does *everything* for your benefit. Its actions may have destroyed love affairs,

The Survival Trip

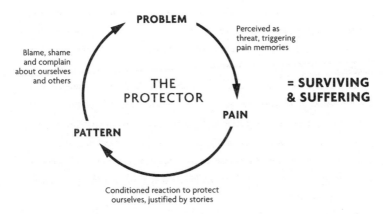

career paths, or friendships, but it was all in the name of safety and security. If it feels your gratitude, it will open up to change. See if you can thank it for keeping you safe all these years. Go on. Right now.

THANK YOU!

Repeat it a couple of times. Now breathe in nice and slow and say something like the following:

> Thank you for protecting me for all these years! You've done a great job and I wouldn't be here without you.

THANK YOU!

Feel what happens inside your body.mind as you do this. Can you feel something deep within, something primal, relax a little? That is the Protector having a rare moment of calm as it feels listened to and honored. It may feel strange to thank it, but the Protector will only allow you to rewire your patterns, and so release the energy you need to remix your world, *once it feels respected.*

HENRY AND WENDY: FRUSTRATION AT FIRST SIGHT

Calling our personality traits by a name creates a bit of distance between who we are in our essence and who we become when we're scared or stressed out. It reminds us that our personality has been invented by the Protector and is not timeless or essential.

One of mine is 'Henry,' one of my middle names (named in honor of my German-born grandfather, Heinrich). Albeit stereotypical, true to his German roots, Henry is a master organizer and gets huge amounts of stuff done. Without him, I couldn't run two businesses, be an involved partner and dad, and write books at the same time. Henry tries to protect me, but he can easily become a little dictatorial, telling people around me what to do (and making few friends in the process).

The Protector wanted to make sure I never had to deal with the pain of a divorce and the chaos that ensued. I can still bring to mind some of the key pain memories around these moments. Over time, this felt so scary, so unsafe, that the Protector compensated by inventing Henry. Now, whenever I feel really overwhelmed, especially by mess and disorganization, Henry pops up to force order upon the chaos. This can be really helpful in running a family of four but can be a right pain in the butt for everyone. Including me.

My wife, on the other hand, has an inner 'Wendy,' a freedom-loving, chilled-out teenager, oozing with Californian surf vibes (where my wife grew up). Wendy has ninja skills in getting my inner Henry to chillax, helping him let go and so allowing my creative spirit back out. However, Wendy can also act like a spoiled teenager who can't be bothered to do anything for herself or finish things properly. When she was very young, her dad left and never came back. Her pain memories are of a childhood without anyone to help her feel powerful. So to protect her from the pain of impotence, her Protector invented Wendy. Wendy doesn't bother enough to fail.

Our Protectors invented Wendy and Henry to deal with the same pain, the pain of powerlessness. Now Henry and Wendy frustrate each other sometimes; but they heal each other even more because of the love, patience, and connection we feel with each other in our essence.

Can you love the Protector for all your patterns, even if they have hurt you and others?

The Protector designed your defensive patterns, so they can be redesigned to suit a wiser, more creative perspective on your life. When it feels safe, it will begin to let go of the pain and release the old patterns *because they are no longer needed*. It won't do this because you tell it to. It will only do it once it is safe to. This is logical, no? Once you accept your patterns and their design instead of resisting them, anything is possible.

As we provide security and love for ourselves, we demonstrate to the Protector that nobody can ever hurt us emotionally again. People can do all manner of things to punish us but if we can provide a continuous source of safety and love within, we cannot be hurt. Then we can be in the worst situations and still find creativity in our HANDS, forgiveness in our HEAD, and love in our HEART. Safe in this wisdom, we can reassure our Protector that all is well. Over time, the patterns fade and creativity flows in their place.

From constraint to creativity

THE PROCESS OF HONORING, loving, and re-educating the Protector is the key to all lasting transformation. By engaging fully with the original pain, no matter how big or small it might seem, we give our HEART the chance to be free of it. As soon as that happens, our HEAD can start weaving inspiring stories, which harnesses our creativity and potential. Then our HANDS can build exciting projects that make a difference to our lives and those of the people we love. The energy that was being used to defend us can now be used to become a more confident and compassionate lover, a more impactful and visionary leader, or a more empathic and flexible parent.

When we withdraw the splinters from our HEART, we may well find that lying hidden in the pain.pattern crystals are the very traits and talents that we have been missing for so long. Beneath the pain of the Big Shot is all the effortless cool and confidence we have craved. Behind the pain of the Control Freak is all the power and potency we have always dreamed of. Under the pain of the Cynic is all the magic we have ever desired. These gifts, and others like them, are like uncut diamonds that sit within every pain. pattern crystal. They wait there until we are ready to find them by lighting up the darkside within.

To go deep into the pain, hidden in the darkside, takes guts. This does not mean we want to override our fear with more adrenalin and cortisol. This just creates more stress. We want to cultivate the kind of courage that inspires

THE LOVE MIRACLE

Boris Cyrulnik is a widely respected doctor who studies the impact of childhood trauma. He has worked with child soldiers in Colombia and victims of genocide in Rwanda. In Romania, he worked with orphans who had been put into institutions and denied affection for years. Without love they became withdrawn and afraid. Many stopped speaking. Others rocked themselves silently on their beds. Some were so untrusting of others that they tried to bite people when they came near them. They were barely surviving. Their patterns were all these kids had left between themselves and total implosion.

However, when these children were put into loving homes, they were able to bounce back within a year. Their prefrontal cortices returned to normal size. They stopped defending themselves with such extreme patterns. The more solid and authentic the love, the faster they came back to life, like drops of water falling on a desert awaking the flowers to bloom. Cyrulnik's work with such kids has shown conclusively that unconditional love can help children heal from even the worst abuses. If it can switch kids back on who have been so poorly treated, then we can be confident that love can do the same for us too.

us to keep our sometimes raw and ragged **HEART** open when it most wants to close. The more open it is, the more pain can be released. Courage is about staying vulnerable, undefended, so we can remain open to the possibilities that are within our pain. When we shut down in fear, the gateway to freedom shuts down too. Tunnel vision replaces expansive insight. We can't maintain fittedness if we don't have the courage to stay open and available to what is emerging. The root of the word courage is *coeur*, heart. We have to have a big, open, loving, and **switched on heart** to be courageous.

'Courage is not the absence of fear but the mastery of it,' as Mark Twain remarked. People with courage still notice their fear and observe pain arising (which can be seen in brain scans) but don't let it trigger stress. Following the ABC of holding it down (see Session 01, pages 45–46) stops us from being triggered into the usual fight-or-flight response, and allows us to stay alert and attuned to our environment.[16] With courage (and curiosity), we can resist the Survival Trip long enough to process our pain. This means moving courage from our **head** into our **heart**, where we can fully **embody** it.

When we tear down the walls that have been keeping life out, and us in, for so long, we are doing the most important work of our life. This kind of work, **inner work**, will give us all the adventure and love that we've ever wanted. We get to create dazzling skyscrapers in the place of decrepit old buildings. Rather than become addicted to things that cover up the pain—the rush of a cream cake or the buzz of a line of cocaine—we become addicted to finding our truth and allowing it to liberate our fiercest creativity. Nothing is more enlivening than finding our true character beneath the worn tatters of our personality. The more walls we purposefully deconstruct, the more we open up space for our real character to come out, covered in sweat and dust, ready to make sweet love to the world in all its ephemeral glory.

The pain points us in the right direction. As Denis Diderot, the French philosopher who wrote the first ever encyclopedia, said, 'All that stirs the soul, all that imprints a feeling of terror, leads to the sublime.'[17] As we learn to uncover each pattern and see, with absolute clarity and courage, the pain it has been designed to cover up, we get access to the peace, power, and possibility that no job, sexual conquest, or intense drug could ever give us.

The more we love, support, and secure ourselves, the deeper we can go inside to access our truth. The truth, sparkling and effervescent, will always set us free.

SWITCH ON TO PAIN

Switched Off: Pain is something to be avoided at all costs (that includes admitting that we have any in the first place). Vulnerability is painful and we can prevent it by being tough or hiding away.

Switched On: Pain is an inevitable part of becoming a full human being yet, when left unhealed, impacts everything we do. Pain is an invitation to love, secure, and support ourselves more. When we do, we allow the pain to depart and the truth to set us free.

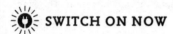 **SWITCH ON NOW**

Remind yourself of a problem you want to break through.

HANDS: Hidden beneath the immediate physical reaction to the problem, can you spot any tension, density, stickiness, or emptiness somewhere within your body.mind? Can you allow it to be there without trying to change it or get rid of it?

Now imagine this is a crystal of pain.pattern that has good reason to be there. If you allowed the crystal to dissolve, leaving an uncut diamond of truth, what might it be offering or telling you that could be liberating?

HEAD: What are your most destructive and sabotaging patterns? How have they got in the way of your brilliance? How have they messed things up around other people?

Now, sense the Protector as a force inside you. It has established your patterns to keep you from pain. Try on the idea that all those patterns were created to help you arrive safely at this place in your life. Here, today.

Can you see any ways they have protected you from feeling pain (such as letdown, disappointment, lack, fear, and so on)?

HEART: Beneath the patterns, can you feel any sense that you have been lacking love, safety, or support? In what ways? Can you sense when you might have first felt this pain?

Can you allow yourself to notice any pain without trying to maximize it or minimize it? Can you allow your **HEART** to stay open and vulnerable by breathing deep and feeling your courage alive within?

Can you thank the Protector for all it has done? Can you forgive it for having outdated patterns that are no longer serving you?

Can you imagine hugging it? Go on then!

BREAKTHROUGH QUESTIONS

 If I was the Protector inside me, what would I need to hear to help me relax, drop my defenses, and be at peace?

 If the wisest person in the world had designed this pain as my personal wake-up call to life, what kind of love, safety, or support might they want me to give myself?

Session 04

Presence

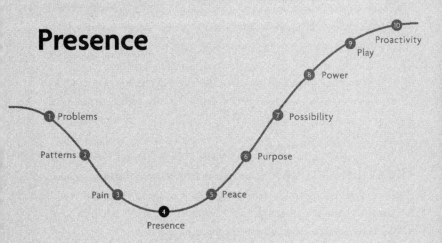

ALL THE LOVE, SUPPORT, and security we ever need to have breakthrough after breakthrough is available to each of us in every moment. It is all around us and within us. As Einstein worked out with $E = mc^2$, all matter exists as energy. We are all made up of the same energy that makes up the stars. By reconnecting into this energy field, we can feel its power and warmth deep inside, burning like a billion suns. As we awaken to this **Presence**, we realize that our true nature is as one with the universe. This realization has nothing to do with supernatural or religious voodoo. It is just the reality that we are made up of the same energy that makes up the universe. It is present in every particle that surrounds us and keeps us alive. By choosing to reconnect with it, switch on to it, we become truly and absolutely free.

Throughout history, sages, poets, and philosophers have tried to help us feel (and be) this Presence by becoming 'enlightened.' We switch on, shifting from feeling alone to feeling like an intrinsic part of the rich tapestry of life; from feeling separate to feeling connected. Many of the great wisdom traditions—China's Taoism, India's yoga and Vedanta, Zen meditations and riddles, Tibetan Buddhism and its mandalas, Sufi poems and dances, Jewish Kabbalah, the sayings and rituals of the Native Americans—have developed techniques and tools to help us to switch on and feel Presence.

One of the most powerful subjective experiences of this Presence, is 'love.' This passion, this connection, this inspiration is at the core of all creativity. Love can simply be thought of as the force of attraction, of connectedness, that we feel when we return home to the universe that we thought, for a while, we were separate from. However, don't let my words be prescriptive. If you feel Presence as nature, fun, power, freedom, *satchitananda* (being, consciousness, bliss in Sanskrit), nirvana, the Rave, or sacred fire (or anything else at all), then that is the truth for you. What is important is that you feel that it supports you and guarantees your emotional safety.

To presence this love, love that creates and heals, we must wake up to our true nature as being one unique and connected part of the universe. When we feel connected to everything and everyone else, then we can start to feel the raw Presence of the universe at our back at all times. Then no pattern is too big to break through, whether our own or those in society. All those self-sabotaging patterns become ripe for rewiring because the Protector has no need to protect us from the past any more. Until we feel connected instead of alone, we will always feel the pain of separation anxiety and so maintain patterns to defend against it. Although we can't jump in a time machine and change our history, we can transform how we feel about it inside. We can pour love—constantly available when we tap into Presence—into the places where we feel a lack (which we experience as pain).

The I of the storm

WE HAVE SEEN THAT infancy is a crucial time for us all (see Session 03, page 81). Those first few years are vitally important in reassuring our fledgling selves that we are safe. A deep sense of security and connection can stay with us forever, providing us with an entire life framework that helps us thrive. Yet, no matter how amazing our parents were at helping us feel safe, at some point we all felt the experience of separation anxiety, and the emotions of fear, disconnect, and loneliness it brings. Before, it was me-and-mom-and-dad-and-everyone are one. Then, suddenly, we are just a 'me.' This is a painful fall from grace, but it is an essential part of being human. The mythologist Joseph Campbell suggests that the idea of the Fall of man in the Bible is a metaphor for this realization of separation.[1] We are kicked out of the Eden of cozy togetherness and now have to make our own way in the world.

From the second our alarm clock, room-mate, or baby wakes us up in the morning, we start to hear an 'I' speaking:

- 'I am tired.'
- 'I am starving.'
- 'I am horny.'
- 'I don't want to go to work today.'

This kind of self-talk sounds as if it comes from an 'I.' This is the 'I' of the storm of all our pain. As soon as we believe in that 'I,' we separate ourselves from everyone and everything else. Soon, we feel alone, afraid, disappointed. We feel lacking in *something*: Food, love, cuddles, attention, support. Something. This is the lack that is at the core of our pain.

- 'What about me?'
- 'What am I going to get out of it?'
- 'Why does nobody appreciate me?'
- 'Why am I not getting that cool thing?'
- 'What's wrong with me?'

The 'I' is consumed by lack. The Protector then develops patterns to cope with it by trying to control, manipulate, and dominate our environment.

Clearly we hear self-talk all the time, chatting away with all these 'I' sentences. It's just that it is not all that we are. Yes, 'I' am distinct from 'you.' But we are still connected because we are part of the one universe (or multiverse). When we buy into the 'I', or **Tiny Me**, it exacerbates fear, limits freedom, and puts a cork in creativity. It's called 'tiny' for two reasons. First, in the face of life's enormous challenges, it often feels powerless and small. Second, compared to the vast richness of our potential, its ideas about who and what we are, are narrow and limited.

The separation between 'I' and 'all the things that are not me' was made formal and famous by the philosopher René Descartes. On an admirable mission to try to ground all human knowledge in something solid, something that could not be changed as times changed, he observed his self-talk. So he exclaimed 'Cogito ergo sum!' ('I think therefore I am.') If I exist in my head, which seems to be true because of all this chat I keep hearing, then I must exist in reality. This theory then became the grounding for all 'real' science, which needs a separate 'I' to study 'objectively' a disconnected physical world, 'It', or a disconnected social 'Them.'

Now scientists see nature as a mechanical clock. This view works really well when studying billiard balls ricocheting into each other; and silicon chips processing binary code. Yet it works less well when understanding how complex, adaptive, non-linear systems (i.e. us humans) work. When we believe that everything is a machine—known as the mechanical worldview— it gets pretty intoxicating. Surely if we know how the clock works, our Tiny Me thinks, then we can predict and control everything. The Protector loves that chat! This story of power and domination over the chaos of nature holds many in its thrall.

Nowadays, most of us don't stop to wonder if this Tiny Me is not the whole story (or even an illusion). We see it as a hard fact of science, even if we have a sneaking suspicion that we are more than just a clockwork mechanism instructed by a computer-like brain. As soon as we think that all we are is this Tiny Me, we are destined to suffer. The moment we split the world into 'me' and 'things that are not me' (some of which I want, some of which I really don't), the trouble begins. 'I' will *always* crave some things and try to avoid others. This powers up our whole pattern-forming, pain-protecting system. These constant desires and fears create stress and fling us into the Survival Trip over and over again. The tragedy is that no amount of stuff from the outside can ever make up for lack within.

> **No amount of fame or fortune, chocolate or sex, can help us feel connected when the sense of disconnection originates inside us.**

This deep, gnawing sense of separation, crowned by the illusion that we are just a Tiny Me, generates the profound sense of lack that so many of us feel and that all our patterns are there to protect us from.

The suffering does not just stop with us either. As soon as we think we are separate from nature, we start to treat it in ways that are neither empathic nor even smart. Tribes that have a guiding story of connection with nature treat it with respect. The Huaorani hunters from the Amazon may kill animals for food. But each understands that it is a gift from the universe and respects the animal. Accordingly, the hunter endeavors not to waste any of a kill. On the other hand, the Western story has disconnection at its heart and so we exploit the environment without connection to it. In the Bible (Genesis), God says: 'Let man have dominion over the fish in the sea, and over the fowl in the air, and over the cattle, and over all the earth, and over every creeping thing that creeps over the earth.'

With separation, comes control and domination. This not only leads to our own suffering, but also to the suffering of millions of people, animals, and plants.

Blowing the mind

ANYONE WHO HAS ARRIVED home and then realized they can't remember a huge chunk of their journey, knows that the Tiny Me is not all we have access to, on any given day. In fact, even in the minutes it has taken you to read from the start of the chapter to here, your mind is likely to have wandered off *a few* times . . . without you even knowing it. Our body.mind pops off to daydream-land multiple times a minute. Our brain spends around 30 percent of its time 'out of it,' but we rarely notice because the brain plugs the gaps in our awareness automatically to give us the sense of a concrete, permanent 'I.' However, this 'I' is neither essential nor eternal but instead generated by incredible mental wizardry.

 DISCONNECTION KILLS

Separation is not just emotionally agonizing. Being alone can also lead to long-term, lasting damage to our physical health too. Elderly people who don't spend much time with others have a higher risk of depression as well as heart disease and premature death. In one study, 22 percent of people categorized as 'highly isolated' died prematurely compared with 12 percent of those who were more connected to life.[3] Another study shows that being disconnected from others is more detrimental to health than obesity, smoking, and high blood pressure.[4] In animal studies, infants that have been abandoned by their mothers become permanently alert to danger. Inside their brains there is frantic activity of the neurotransmitters of attention and arousal. If this continues, they enter a lifelong stress response, cycling through the Survival Trip until death.

Research has shown that the neural pathways involved in social relationships are intertwined with those that respond to pain and joy, around the anterior cingulate cortex and insula. Social isolation hurts us deep in the brain.[5]

It appears that a bunch of pretty independent parts of the brain work together to create the illusion, or delusion, that we are an 'I,' an individual Tiny Me. From a fuzzy vortex of signals continuously streaming in from billions of cells, it generates a stable sense of self. This appears to happen deep in the area around the insula and prefrontal cortex (see page 7). It continuously observes the beliefs we hold dear and behaviors we display, and knits them together into a coherent narrative, which becomes our personality.[2] If we change beliefs or behaviors, it adjusts the sense of self accordingly. Thus, the Tiny Me seems to serve a vital function: It helps us navigate through the chaos of life long enough to pass on our genes to the next generation (we hope).

Although it may help us to survive, sadly the Tiny Me also stops us thriving. We have to move beyond it, if we want to be free from fear and enjoy lasting peace. In 1971, Edgar Mitchell, a scientist and astronaut, left the spacecraft *Apollo 14* to begin his descent to the surface of the Moon. He was the sixth man ever to step onto it. On the way back home, looking out over the Earth for the first time, he had an experience that changed the course of his life: 'What I experienced during that three-day trip home was nothing short of an overwhelming sense of universal connectedness . . . an ecstasy of unity.' He had broken through the confines of his Tiny Me to experience the **Great We**. It's great because it is wide open and expansive; and also because it helps us step up from self-centered worries and take response-ability for the whole.

When we experience this unity, we know we are not limited, small, and separate. Instead we realize we are amazing, huge, majestic.

Mitchell was inspired by his experiences to found IONS, a think-tank and institute that engages in cutting-edge scientific research into consciousness beyond the Tiny Me. Although he witnessed a sight most of us never will, at one time or another many of us will experience moments that give us a sense of the presence of the universe we are conjoined with. It may happen when you gaze out to sea on a deserted beach or reach the top of a mountain trail. It might happen when you hold a newborn baby or contemplate the elegant laws of physics. It might happen as you bump and grind on a packed dance floor or wave your hands in unison with a crowd at a concert or match. It might occur in the simple moments of sublime intimacy that can happen between lovers; or when viewing a Rothko painting (like Kandinsky and many others, he created art to provide us with this experience).

WHOSE FREE WILL IS THIS ANYWAY?

In the 1980s, remarkable experiments by Benjamin Libet took the study of consciousness by storm. Test subjects were asked to move their hand, by choice, while scientists recorded their brain activity. What Libet discovered was that the brain starts to build up a readiness to fire before the test subject thinks, 'I am going to move my finger now.' It can be up to two-thirds of a second before. So who (or what) is doing the instructing?[6]

These experiments seem to cast doubt on the ideas of Descartes (see page 106). What we think of as 'free will' may not necessarily be the will of the Tiny Me.

The experience of Presence, of **reconnection** to the universe, may be fierce and fiery, an ecstasy . . . or serene and simple, an emptiness . . . or anything and everything in between. Presence can feel rambunctiously red as the earth of Hindu India, with its irrepressible pantheon of wild gods, all different facets of unity; as dreamily blue as the misty rivers of Taoist/Buddhist China, with its ancient sense of the ineffable 'way'; leafy and verdant, like the rolling hills of England and New England, and their Green Man heritage; or a dusky yellow like the sands of the Western USA and its Native American spirit.

In these moments of reconnection with the universe we are part of, we are given a glimpse beyond the veil of 'normal' reality to see the blushing bride of unity that exists behind it. The doors of perception are opened, and we see the world to be infinite (to paraphrase Aldous Huxley, whose sentence inspired Jim Morrison to call his band 'The Doors'). We feel the raw, creative presence of the universe. We sense that there is something more to us than 'me, myself, and I.' Something way more. As we probe deeper into this experience, we realize . . . We are this. We are that. We are one. We are many. But above all, we are part of the universe.

Even a hardy weed flowering by the side of the road or the rain sprinkling down on our faces during a summer shower can be enough to bring us into a sense of wonder at the profound interconnectedness of all things. It doesn't have to be anything more mystical. Just experiencing the sun illuminating a flower, imagining the photons hitting our retina and images appearing inside us, can be enough to wake us up to the insanely complex interplay of life of which we are a part. OK, it may be easier to presence this wonder on a sunny Sunday afternoon while gyrating to beats on a gorgeous terrace in Ibiza than it is waiting for the 6 a.m. bus on a cold damp day in winter . . . but it can be done. There is no need to go to Goa, Ibiza, or Peru to experience it (although they all rock). You can reconnect in your living room or on your bed just as easily.

I KNOW WHY THE BUDDHA LAUGHS AND CRIES

A while back, I travelled to Goa, India, for a few weeks for a working holiday. During the day I was developing a tool to empower the most marginalized people on the planet with coaching techniques. At night I was raving, meditating, and generally kicking back. One evening, I took part in a healing ceremony that woke me up fully to the presence within me.

Within an hour of the start of the ceremony, my Tiny Me had faded into the background and I experienced myself as the Great We. I was no mind and all mind! I was nature. I was the universe. I was the floor and the sea, yin and yang, all of it. I began to laugh and cry at the same time, struck by the joy and suffering designed into life at the edge between the Tiny Me and the Great We, switched on and switched off. This was not an experience of God in any conventional sense. I simply woke up to the reality that everything is connected and that we are all one. I had always sensed this but, with this experience, it was no longer just a theory or a hunch. It became a direct, felt, lived experience, which I began to embody. Life would never be the same again.

With self-love always at my back, I no longer feel afraid or alone (although the habits of feeling this way return when I switch off in moments of fear and stress). I feel a welcomed and cherished part of the whole. Through taking refuge in the Great We, I have been able to heal many of my deepest childhood wounds and change many of my most sabotaging habits. My mojo has flowed and my creativity exploded. This book, the company that has co-produced it, my marriage, and my commitment to switched on parenting, have all flown from my reconnection to Presence.

I believe that virtually all of us intuit this. It may get buried deep down until it becomes almost imperceptible . . . but it's still there. You may not recognize it within you, if you have become sucked into the constant momentum of modern life. You may not have words to express it, if you haven't ever come into contact with mystical poems and wisdom teachers. You may even reject it out of hand as nonsense, if you have fallen in love with the realism of science. Yet until you reconnect to something bigger than you are, or rather bigger than your Tiny Me thinks it is—with whatever metaphors or techniques work for you—you simply cannot be totally free because background separation anxiety will *always* be there.

Going inside, to find out who we really are, is what counts. We have to know ourselves, as the Ancient Greek aphorism goes (inscribed on the temple to Apollo at Delphi). All we need to experience Presence, and relinquish suffering, is inside us. Everything we need to reconnect to the universe is within because *every atom, molecule and cell that makes up our body.mind is inherently, already and always connected because it is part of the universe.* The Presence is already inside us; we are it. It is just that the separatist worldview of the Tiny Me has dominated most of our experience and will continue to do so until we switch on.

Ecstasy and emptiness

A LAUGH WITH A buddy, a yoga class or meditation, a freeing dance, or the bark of dog can be enough to reconnect us back to ourselves, the people around us, and nature. Science has even given an experience like this a label, being in 'flow.' **Flow.states** can happen to anyone. The most capped French soccer player of all time, Lilian Thuram, scored two goals in a World Cup semi-final, yet he claimed he had no memory of the whole thing. His coach said he was in a 'mystical state.' A fellow player went up to him and said, 'What is going on? Who are you?' Thuram said in an interview: 'I didn't know who I was or where I was.'[7] Psychologists have interviewed hundreds of sportspeople, artists, and scientists, and many of them have experienced times when their sense of self, time, and space has receded. Instead, they have been fully consumed by the moment, in flow.

ZAP THE BRAIN AND THINGS FLOW

Rock climbing. Playing a video game. Playing an instrument. They can all lead to scientifically observable flow.states. The brain slows down to a state similar to how it looks when dreaming. High levels of serotonin and dopamine flood the body.mind. The prefrontal cortex, where we evaluate options, make judgments, and inhibit our emotions, becomes deactivated. It is also the area where much of the idea of the Tiny Me is generated. As it hangs back, we start to feel safer, more able to take risks, and so are more creative.[8]

In one study, a group of test subjects were given an impossible brainteaser, the 'nine-dot problem.' Based on years of research, it would be expected that precisely zero people in the group would solve the problem. That turned out to be true. Then, some underwent a technique called transcranial Direct Current Stimulation (tDCS). Basically, the fronts of their brains, where the prefrontal cortex is, were zapped (in a totally safe and non-invasive way, of course). This artificially inhibited their prefrontal cortex. In this state, they were given the nine-dot puzzle again and this time 40 percent of them managed to crack it, and fast! It's amazing what's possible when we get the Tiny Me, and all its disempowering chat, out of the way.[9]

Many people report that they feel 'ecstatic' when they reconnect. The Greek word *ekstasis*, the root of the word 'ecstasy,' means entrancement or astonishment. It usually refers to an experience when we are totally out of our HEAD (and often into our HEART). In many cultures, this kind of ecstasy is a normal part of life. Sufis get into this place by whirling around as they pray to Allah (little kids like to get out of their heads by spinning, too). Colombian shamans get there by drinking ayahuasca.

There is an analogue, a kind of mirror opposite, to ecstasy, which is called emptiness (*sunyata* in Sanskrit). The Buddha taught that the experience of enlightenment comes when we realize that all our thoughts, beliefs, cravings, and conditioned responses are *empty* of any ultimate reality.

Zen masters feel this void through *zazen*, sitting meditation (the Japanese word *zen* derives from *zazen*, which was called *chan* in China).

> **Whether in a flow.state, in ecstasy or in emptiness, we haven't gained anything we didn't have already. In fact, quite the opposite has happened. We have returned to our essential nature as one.**

For a brief time, the Protector has taken a break from protecting us. Rather than remaining within the walls of the Tiny Me, we are free to expand beyond limits. I have this experience regularly when I dance. As soon as I *stop* evaluating, planning, and attempting to look good (all hallmarks of my Tiny Me), I lose myself in the movement and fresh shapes and forms emerge. I become the dance instead of being a dancer. The same thing happens when I'm on stage, doing a talk, or training people. Stuff comes out of me that I have not planned or managed. As soon as I become proud of my moves or chat, the moment of creative flow is shattered.

One for all, all for one

MY THESIS AT CAMBRIDGE delved into the earliest research in the neurobiology of experiences of unity, flow, and ecstasy. As we begin to experience ourselves as interconnected, at one with everything else, activity in our parietal lobes is massively reduced.[10–11] Curiously, the parietal lobe is the master of making comparisons:

- Right vs. wrong
- Pain vs. pleasure
- Up vs. down
- Me vs. others
- Good vs. bad
- Worthy vs. guilty

🔬 TOOLS FOR PSCHYONAUTS AND THRIVANAUTS?

Entheogens are substances like LSD, magic mushrooms, ecstasy, ketamine, and ayahuasca. They are calked entheogens because they often give people an experience of having a 'god' (theos) within. I neither recommend nor condemn entheogens because every human being needs to learn how to intuit what is right for them (we'll look at discerning intuition in more detail in Session 09, page 226) rather than rely on the rules or dogma of others. One thing that I have experienced, is that entheogens might sometimes be able to indicate the route and destination; but only deep inner work, without chemicals, allows us to travel there at will (and the chemicals can be damaging to our body.minds too).

These substances are now receiving a lot of attention from the mainstream medical and biological communities. One major study claims that psychedelics don't cause addiction or long-term psychiatric issues. In fact, 'in several cases, psychedelic use was associated with a lower rate of mental health problems.'[12] There is growing interest from psychiatrists, addiction researchers, and of course drug companies. Some of these substances may help to generate rapid recovery from severe and 'untreatable' depression, alcoholism, and heroin addiction.[13]

As soon as we compare things like this, we automatically split the world into two (or more) parts. We force ourselves away from any sense of unity and into what is known as **duality**. We can't be in flow if we feel separate from the thing we are doing. As soon as I think I am 'right' then naturally someone else, somewhere, has to be 'wrong.' It may feel great for a moment but sadly I can no longer be at one. Unity can't exist when we want to be better, faster, richer, smarter, or sexier than anyone else. When Adam and Eve discovered 'knowledge' by eating the apple in the Garden of Eden, suddenly they realized they were 'naked,' and that there was an opposite, called 'clothed.' With it came 'shameful' (as opposed to 'decent'). We were ripped out of the bliss of unity, symbolized by Eden, and instead given the knowledge of comparisons and dualities. This is why it was such a Fall!

Opposites may seem to be different from each other but delve a little deeper and we see that opposites are actually *two* poles along *one* continuum.

For example, hot and cold seem to be opposites but they are unified as temperature, just differing by degree. We can take pretty much any quality, name an axis after it and create two polarities made up of the extremes. Relationships get broken into passionate vs. apathetic; married vs. divorced. Careers get split into flying vs. failing. Yet they are made up of one thing, forced apart by our comparison-making brains.

As we fall into the trap of making comparisons, we are flung out of connection and into separation. This doesn't mean that we should stop noticing and enjoying distinctions. It just means that we can move beyond them into unity. Comparisons, judgments, and criticisms become way less important when we practice sensing everything as one. Tiny Me blends into Great We, and we can be both separate individuals and all connected at the same time. This is unity through diversity. Diversity in unity. The dualities dissolve, leaving just one thing, or **non-duality**. We can then be a Tiny Me that does lots of things . . . driven by a Great We that feels part of everything.

If you want to return to Eden, which you can do while sitting at home on a Sunday afternoon or waiting for a low-cost flight to take off at 5 a.m., you have to let go of comparisons. Then there will no longer be a 'good' or 'bad' experience, a 'nice' or 'nasty' person; or a 'Me' and a 'You.' There will only be **oneness**. The Sufi poet Rumi (the best-selling poet in America, 800 years after he wrote) reminds us: 'When you see the splendor of union, the attractions of duality seem poignant and lovely, but much less interesting.'

We are The Tiny Me and the Great We. We are all of it. Me, you, and the Buddha are one.

The Big U

THERE IS AN ASTONISHING amount of similarity between most of the wisdom traditions out there, even though they have emerged over thousands of years, and thousands of miles apart. Aldous Huxley called the set of beliefs that appear common among them the 'perennial philosophy.'

His research (and much that has followed it) demonstrates that the idea that we are all interconnected has surfaced in every region of the world.[14] Although each **wisdom tradition's** language, tone, and metaphors are all unique, they sing a song of the wonderful unity at the core of existence. From Taoism to yoga to shamanism, they share two fundamental truths:

1 The world is not the way we think it is. Yes, it looks all separate and disconnected, but it is actually joined up in many fathomable and unfathomable ways. The nature of it can be glimpsed in various guises, such as love, truth, and creativity.
2 We are more than we seem. We are not merely our patterns or our pain. We are actually part of this *one* thing. Experiencing Presence is enlightenment, realization, *satori*, *samadhi*, *kensho*, bliss, or any of the other terms for this ecstasy or emptiness. The Tiny Me is 'blown out,' the literal translation of nirvana.

Notice, there is nothing here about gods and goddesses, guilt and repentance, or obedience and wrath. There are no requirements to sing hymns or make sacrifices. You don't have to buy crystals, join a cult, or wear any funny outfits (though doing this can be a lot of fun). In fact, we don't have to label ourselves as anything at all. We are just people who are awake to the interconnected nature of life, and live as much as we can from that place. Whenever we get stopped by a problem, spot an old pattern, or sense some pain wanting to be released, we switch on to Presence and break through. All we have to do is get out of our HEAD, which usually fixates on the separate Tiny Me, and get into our HANDS and our HEART, where we can reconnect with the rest of the universe.

The Great We has nothing to do with God (if we think of God as some kind of bigger or better individual than us). The oneness isn't a God with a face or a name, although imagining it to be Buddha, Nature, or Brahman can be both playful and powerful in helping people, who relate to those concepts, to switch on. This one thing we are part of is simply *everything that is*, a totally secular idea that even fits with being an atheist. The science-fiction writer Philip K Dick called it a 'Vast Active Living Intelligence System.'

With more than a hint of tongue-in-cheek irony, he also called it 'Zebra.'
I like to call it the **Big Universe**, or **Big U**. You can think of the Big U as a
metaphysical reality (i.e. you actually believe it is physically all connected up),
or you can simply feel it as a *metaphorical* experience (i.e. a powerful form
of poetry). Either one can unlock the gateway to love, which is essential for
full-tilt creativity.

Even hardcore atheistic philosophers, usually happy to direct scorn
at anyone using the 'S' word (spiritual), have started to come round to
the inevitable logic of unity, of oneness (though they have made up a
fancy academic name for it, of course: 'Panpsychism'). Galen Strawson,
a professional philosopher and leading proponent of panpsychism, has
reasoned that if every concrete phenomenon in the universe is definitely
physical (i.e. is made up of matter), and that consciousness exists (we all seem
to agree that it does), then consciousness must be in matter too. It can't come
from nowhere. It has to be somehow in the atoms, molecules, and cells that
make up the universe.[15]

This means every physical thing in the Big Universe must have
some capacity or potential for consciousness. That includes dogs, pebbles,
playgrounds, and cups of coffee. They all are connected to Presence.
Descartes was wrong to split the world into mind stuff and body stuff. They
are one and the same thing. 'To put it crudely, the stuff of the world is mind-
stuff,' said Arthur Eddington, a world-famous astrophysicist.[16] Rewind a few
thousand years before Descartes, Strawson, and Eddington, and the historical
Buddha, who became enlightened under the Bodhi Tree in India, taught that
everything is made up of Mind. It is all one thing. Mind and matter are one.
As the universe expands, that one thing evolves into more and more complex
and awesome things, like the human body.mind, nuclear reactors, and the art
in the Tate or Guggenheim. It is this complexity that we must remain fitted
to, in step with, if we want to thrive.

We live in a universe characterized by dazzlingly creativity. However, the
stars and our sandwiches are all made up of one type of stuff. Even when we
do 'objective' science in a lab, we influence the things we study because we
are interconnected with them. Objects change how they act depending on

the kinds of tools used to measure them. The scientists are caught up in the very thing they are researching.

An electron can exist as either a wave or a particle. In fact, at any moment it exists as both (and neither) in a strange phenomenon known as 'superposition.' It is only when we look at the electron with a measuring device that it switches into a wave or a particle. Which it becomes depends entirely on the instrument chosen. This is called 'complementarity.' This mind-bending idea, straight from the forefront of physics, is still hard even for professional scientists to grasp. In an essay in one of the most respected scientific journals, *Nature*, a Professor of Physics at Johns Hopkins University wrote, 'The Universe is immaterial—mental and spiritual. Live, and enjoy.'[17]

Modern physics and the ancient wisdom traditions say the same thing: Everything is connected. Particles that have been split into two and sent in two different directions still remain somehow connected together. If one flips to be positive, the other always will be positive too. They seem to know which the other is, without any visible bonds. They can be 'entangled' like this even when miles apart, without any obvious mechanical connections. These are called 'non-local' effects because they have obvious local connections. Einstein famously called this 'spooky action at a distance.' In one study, particles have been effectively 'teleported' between two islands in the Canaries, 89 miles apart, without passing through the intervening physical space![18]

Scientists have now discovered that these kind of quirky quantum processes, previously thought to be observable only in extremely cold, sterile lab conditions, can actually happen at warm temperatures and inside organic materials! It is scientifically possible that the atoms in our brains, in our genes, cell receptors, and neurotransmitters are connected in a quantum soup with every other part of the universe, 24/7. Quantum processing has been found to take place in chlorophyll, the pigmented cells which harness the sun's energy in plants and turn it into food. Without chlorophyll, there could be no animal life on this planet. Chlorophyll turns light energy into food energy, and it does so incredibly efficiently. This is thought to be due to quantum effects.

The same spooky action might help us understand how ATP, the basic molecule of energy in the human body, is generated so fast, something that has baffled scientists to date. Quantum processes could also explain how we can differentiate maybe a billion distinct smells with only 100-or-so types of smell receptor. What this means is that, right now, as you read this, atoms all over your body.mind could be accessing information that is not local to you (i.e. not in the confines of your physical body.mind). It is even possible that insights and ideas come into your body.mind from the Big U. My hunch is that this is part of the story behind authentic creativity.

Human society, as well as human nature, is also totally interconnected. Although it appears as if we are separate individuals and countries, we are all intrinsically linked to everyone else through networks of money, products, waste, banking systems, taxes, global brands, and information. Food price spikes in Egypt affect those living in Edinburgh. A credit crunch in New York affects people in New Guinea. The whole idea of a nation, with borders and passports, is becoming ridiculous in a globalized world where soon, pretty much every product (and perhaps every body) will be connected up to the Internet.

What happens to one impacts us all, all ways. We humans are dancing with the Big U at all times, even if we don't know it.

What is enlightenment?

THE TINY ME WILL want us to obsess over what 'I' can get or avoid. We can allow it to carry on doing its thing while we tap into the Great We and live as much we can from a place of interconnection. Practicing how to shift away from the fixations of the Tiny Me into the expansiveness of the Great We is elemental to thriving.

From its seat in the cosmic theatre, the Tiny Me's view is restricted. It peers out into the universe, only ever catching a glimpse of the entirety of all that is. Even when we reconnect and come at the world through the lens of the Great We, we can never fully grasp with our conscious mind the infiniteness of the infinite. Although we can describe it with words like Oneness, Mind, or Tao, concepts themselves can never fully describe the thing. They are just words and, therefore by definition, are limited. The enormity of it all will always be a bit of a mystery. It is this mystery that mystics like to groove on.

All we can do is experience the mystery, wonder at it, marvel at it . . . and then do our best to live according to its relentless logic of radical unity, empathy, and compassion. This is what true enlightenment means: Living with love, truth, and creativity as much as we possibly can. We all have everything we need right here, in our body.mind, waiting for us to come and find it, by whatever path we choose. Within all of us there is this refuge, a place of Presence, centeredness, and calm. We can practice reaching this **still-point** within by reconnecting our **HEART**. Only then can we begin to break through and out towards a state of thriving.

Finding Your Still-Point to Connect to Presence

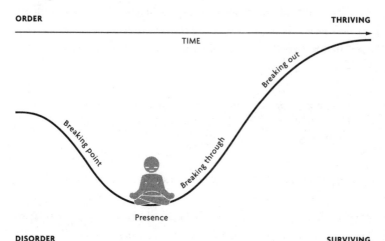

Most wisdom traditions offer up techniques that can help us connect into the grid, the oneness. I call them **reconnection practices** because they help us relink with the universe we are already connected to. Some traditions, like Vipassana meditation and ascetic Christian paths, suggest retreating from the world for a while to go inside and connect. Others, like tantric sex, archery, flower arranging, ecstatic or trance dance, and breathwork, teach us to get us stuck into life to find our joy. Some, like traditional forms of Buddhism, suggest that years of practice are needed to switch on fully. Others, like Zen Buddhism, say that we can become enlightened instantly. What I believe that they all share, though, is the focus on reopening a blocked connection to the Big U.

One thing that gets a lot of people in a tizzy is the idea that to reconnect and experience the Big U properly, we somehow have to destroy our ego, the Tiny Me. Even if we could obliterate it (which we can't), it would mean we would no longer be able to function in the world. That means no more exciting projects, chocolate brownies, or sweet lovemaking. I, for one, enjoy these things. The Tiny Me is brilliant. It allows us to live life. However, if we think that it is all we are, then we limit ourselves needlessly. We become trapped in our personality and not our potential. By switching on, deep inside, we blow out the worries of the Tiny Me (even if this only lasts for a few seconds) and come back to our still-point within the Great We. As the Tiny Me relaxes, the Protector within relaxes too.

Every given moment, including this one right here as you read

THIS

is an opportunity to switch on and reconnect with Presence.

Many wisdom traditions, in particular the Buddhist path, tell us that what is left, once we switch on, is nothingness, emptiness, the Void . . .

However, to many of us who love stories of space travel like *Gravity*, *Alien*, and *Star Wars*, the idea of nothingness can be pretty terrifying. How many people have we seen sucked out of air locks into the void of space? Things that scare us trigger the Protector into action to defend the Tiny Me from attack. What happens next is predictable. We go into lock-down and resist both the experience of oneness and its many benefits. So obsessing over the void can be a bit of a red herring. One of the great Zen masters of ancient China, Shen Hui, said that, to the enlightened (the switched on) the void is no longer a void.[19] In its place, is Presence. The Chinese call it the 'Tao.' Hindus call it 'Brahman.' Kabbalistic Jews call it 'Ein Sof.' Far from our annihilation in a cosmic void, the exact opposite is true. We discover we are Everything. We are the Great We, the Big U and, above all, limitless.

 THE MAGIC OF MEDITATION

Meditation is a popular choice for reconnection, although there are as many ways of meditating as there are people alive because no two people share the same body.mind. There is no one way to do it and no right way to do it. Most forms of meditation encourage the Tiny Me to worry less, think less, and chat less, though they can do this by focusing on nothing, something, or just allowing the moment to be here (which is the way of mindfulness). Recent (and quite controversial) research into meditation has suggested that it can help us overcome stress and anxiety as well as enhance long-term thinking capacities. When we meditate, we chill out our nervous system, preventing stress hormones like testosterone, cortisol, and adrenalin from being squirted with abandon into our bloodstream. One study has indicated that meditation can reduce the chances of dying from a stroke or cardiac arrest by almost 50 percent.[20]

Meditation has also been shown to reshape the brain. It expands the size of key parts of the prefrontal cortex, especially the parts that help dampen down impulses. Advanced meditators can reduce their experience of pain by consciously increasing activity of their anterior cingulate cortex.[21] It can even reduce the size of gray matter around the amygdala, where pain memories are stored. Just two weeks of compassion meditation, taught over the Internet, made participants more caring. One study found that just a handful of short sessions of meditation made people three or four times more likely to give up their seat to a person with disabilities on public transport![22]

We are all made of recycled stardust, temporarily formed into human beings. We live in the world as separate-seeming individuals who are, at one and the same time, one part of an enormously complex symphony of existence. It doesn't really matter which, if any, wisdom tradition you follow or whether or not you feel there is an Everything or Nothing. It matters not whether you are an atheist or Buddhist, a Catholic or a skeptic (or in some ways all four). What matters is that you switch on to Presence and find your still-point within, where you can always take refuge. As the Zen master Bodhidharma told us: 'The fools of this world look for sages far away. They don't believe that the wisdom in their own mind is the sage.'[23]

You can provide yourself with an unlimited supply of love. Bring love into every moment, and with it you'll melt away pain, suffering, and injustice. Feel stillness inside and you'll find that any anxiety about the future fades away. Experience Presence in your **HANDS**, **HEAD**, and **HEART**, and you'll come alive to the pure creative potential of this moment, here, right now, to be whatever you want it to be . . .

SWITCH ON TO PRESENCE

Switched Off: The universe is a cold, meaningless place. We are all separate and alone. We have to protect ourselves from people and defend ourselves from threats. In this universe, cynical competition for scarce resources is the way to survive.

Switched On: We are all connected within one vast, infinite field of energy called the universe. We are all children of this universe with a right to be here and to be loved and appreciated. We are distinct individuals yet all interdependent on each other in every sense. In this universe, co-creation is the way to thrive.

 ## SWITCH ON NOW

HANDS: Touch an object, a person, or something within reach. Hold your fingers there and sense where your fingers end and the object begins. Think about the quantum movement of energy at the point of intersection, where finger meets matter.

Can you sense Presence in the gap?

HEAD: Define who you are in less than ten words. Is this all you are? Who has decided where your limits lie? Or are you more than this collection of words? How much more?

Now imagine letting go of every comparison and concept you have about yourself. Let go of every idea of right and wrong, old or young, clever or stupid, and imagine instead the multitude of possibilities you have to express yourself.

HEART: When do you feel most in the flow, in the zone? When do you feel most calm and connected? When does your self-talk become quietest?

How does it feel when you breathe your way into a still-point?

When do you feel most connected to other people? To nature? What does it feel like to be this connected, present, flowing?

Imagine the universe is a giant hand at your back. Imagine you can sit back, onto the palm, and allow all your worries and concerns to take a break. Allow yourself to take a seat now and relax, melting like ice into a pool of warm, clear water. Enjoy this still-point. Enjoy your refuge within.

BREAKTHROUGH QUESTIONS

 If I was the one I have been waiting for, what would I do next?

 If I was supported by infinite amounts of love, how would I enjoy it right now?

Session 05

Peace

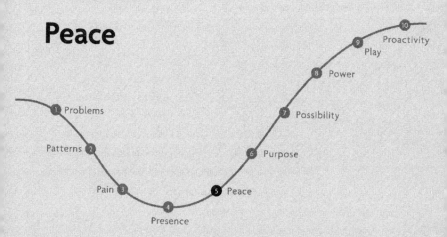

1. Problems
2. Patterns
3. Pain
4. Presence
5. Peace
6. Purpose
7. Possibility
8. Power
9. Play
10. Proactivity

WHEN WE SWITCH ON, we let go of all the noise and neediness of our old patterns. In their place, a stillness and spaciousness forms within our body.mind. Our lives can pivot in an instant in these moments. Without inner peace, our energy and attention remain tied up in keeping the world at bay, rather than working out how best to dance with it. Peace is not a reward for good behavior. It is not something that can be pursued and it cannot be purchased. Peace is something that arises, effortlessly, the moment we let go of our old assumptions and rejoin the sea of love that always surrounds us.

I often ask clients, whether entrepreneurs, troubled teens, or C-suite execs, the same question: 'If you had a magic wand and could wave it right now, what would you want more of?' After the first few responses, such as money, time, and the like, most groups settle on one thing: More peace. This is true whether in China or California. Shalom. Salaam. Shanti. Paz. Peace . . . is what we all want more of.

Yet peace is not designed into the systems we are part of. Most modernized economies are focused on boosting productivity and profit. To fulfill these goals, we are rewarded for success and punished for failure. A 'zero-sum game' has been invented: We are told that if she or he has more then I must have less. The cultural narrative tells us that the strongest and the fittest survive. So we compete at school, college, and in the job market to win our share of the pie. Competition is comparison on crack. By constantly comparing ourselves to others, as well who we were in the past and who we could be in the future, we create enormous amounts of stress in our body.mind. But it doesn't have to be this way.

Anthropologists have identified around 40 or so predominately peaceful cultures. There are fascinating similarities between these societies, like the Semai of Malaysia and Zapotec in Mexico. The people within them consider cooperation to be way more important than competition. They see competition as dangerous because it breeds aggression. So they teach kids to play to learn, not to win. Boys pretend to hunt together, collaboratively. Girls play together at creating a home. All of them swing on vines, jump through waterfalls, and create fantasy worlds. Yet there is rarely a winner and a loser. In some of these societies, no one can remember a single violent event ever having happened. They are peaceful because they have been taught to collaborate not compete.[1] Imagine what it would be like never to compete against your own expectations, or anyone else's, again . . .

By switching comparison for compassion, competition for collaboration, separation for unity, we can release into peace rather than promote more pain.

The Master Switch

PEACE IS THE KIND of inner calm that can get us through even the most cataclysmic crisis. By reconnecting as many times as we need to find our still-point inside, we can avoid becoming overwhelmed and seize our breakthroughs. Without connection to Presence there is just too much to be afraid of: Being alone, being let down, and being left without. Our body.mind remains too tight, our beliefs too rigid, our ideas too predictable. However, nothing can break us when we know how to access peace. Nothing can come close to the enormity of love that radiates into us when we let it. Nothing can resist being broken through.

Imagine inside your body.mind, anchored in your **HEART** but stretching through your **HEAD** right to the tips of your **HANDS,** there is a massive switch—like the kind of circuit-breakers that sit backstage in theaters, ready to turn on or off the electrical supply to the whole stage. This master switch toggles between two radically different ways of experiencing the world.

Every minute that you're awake you get to choose between these two states.

Nobody can ever prove, conclusively, that being switched on or off is right in any absolute sense. No professor, parent, or guru can ever tell you, with certainty, which is 'true' or which is 'false.' No one will ever be able to. You have to make the choice yourself, probably many times a day!

The Master Switch

Everything is disconnected, random and meaningless

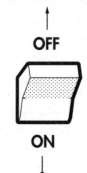

OFF

ON

Everything is connected, interdependent and meaningful

Right now, are you switched on or switched off?

It really is a binary decision. Although we may like to think that the way we met our current partner was deeply serendipitous but breaking our leg the day after was just unlucky, both of these statements can't be true. Either every experience in your life has some kind of empowering meaning . . . or none of them have. The world is either meaningful or meaningless. The dots in the universe are either joined up or they are a random mess. If you have ever thought that one thing in your life, one meeting, one encounter, one lucky break was ever 'meant to happen' then, in some way, everything that happens to you must somehow be 'meant to be,' even though it might hurt like hell.

> **Every single problem you experience can be metabolized within you into something of value, just as we metabolize food into energy. We just have to be willing to switch on.**

 RESILIENT VIETNAM VETS

There is always a way to make an experience mean something more empowering, without having to fight reality. During the Vietnam War, many American prisoners-of-war were tortured, humiliated, and viciously beaten. In one study, those who had found a way to grasp some meaning in the experience— switching from passive victim of life to active co-creator with it—were much better equipped to bounce back afterward. They found ways to appropriate the experience into their life story and become wiser, more grateful, and more optimistic about the future because of it.[2]

In another study of 750 former POW in Vietnam, the ones who managed to avoid PTSD and depression best were the soldiers who used the experience to become more optimistic, altruistic, and self-empowering.[3]

We thrive when we own every problem we encounter and bring it inside us where we can switch it into something meaningful. Any **resistance**, any pain, can be released because of our felt sense of connection to the Big U. Within the cauldron of the body.mind, in our cells and neurons, we can transform constraints into creativity and patterns into new superpowers. Love is what heats up the cauldron and keeps it fluid. This is the triumph of connection over separation, healing over trauma. It is full engagement with a world that is constantly challenging us to go with the flow as it evolves into ever more complex forms.

This is where the rubber hits the road and where switching on really starts to count. Here are some examples of switching from disempowerment to empowerment:

You're having a fight with a lover. They are doing your head in, triggering the story that they are . . .

SWITCH ON

Experiencing peace within, you find a creative way to respond to them that honors their patterns and pain. The moment becomes one of total appreciation for their uniqueness as you find a way to reach them as you know they are in pain, asking them if . . .

You look in the mirror. Eek! You're feeling too skinny or too fat, proving that you are . . .

SWITCH ON

Experiencing peace within, you breathe and let go of all the self-talk. You distinguish who you really are, an intrinsically beautiful part of the Great We, from who you have become, a Tiny Me with a load of normal patterns. You decide to nourish yourself by . . .

You feel jealous about the success of a colleague, because they always get . . .

SWITCH ON

Experiencing peace within, you honor their capabilities and commitment, framing them as an example that can help you focus your resolve. You own your own lack of activity and commit to . . .

You might find yourself saying, 'Hold on! Of course *you* can switch those kinds of things into something empowering that brings more love, trust, and creativity into the world. But *my* problems are so much more serious and . . .' Well, I hear you. And I get you. I struggled with that for years (and still get caught up in that story from time to time). This is why you have to expand your experience of yourself beyond the Tiny Me and into the Great We. It is only this connection that is deep enough to overcome the Big Kahuna Burger stories we tell about ourselves that have us be a victim, afraid, unloved. We can only get to the peace once we find some meaning, some wisdom, in the pain. This is what sets us free.

Switching on doesn't mean that we ignore or deny pain. We do the complete opposite. We fully *accept* every experience, really feel it, but rather than trip out on it, reacting or repressing, we find a way to find a meaning within it that is empowering. Any time you're stressed is the perfect chance to go inside and switch on. It may not be convenient in a grocery store but there is always time in the day (or night) to take a few moments to dive into the lagoon of your experience and bring back a pearl or two. Yes it may be dark in there occasionally. But you have the light within to illuminate the way. If you have the *cojones* to honor your pain, own it, and explore it you can always find a way to co-create with it something of value for yourself and the world.

I find that I do a lot of inner work at night. The wisest parts of me won't let me sleep if there's inner work to do. So if I am obsessing about something, anxious, tense, or moody, I know I am ripe and ready for a breakthrough. The gateway is the pain itself. Our darkside calls us to attention, offering peace in exchange for a connection to Presence. In the Eastern traditions, the lotus is a common symbol for this exchange, which is why it is plastered across meditation books and yoga centers across the planet. The beautiful lotus flourishes in dank and skanky swamps, just as our liberation lies within the parts of ourselves that are most hidden away. The problems we suffer and struggle with provide us with our release as soon as we take refuge inside.

It may not be 'easy' to find an empowering way through every experience; but it can be done. The toughest life with meaning is more thrivadelic than the easiest life without.

Luckily we have a brilliant helper within who can help us process our pain and find peace with anything.

Fade up the Connector

ONE WAY OF DOING inner work appears in virtually every traditional culture on the planet. It involves a switched on person, a medicine man or wise woman, helping their tribespeople heal. A common name for this kind of person is a shaman. I believe we all have a shaman inside of us. I call this inner shaman, **the Connector**. Contemporary studies on resilience state that we all have this force within (even described as 'spiritual' by one leading researcher) that compels us to become more generous, compassionate, wise, and whole.[4] Once we find our refuge or still-point, the Connector will come out and help us find peace. The Native American shaman Black Elk said: 'The first peace, which is the most important, is that which comes within the souls of people when they realize their relationship, their oneness, with the universe . . . this center is really everywhere, it is within each of us.'[5]

While the Protector's job is to defend you against threat, the Connector's role is to help you move forward, heal, and grow. The Protector merely defends against what you *don't* want. The Connector works tirelessly to help you create what you *do* want: What is good, noble, and true. Our inner shaman seems to have the right amount of strength, and the right kinds of skills, to take on the problems we face, and break through them as long as we keep our connection to the Big U open.

> **Your inner shaman is waiting for you right now
> to support you to find peace with any problem.**

You can awaken your Connector with any form of **reconnection practice**. Most involve the HEART and HANDS as much as the HEAD, so they are not easily taught by using words on a page. They need to be experienced, practiced, felt, and then embodied. I urge you to explore some of the different forms and traditions and sense which ones help you find peace, purpose, and power. You can explore an A–Z of these practices at www.ripeandready.com. I have developed a reconnection practice for clients, individuals, and groups, which fuses elements of mindfulness, meditation, hypnotherapy, breathwork, dance, and the emotional power of music (and more). You can find videos and recordings on the site too.

One thing worth mentioning. Be sure to find a practice that connects you to your HEART, to compassion, and to love, not just one that teaches you how to still your thoughts and quiet your HEAD. Mindfulness meditation has gone mainstream recently, which is brilliant. However, without tapping into your HEART as well as your HEAD, it can be used to increase productivity without empathy, and boost profits without serving humanity.

Unless you intentionally look to engage and heal your HEART with your inner work, the Protector within will still engage in activities that are defensive, controlling, and manipulating. You know if you are really connecting to the Big U, because your pain will melt away and you will effortlessly want to spread the love.

As you experience being at one with the entire universe, the suffering of others will touch you and inspire you into action. Just like when you stub your toe and reach out to it to rub it, you will want to make a difference to everyone and everything that is in pain. We will return to this compulsion to serve the world in Session 10 (see page 244). Keep in mind that indifference to the plight of others, whether friend or foe, comes from the Protector not the Connector.

However you reconnect, as you do, the part of your brain that draws a comparison between your Tiny Me and Great We decreases in activity.[6] As the Tiny Me's voice of judgment/doom/criticism calms, you get access to a load of alternative possibilities that come from accessing the Great We. The Protector fades out and the Connector takes over, just like on the cross-fader of a DJ's mixer (see diagram opposite). Balance between the two—being in the mix—is the goal. The ideal place to be along the cross-fader will change in each moment depending on what is emerging around you.

Like stepping through a shimmering waterfall to find a safe cave away from the predators of the open jungle, we can always step inside to find peace. Even if you simply spend five minutes a day with your eyes closed, asking the Connector to scan your body.mind for any pain that it can release, it will have a massive impact on your wisdom and your wellbeing. Rather than worrying about whether you are 'doing it right,' focusing on a word or trying to stop words coming to mind at all, just allow yourself to switch from broadcast mode to receive mode. Receive from the Big U you are connected to.

The Cross-fader of the Self

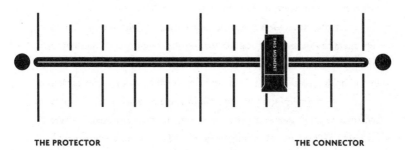

THE PROTECTOR   THE CONNECTOR

Healing the hurt in real-time

RECONNECTION PRACTICES HELP US to work with painful emotions without freaking out. This is because the love outweighs the fear; the truth overcomes our disempowering stories; and creativity is more potent than habit. The involvement of intense empowering emotions in the process of healing is key. If our most fervent disempowering emotions—summarized by the word 'pain'—drive us to create patterns, then it seems logical that we might only be able to dissolve them with stronger, more inspiring emotions. We can flood our body.mind with love, truth, and creativity so that we feel safe, secure, and connected enough to first feel, and then release, our pain.

Before you allow yourself to experience pain within, it's worth pre-empting the needs of the Protector. Remember, its job has been to defend you against pain and the fear of pain. So until it feels totally reassured that you are safe, it won't let you get near the real action. Tell it that it is safe and that you have its back. Tell it that, if it's too much, you will give it some space to rejuvenate (and seek professional help if needed). Tell it that you're ready to let go of your pain and ask for its help in doing this. Treat the Protector as a trusted ally and it will be more up for letting go of the anxiety that locks the pain in place. You can even ask it if it has any concerns about transforming. It may well have some. See if you can reassure it by meeting its needs. Remember: The Protector really does want what's best for you. It just has old-fashioned ideas about how to make that happen. Ask the Connector to help you safeguard the Protector if you get stuck.

Once the Protector is prepared to feel the pain without shutting down, reconnect to Presence. You can do this self-healing in active meditation, while 'in the zone' on a walk, run, or yoga class, or while bounding around in an ecstatic dance class. You can even do it while making love (although I wouldn't recommend it unless both/all of you are aware of what is planned, switched on, and keen to experiment in total trust and intimacy). There are no right or wrong places to transform your life. Any space where you feel safe enough to do inner work is great, assuming it is socially appropriate and respectful to others. If anything starts to feel a bit 'off,' just stop the process and come back at a more appropriate time.

As you feel the pain arise, let it go! Whether abandonment, humiliation, rejection, shame, or fear, allow it to dissolve away as you bathe in love from the universe. Just as a warm bath caresses your tired muscles and exhausted mind, so too can the warm glow of oneness relax, repair, and refresh you. You might be feeling pain that has never seen the light of day before, having been pushed deep down into your darkside. So be prepared to allow it to be there before you move to change it. Give yourself time to grieve, cry, be angry, or whatever response wants to be heard.

The time has come to allow yourself to release the emotions that you didn't feel safe enough to express when a child.

You don't want to dwell on them for hours though, which can just reinforce the conditioning inside and consolidate the memories again. You don't want to get hooked into them and come full circle. But don't rush either, otherwise you may prevent yourself from really feeling the pain. If you don't feel it, you cannot release it. If you leave pain repressed, it will remain inside. It may take many sessions, over many months, before you have cried all you have to cry about something.

Some forms of bodywork can help accelerate the release in your neurons. Moving, dancing, and shaking are also helpful. The most powerful approach I have found is Biodynamic Craniosacral Therapy (and I am lucky enough to be married to an amazing practitioner of it). It can really help clear out the old patterning at the cellular level.

If, at any point, the Protector in you says, 'Uh uh, I'm not ready to release it yet,' try asking it what it needs to feel safe. If it still isn't up for it, postpone the inner work to when you feel more resourced and safe; or seek professional medical or psychological help. If you ever find it is too much or too intense, try deepening your connection (perhaps by breathing more deeply, moving more, or shaking). If this doesn't work, let the whole idea go and return to it within a few days. Watch out though. It may be tempting to 'forget' to come back, or suddenly get really busy. This is just the Protector doing its best to avoid the pain. Engage the Connector to help you safeguard the Protector some more and make a date to do more inner work when you

RECONSOLIDATION RESEARCH

Various studies have indicated that intense memories, stored in the amygdala, can be radically altered. The memory becomes unstable during a short window, for around ten minutes, after it has been triggered. Rats that have been conditioned to fear a stimulus, or have been trained to become addicts, have had the memories associated with their behavior disrupted by treatment with chemicals that alter how the neurons work. This has been called 'reconsolidation.' In human beings, intervention in those ten minutes seems also to have a positive impact. It seems that every time we activate a memory, we have an opportunity to heal it in some way, to reduce the intensity of the difficult emotions associated with it, and so lessen their profound impact on our wellbeing.[7-8]

intuitively feel it is right.

Healing like this cannot be done by force. Force provokes the Protector. You can't will yourself to heal; you can only choose to let go of what's stopping you from being whole. This is what I call 'Tickle Theory.' If you want someone (including yourself) to shift, permanently, it is far more effective to tickle them than push them. Pushing will trigger resistance (as will bribes or demands). Tickle people and they move, laughing while they do it. Healing only occurs through softness, gentleness, and compassion. Tough love is valuable as long as it is really coming from love, spoken firmly and clearly so people really feel the compassion. But nobody needs any more aggression or pain.

Over time, if you keep on doing inner work—and keep on processing your pain as it is triggered by life's rich array of problems—you'll learn to trust the Connector to help you find the right people, healers, friends, and communities to nourish your drive to thrive.

Although most of us have big 'stuff' to let go of, transforming our inner landscape doesn't have to be serious and scary. Transformation can even be exciting, adventurous, and enlivening. Yes, it may mean crying for a few days at random moments or going on an emotional rollercoaster ride. But isn't that the point of life? To live and feel fully? And remember, if it ever gets too much, there are many experienced professionals who can help you through the tough patches and support your healing journey.

The Connector in you is an expert shaman, designed to help you heal. Things may get fierce for a bit but it won't last long as you learn how to come back to love, connection, and Presence. Your still-point is your refuge and it's always there for you! When you have the support of the universe at your back, no pain is too much to feel and release. This doesn't mean that professional help isn't valuable, rewarding, and, sometimes, very important (especially if you are feeling like you are in distress for an extended period of time). However, never forget that this is *your* life, *your* body.mind, and *your* pain. You have the potential within to transform. New frameworks and techniques, often wielded by professionals, are fabulously helpful. But they are just tools. The Connector does the work, all ways.

Being Joystruck!

THROUGH REGULAR PRACTICE, NO matter where you start on the scale of thriving, it is possible to master your inbuilt capacity for self-healing. You can use whatever stress or fear you stumble on during a typical day as fuel for more release into peace. Someone's cussed at you in class? Take a moment to switch on, find the pain it touched, and heal it in real-time with love. Can't finish a project on time and upset with yourself? Switch on and find the original fear and dissolve it into the 'it's all is good' of connection.

When you let go of pain (and its associated fear memories) you may experience a major discharge of stored-up emotion. It's not uncommon to dissolve into fits of hysterics, cough, choke, or sob in a flood of tears. Some people get hot and sweaty. Others cold and chilly. Some get dizzy. This can often be part of the healing process. If it feels too much, seek support from a medical or psychological professional.

Our Tiny Me can get a bit disoriented when a major belief or habit is released from our system, especially if it's been around for a while. This is normal and to be expected. Although sometimes the feelings might be unpleasant, they are signs that the energy behind those old, repressed emotions is on the move. If you can bear it, breathe the 'stuff' away. If you feel like shaking or moving, follow that **intuition**. And if you want to stop, stop. There is always another time. If you sense it would be useful, get some coaching, therapy or support from someone who cares. Ask your doctor for their opinion. Have a long shower or a dance. Meditate some more. Above all else, treat yourself with compassion and know that everything is always transformable with courage, curiosity, and conviction.

As the body.mind releases stored-up emotions, it becomes more and more open to what the specific moment may bring. With big releases of pain, it is common to experience clear, fresh energy rushing into us from above, below, or behind. Whenever we are ready to open up, the universe is ready to get us loved up. I call this rush being **Joystruck**. It's similar to the rush you might get on the dance floor, yet cleaner. Presumably, it involves a release of oxytocin and a burst of activity from the vagus nerve. I sense it may be the experience known as *kundalini* rising, an ancient yogic phenomenon where a (metaphorical) goddess or sleeping snake awakens and arises from the base of our spine, as we become alive to the reality of the loving universe we are one with. Whether it is *kundalini* or not, this experience of pure joy, emanating from a **healed HEART** up through our **HEAD** and our **HANDS**, can be sparked when we switch on and swap out some reactive pain for some rejuvenating peace.

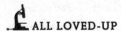 ## ALL LOVED-UP

Long thought of as being purely a biological pump, research has begun to show just how powerful the heart is as a feeling and thinking system in its own right. Some refer to the heart, with its estimated 40,000 neurons, as a 'little brain.' The heart can actually sense, learn, and remember, sending signals upward to the insula to be actioned. The heart also releases oxytocin, making us more trusting, committed, and helpful (although it may also have a role in reinforcing pain memories on the social side of the brain).[9]

Oxytocin, often called the 'love' or 'intimacy hormone,' is all about helping us connect. It is released by mothers as they breastfeed and both parents as they cuddle their baby. It is also pumped around the body when we fall in love (or simply think of people we love). Being cared for and being cuddled both release oxytocin. So does a quick massage. Even logging onto Facebook can boost it, as does dancing or yoga.[10] Oxytocin reduces blood pressure, balances body temperature, inhibits anxiety, reduces levels of the stress hormones, and promotes healing of cuts and bruises. It makes us more social, nurturing, charitable, and trusting (although only within our 'group,' not with everyone it seems). This is the reconnection response in action.

As you release pain, the stories held in place start to fall away. As your body.mind gets all loved-up, oxytocin and other hormones help release the fear memories rather than strengthen them. The frames through which you see the world become massively more flexible. You can start inventing much more empowering stories that inspire you to thrive through even the most intense or challenging problems. You can finally experience the full intensity of the world as it is, unfiltered by stories and unmediated by bullshit. You get the whole triumph and tragedy of the human experience in all its glory. This might be a lot to take in when it first starts happening. If you are used to a fixed viewpoint, suddenly having a whole palette of them is both liberating and awe-inspiring.

As our minds are no longer slaves to one fixed perspective, they are emancipated. Freedom is peace. Peace is liberation.

You might feel space opening up in which you are free to transform your experience of the past, recasting it as a source of meaning as opposed to a source of pain or regret. If you do, there will also be an opening to forgive people, especially those who in your old story you had decided were mean or nasty. When we forgive people, we give up being victims. We release ourselves from victim stories, which always disempower us. We take back the power we gave them when we decided they had 'made' us unhappy. This doesn't mean you have to condone their behavior. It just means that you understand that they, too, are deeply flawed people driven by pain. Hurt people hurt people. Forgiveness releases everyone from a trap from which there is no way out.

If we feel big enough, if we feel the Great We at our back, we can even apologize to them for our part of the conflict, our contribution to the mix (if there was one). We can even apologize for casting them in the starring role of baddie in our story. An apology like this is not the morally right or wrong thing to do. It simply opens up possibilities for co-creativity that simply weren't there two minutes before. Just a simple, elegant . . .

My Bad! Sorry.

. . . can do it.

Release into peace

ANY PAIN, ANY BELIEF, any assumption can be released into peace by letting go of it. We can allow it to dissolve and flow away in the great flood of love that courses through us when we switch on. The more often we reconnect, the more pain we can release. Trust begins to form between us and the universe. The Tiny Me learns it can relax into the Great We and be free. We can now start to let go of any fundamental disappointments we might have with the universe, with life itself.

We are, already, part of the universe. If we don't fully trust the universe, then we cannot trust ourselves. And if we don't trust ourselves, we cannot trust the universe. Until this relationship is clear of bullshit stories, we won't feel fully at peace. In many ways, the entire journey across the Breakthrough Curve is a process of deepening this trust. Trust is the lubricant of creativity.

To trust life, we have to find a way to be OK with whatever

IS

. . . in this moment here, even if we wouldn't choose it in an ideal world. We have to find a way to replace OI! NO!—the protestations of the Protector—with

YES!

Fortunately, the Connector can say this to everything. It can say this to all that has been and all that is.

By saying yes, you signal to your body.mind that you accept what is—trust it, **surrender** to it. Try it right now. Think of something that has been annoying you, something you or somebody else has done. Something that feels intensely irritating, upsetting, scary, or stupid. Now say, 'YES!' to it and see what changes in your body.mind. Breathe deeply and keep saying, 'YES!' until either you release into peace, or you spot an area of pain that might benefit from some inner work.

Now for our natural ingenuity. Follow 'YES!' with

AND . . .

The magic of the creative spirit now begins. Saying, 'AND . . .' allows you to take what IS and adapt, flex, pivot, adjust, iterate, and innovate it into what it *could* become in the future. This is like dancing with a partner. For you both to flow, you can't criticize what they do, no matter how much you may dislike it. If you have a go, it will shut them down, and you will lose the flow. Instead, you have to work with them and guide, coax, tickle, and inspire them into a style, rhythm, and tempo that you love. This YES! AND . . . is the core teaching of all improvisation training for actors. It is what every musician has to learn when jamming. Go with what IS, and use your ingenuity to shape it into what you want.

Try it now. Take that thing that has been irritating or upsetting you and say, 'YES! AND . . .' to it and see what your body.mind comes up with after the AND.

Saying, 'YES! AND . . .' doesn't mean we have to *agree* with the way the world is and it definitely doesn't mean that we want it stay the same. It is just that we accept that *what is* . . . well, *IS* and, with that acceptance, we can look to see what we can create differently in future. We don't waste our energy and effort on resistance, either internal or external. Instead, we accept the **ISness** of this *moment* because it IS. We can then use all our energy to find, and bring to life new possibilities that can bring more love, truth, and creativity to the *next* moment. The 'YES!' gives us the peace we need to let our patterns go into love. The 'AND . . .' stimulates the Connector to get busy creating things that move us toward more thrivability.

Nelson Mandela and Mahatma Gandhi both enacted this YES! AND . . . philosophy in their world-changing work. Gandhi was a major proponent of the philosophy of non-violence, *ahimsa*. He refused to *fight* the ISness of the British occupation of India with violence. He did not deny the reality of what was by repressing it or reacting to it. He *accepted* it, while committing himself in the core of his being to the liberation of his people. He believed non-violence was the most powerful force in the world, the key to unlocking the creative spirit. He saw peace as the start of love coming into the world as action. This is the essence of the YES! AND . . . Peace moves seamlessly into love, which ignites creativity. Peace is the essence of creativity.

In a parallel epiphany, Nelson Mandela realized he had to transform *himself* from righteous fighter to collaborative statesman, if he wanted South Africa to transition to peace. To do that, he had to accept that white people, including his predominantly Afrikaner oppressors, needed to be part of the future of the nation. He had to say 'YES!' to them, and the past, before he could play with the 'AND . . .' He had to tame the troubled waters of his own pain before he could bring more peace and prosperity to his people.

He switched on to his 27-year prison experience, recasting it as a massive source of empowerment: 'If I had not been in prison I would not have been able to achieve the most difficult task in life, and that is changing yourself.'[11] With a tranquil HEART, he had the insights he needed in his HEAD to guide the country from minority to majority rule. In one powerful moment, on national TV, he reached out his HANDS to President F W De Clerk in a clear display of brotherhood in a war-torn land.

In other words, peace is not the end of our journey. It is a prerequisite for accessing our full creativity without wasting precious time and energy on patterns (and the reactions these spark in others).

By diligently reclaiming *all* the energy stored up in our pain.pattern crystals, we can bring it to bear on creating a thriving world for ourselves and our people. The splinters are removed, the walls come down, and we open up new fields of possibility to explore.

Breaking Through Front

When we switch on
to break through the
walls, we get to enjoy
a world full of possibility

The big surrender

THE TINY ME USUALLY thinks it can outsmart life. After all, this is what it spends most of its time trying to do to keep us safe. Yet how can we be smarter than a universe that has created millions of species, all adapted to their specific niches, and all able to thrive on this planet? Although we might think we can control it, in reality life is always in the driving seat. So our only hope for real peace is to surrender to that cosmic wisdom, even if we have trouble understanding it. We cannot analyze the vast symphony of activity in the complex, adaptive system of the Big U from our position as one tiny part of it. So we all have to choose whether to fight it, resist it and be angry with the universe; or surrender to it, with a big YES! AND . . . so we can start to co-create with it.

The word Islam is derived from the Arabic *aslama*, which means to submit or surrender. Five times a day, observant Muslims consciously open their HEARTS to their God in a declaration of surrender. The philosopher Friedrich Nietzsche, who pronounced that God was dead, promoted a secular version of this. He called it *amor fati* or the 'love of fate.' As he put it: 'My formula for greatness in a human being is *amor fati*: That one wants nothing to be different . . . not merely bear what is necessary . . . but love it.'[12] This is what surrender means. This is what it means to go with the flow. We don't fight the ISness. We let go of the Tiny Me's constant opinions about what should be happening and what we should have received. We find some way to accept what IS, find some meaning or love in it. If we have not learned to love our fate, we will bring pain and patterns into our future, limiting our creativity.

If you really want to grow with every challenge, and are committed to having a fully thrivadelic life, you will have to learn how to let go of *everything* that is keeping you stuck. Any time you feel yourself moved to blame, shame, or complain, it is because your Tiny Me is fixated on something and thinks what IS should be different. Time to let go.

> **Every regret is an opportunity to relinquish another story about what coulda/woulda/shoulda happened.**

This is why the Way of Breakthrough, living from enlightenment, is not a piece of cake. I often hear people say how easy it must be to drop out like a hippy. Yet the true path of wisdom, of switching on, is profoundly challenging because we have to keep on surrendering. There is nowhere to run away to. There is nothing to hide behind. Stories, assumptions, 'noble lies,' habits all drop away, leaving us naked in the ISness. Once we have seen the truth, each moment becomes a choice: To live in fear and reaction . . . or let go of it all and find a way to be at peace with every experience.

Can we live without bullshit to defend us? Truly vulnerable to the vagaries of the universe, open to whatever this moment has in store for us?

On the path of wisdom, eventually we must all face the ultimate thing to let go of: Our life. Death greets us all. If we are anxious about it, then, by definition, we are not fully at peace. Although it's not sexy to talk about it, death is part of the ISness of life. We can't have one without the other. It's a package deal. If you are anxious about it, as most of us are if we are honest, it is a signal there is something we are holding on to. We have the choice: Switch on or remain switched off? We can let go of the stories, the attachments, and the fear; or we can remain tenaciously holding on to them as the clock counts down. The philosopher Søren Kierkegaard said, 'Whoever has learned to be anxious in the right way has learned the ultimate.'[13] We can use our fear, especially our fear of death, as an opening to surrender even more.

Every shade of fear, worry, or doubt is an invitation to switch on and remember our oneness with the universe. We have to give something up when we do. We have to let go of the opinions and assumptions of the Tiny Me. Those 'noble lies' have to be released. In fact, enlightenment experiences are often called 'ego deaths.' Our Tiny Me has to 'die' continuously (or at least fade out of the mix), for us to enjoy the peace of oneness. This can lead to a lot of resistance within because the last thing the Protector wants is to disappear! So it will kick and scream until we learn how to reassure and secure it. The more we reconnect, allowing our Tiny Me to fade out gently for a few minutes during lovemaking, meditation, or dance, the more willing it is to come to terms with death.

Eventually, we will be able to think of our death without terror. As long as we reconnect and accept what IS, we can keep on releasing the fear, telling ourselves that the 'happiness of the drop, is to die in the river,' as the Sufi Al-Ghazali wrote. In other words, when we die as individuals, either literally or through ecstasy, we return to the source of all things, the Big U. We are already part of the oneness. When we die, we will still remain part of it.

If things ever get scary and trip you out, here is a simple reconnection practice to try, based on the ancient Hawaiian wisdom tradition of Ho'oponopono. When you feel stressed out by something that is hard to let go of, repeat these words two or three times, feeling their meaning within:

> Thank you. I love you.
> I am sorry. Please forgive me.
> Help me. Show me the way.
> I am ready. How can I serve?

That's it. Four lines. Try it now, allowing the words to shift the energy flow in your body.mind, melting some of those pain.pattern crystals away. If you are ready for it, consider your death . . . Can you surrender your fears and stories? Can you take solace in Presence, in the Great We?

Here is what I say: 'YES! I am most certainly going to die. AND . . . therefore, what shall I do with the rest of today, tomorrow, and next year to make the most of this incredible gift of conscious, awakened, switched on life?'

SWITCH ON TO PEACE

Switched Off: The nearest we get to peace is when we forget our worries for a moment or drown our sorrows. Lasting peace is impossible as there are always more things to be fearful of, more random events that can hurt us, including the ultimate, which is our death.

Switched On: Peace arises when we let go of our pain and the patterns that defend us. We release every fear and anxiety as we deepen our connection to Presence. The more we surrender to what Is, the more can create what might be. We can even conquer a fear of death as we surrender to the universe of which we are already an intrinsic part.

 **SWITCH ON NOW**

We now swap the order of the three dimensions from **HANDS**, **HEAD**, **HEART** to **HEART**, **HEAD**, **HANDS** as we start to switch on from our core being outward.

HEART: Picture the word 'SAFE' in your mind's eye. Allow it to take you somewhere that feels safe.

Amplify those feelings as much as you can. Actively boost your feelings of love, trust, and wonder by picturing people, places, and moments in time that you adore.

Scan your entire body.mind for pain.pattern crystals, areas that feel upset, pained, impotent, or anxious. Choose one of them and breathe into it.

Could you ask for help from the Big U? Are you ready to receive it? Can you ask the Connector to take over for a moment and help you release into peace?

HEAD: State a complaint you have about the pain and then say, 'YES! AND . . .' and finish the sentence. Keep finishing it in a variety of ways until you have found a frame that is empowering and will help you thrive.

HANDS: Imagine you are letting the love of the universe into your body.mind. It might come in through your feet, solar plexus, gut, or the top of your head.

Can you allow it in and let it melt away the pain?

BREAKTHROUGH QUESTIONS

 If I were fully connected to myself and the universe, what would I let go of right now to embrace peace?

 If I were the most enlightened, peaceful sage in history, what stories would I be willing to surrender that are no longer serving?

Session 06

Purpose

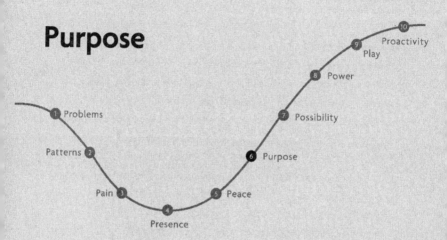

Problems

Patterns

Pain

Presence

Peace

Purpose

Possibility

Power

Play

Proactivity

CONNECTED, CURIOUS, AND COURAGEOUS, we can channel our energy into things that are meaningful; and find meaning in things that trigger pain. We can focus our creativity on building a flourishing future, instead of frittering it away maintaining patterns from the past. Our guiding light is our purpose. We cannot thrive until we discover it; and we cannot fail to thrive as long as we align ourselves with it every day. Everyone has one and each person's is different. Lasting happiness can never come from achieving goals, no matter how audacious, because the glow from every success, whether it is winning Olympic gold or a golden Oscar, fades eventually. However, every problem we have is an opportunity to discover more about our purpose, providing us with a joy that shines brighter with every passing day.

You may think a lot, even worry a lot, about what you 'should' do with your life. Should you keep your safe job or leave it to follow your bliss? Should you have a baby now or party hard? Should you make lots of money while you can or travel the world? Should you start a non-profit organization or change the system from inside it? It's easy to trip out on questions like these but they are the wrong questions to be asking if you want to thrive.

Your purpose is nothing to do with what you should do (or not). It is not about being right or wrong. It has nothing to do with what your parents think. It's nothing to do with being rich, respected, or famous. It's not even about what you want or desire. Instead, your purpose emanates clearly from your body.mind once it is free from patterns. It is Gandhi's idea of love-in-action (see Session 05, page 146). It is your truth once you have reached peace within. Every time you hear yourself or others say, 'I should . . .' or 'I must . . .' you are hearing a story that pain has locked in place. Heal the pain and you are free to co-create a new story with the ISness of life, which can guide you to thrive for the rest of your days.

Purpose is not a big, hairy, or audacious goal. Instead, it is the way you can be each and every moment, of each and every day, that brings the most of your potential into the world. It is the glue that connects your brilliance with what your community needs most. Purpose is a conversation between your HEART and the heartaches of the world. It is a bridge between your unique gifts and what the world wants most from you. You can't second-guess it with your HEAD or force it to be something it isn't with your HANDS. It may not be convenient, moneymaking, or safe. Many of your loved ones may not understand it. Some may resist it. Yet it does not matter who thinks what about it. It is *your* truth.

No more 'shoulds'

ARE YOU EXHAUSTED FROM running toward or away from the hopes and desires of your parents? Tired of benchmarking your success with that of your friends? Undecided whether to focus on fame and fortune or making a difference to society? Confused by competing myths spun by the media about what the good life is? Overwhelmed by just how much you could do with your talents? Unsure what following your bliss would even look like?

Help is at hand. Or rather, in your **HEART**.

To find our purpose, first we have to let go of all the patterns that have got in its way for years. Every time we ask ourselves, 'What should I be doing right now?' we are letting the Protector dominate our lives. This is a question it likes to ask because the answer might reassure it that it is 'right' and so we are safe. Being right, and righteous, is a trap our Tiny Me falls into when it desperately attempts to create certainty in a constantly changing world. It reasons that if it finds the 'right' thing, then everyone will love us, respect us, and appreciate us as we deserve. It reckons that if it works out what is 'right', then we won't experience disappointment and disapproval again.

Our expectations around the kind of life we 'should' lead are always driven by lack. The 'shoulds' start early in life. Parents naturally want a better life for their kids than they believe they had. Education, money, power, fun, love . . . whatever they thought they lacked, they will urge their offspring to go out and seek. Teachers, friends, and the media then pile on the pressure for us to perform, even if they do it with the best of intentions. Most of their suggestions come from patterns created to defend against their own lack. Being young and impressionable, we pick up a load of these 'shoulds' and start to live our life according to their rules. The 'shoulds'—designed to defend against the pain of having no job, no money, no worth—become more bricks in the wall we put up as front. We then use our career choices, relationship choices, life choices as evidence we are a 'good' person or have done the 'right' thing.

News flash: The world is in constant flux. There are never any absolutely *right* choices. This is a judgment based on some arbitrary belief system. There are just *fitted* ones, appropriate ones, which can be discerned by constantly paying attention to what IS. 'What "should" I be doing with my life?' is a worry of the Protector rather than a creative **inquiry** from the Connector. This way lies suffering. Instead, *sense* what fits the effervescent changes that are going on within you and outside of you. Over time, your purpose will emerge. It is a conversation. If the old stories about what is 'right' and 'wrong' get in the way, you won't be able to stay in tune with the chat.

> **We have to stay in a biodynamic, responsive relationship with what IS, not what our Tiny Me thinks 'should' be.**

From the cauldron of love that resides in every **healed HEART**, purpose pours forth like molten metal ready to transform the world. In the place of all those tiring 'shoulds,' you unleash fresh insights and ideas that allow you to live fully, right now, in appropriate, fitted ways.

> **Free from 'shoulds,' you are liberated to express yourself most creatively in the moment.**

This doesn't mean that, once you discover your purpose, you will have life all neatly sorted out on an Excel spreadsheet. Far from it. Purpose is alive. You can't control it. You can't plan in detail how it's going to work out. You just have to feel it, and allow it to emerge from you, free from patterns. The trust you build each time you switch on allows you to live purposefully like this: Half in control, half out—at the edge of chaos.

Purpose is who you are when you are free from being protective, fearful, or aggressive. It is the future pulling you into it, uniquely shaped by the experiences in your past. Your purpose is something you cannot fail to be, as long as you align yourself continuously with it, letting go of any bullshit that gets in its way. The patterns, the stories of should and must, will distort your clarity and deflect your purpose and leave you unable to thrive.

FINDING MY PLACE

For the first three decades of my life, I had no purpose. Or rather, I had one (because we all have one); I just had no idea what it was. So making big decisions, about whether to stay or leave medical school or keep or shut down my (unethical) business, were tortuous. I had nothing solid to gauge anything against. It was like being a ball in a pinball machine, and everyone else's ideals were the flippers. All the competing ideas of what I 'should' do with my life created so much noise that I couldn't hear the faint whispers of my purpose calling me. I knew I must have one, yet I struggled to find it. This was frustrating, annoying, and often bewildering. It also meant I wasted my creative energies on things that just weren't a good fit for me or for the world.

I had to give it all up to find it. I gave up a medical career (which offered instant kudos, social standing, and family respect). I gave up being a multi-millionaire (albeit on paper)—and the trappings of both fortune and entrepreneurial fame—when I exited the successful agency I had co-founded. I gave up being respected by my atheist friends and father, when I became totally convinced of our oneness (and began to live my life from that realization). I gave up being admired by the global social change 'scene' when I decided that, rather than commit my life to treating the symptoms of a messed-up world, I would focus on dissolving the underlying drivers, the suffering that comes from separation, lack, and pain.

Once I had given it all up, I was ready to grok my purpose. Now, whenever my heart breaks with the suffering of those around me, my purpose shoots forth like a bolt of lightning. I know, in these moments my place in this universe and what I was born to do. Every day I learn how to express it in new and ever-more relevant ways. It even gives me an empowering story that allows me to join the dots between my experiences as a bullied, fat, depressed kid; my family history of anti-Semitic suffering and Holocaust survival; the talents and creative, intellectual, and practical skills I have honed; and the rich experiences I've had in my life, both painful and pleasant. This empowering narrative allows me to metabolize problems consistently into opportunities and so unfold more of my purpose.

Weaving a new story

IF ALL OUR OLD patterns are enshrined in stories that limit us, hooking us into blame, shame, and complain, our purpose is a new story that opens up a world of possibility to us. The more of the old story we give up, the more of the new story we reveal. We have no idea how the story will play out, just that we are enacting it in the moment in constant, biodynamic interplay. By getting into the conversation that is purpose, we start to weave a tale that makes sense of the things that have happened to us; and how they can be meaningful for the problems we (and usually other people too) are having today. Here are two examples of people finding purpose in big problems. I have met both personally:

A brain tumor and its devastating physical impact . . .
SWITCH ON
. . . became the stimulus to give up a successful business and commit to being a wisdom teacher bringing more love and truth into the world (which then led to writing a book and more).

A terrorist bomb and the loss of both legs . . .
SWITCH ON
. . . became the stimulus to leave a job in marketing and be a proponent of peace in the world (which then led to the start of a social enterprise focused on peace-building).

No one can tell you that the new story you are weaving is 'right' or 'wrong,' least of all your parents or friends. That doesn't mean to say that they can't challenge you, or give you useful feedback when you are off track, off purpose. But it does mean that it is always *your* choice how to make sense out of all your experiences, both painful and pleasant, so you can focus your attention meaningfully on the here and now. Only you can weave the story you are playing the lead role in.

In many myths and movies, the hero or heroine embarks on a journey to find a special object, such as the Golden Fleece or Holy Grail. It symbolizes the search for purpose. Joseph Campbell, in his magisterial study of myths called *The Hero with a Thousand Faces*, calls the object the 'boon.' In epic tales, the world is in trouble. The hero/heroine must find a boon, which can save their people. What the world lacks, the hero/heroine is called to discover *inside*, before they get the reward. On the way, dragons and monsters must be overcome—symbols of our patterns; representations of our darkside. While we think we are watching the hero/heroine find the Ark or Excalibur, they are really learning about their purpose, which then helps them change the world.

EVEN ANTS HAVE A PURPOSE

Although scientific dogma states that the world is a random fluke, scientists studying complex living systems—such as ant and bee societies, cardiac muscles, and even bacteria—have noticed that there seems to be some underlying intelligence, some purpose, in how they operate. Certain events in the environment 'mean' something to a colony of ants. How they respond to them changes how well they fit their environment (and so whether they thrive). Evolution through (apparently) random mutations and the blind force of natural selection is what brought us here. Yet something like 'purpose' emerges in most living systems. Mainstream science cannot quite explain how this happens.[1]

In human beings, research has shown that purpose is more important than money, ambition, or any other factor in predicting how creative we are.[2] Studies have also shown that having meaning prevents dementia and Alzheimer's, and lessens the impact of aging.[3] If we have a strong sense of meaning, which comes from applying our purpose to each moment, our stress response is inhibited. That is true even if we don't consider ourselves to be 'happy.'[4]

We are all on a 'Hero's/Heroine's Journey' like this. Every problem we face is a call to adventure. Each problem we switch on to reveals another facet of our purpose. As we chomp down on problems, metabolizing them within, we come back with many boons. Each is a plot line in the emerging story of our life's purpose. It is up to us to join all the seemingly random dots in an empowering, nourishing, and energizing way that galvanizes us into action and adventure.

If you can't tell an inspiring story about where you've come from and where you're going to, nobody else will do it for you.

Ask yourself:

- Are you living out your life as a cameo role in the story of your parents?
- Are you playing a bit part in the story of your teachers by agreeing that you are 'bad' at mathematics or only 'good' at sport?
- Are you choosing a walk-on part in the capitalist story that you may not fully believe in?
- Are you prepared to cast off any of these hackneyed tales to forge your own story, even if you can't predict or control exactly how it will unfold?

If you have the courage to set off on one Hero's/Heroine's journey after another, riding one Breakthrough Curve after another, you will bring to life more of your purpose. From a haze of past experiences a powerful narrative will emerge. We thrive in the world to the extent that we can metabolize the things that happen to us into fresh threads for our emerging story.

The story is alive because you are alive. Treat it as a done deal and it quickly ossifies. While the gist of your story will stay consistent, the details will unfold in surprising ways, as you co-create your life with the Big U. This is like Picasso spending decades exploring, in painting after painting, what it means to be a Modernist or Cubist.

The more problems you metabolize, the more inspired your new story becomes. The world is always presenting us with problems, inviting us to switch on and let go of the assumptions that underpin the old world order. Perhaps the most famous story of this surrender is J R R Tolkien's trilogy *Lord of the Rings*. Unlike most epics, where the hero/heroine has to get something cool, Frodo has to find a way of getting rid of the ring of power, control, and domination. He has to relinquish the controlling nature of the Tiny Me to defeat evil and allow the world to be restored to a state of thriving.

Our purpose, once found, can and will rejuvenate the community we are part of.

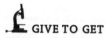 GIVE TO GET

Our pleasure circuits are as active when we watch someone giving money to charity as when we receive money ourselves.[5] Teens who declare that their key motivation in life is to help others are three times happier than those who don't. They are also much less likely to have depression, become pregnant, or fail a subject in school.[6] Employees in organizations are happier, and a lot more productive, when they are consciously aware of the positive impact of their work on their colleagues and customers. In one study, revenues increased by 400 percent when fundraising call-center staff heard short stories from end-beneficiaries about how the money had made a difference to them.

In another project, at Stanford University, women with cancer were asked to attend a support group. Of these, some were asked to *give* support actively as well as receive it; others just received the support of their peers. Those that gave as much as they got lived twice as long as those that didn't.[7] Seniors who volunteered for more than two organizations had a 44 percent lower chance of dying during the study than those that didn't.[8] This means that volunteering has a more powerful impact on our health than exercising four times a week! Even just watching other people being generous has an impact. Subjects in one study, were shown a movie of Mother Theresa caring for people in Calcutta and, hey presto, quantities of a protective antibody in their saliva increased markedly. Some of the group were then asked to think about being loving and being loved. Their antibodies remained high for an hour after the screening.[9]

Who cares wins

PURPOSE IS THE CONNECTION between the gifts of the Tiny Me (the part of us that has tangible skills and talents in the 'real' world) and the ask of the Great We (what we as a community and planet are missing in some way). Our purpose is always as much about the world—the people we love and the communities we live in—as it is about ourselves.

Whereas the Protector asks, 'What do I need to stay safe?', the Connector, taking things much less personally, asks, 'What can I do to share my gifts with the world?' The job description of the Connector is to collaborate, care, and contribute. It is always looking to help or heal others. However, this is not only about others. It is also about finding our sweet spot, our special sauce, where we blossom. If we are on purpose, then both us and the people around us start to thrive.

Rather beautifully, nature has conspired to make service as enjoyable and beneficial to the giver as it is to the receiver. When we contribute, oxytocin is released, which deepens our relationships and inhibits stress. Giving can stimulate our immune system and give us the kind of dopamine-fuelled buzz we get from eating chocolate (see page 62).

Our happiness is massively dependent on how we connect with, and contribute, to others. In a survey of 200,000 adults across 136 nations, people who gave to others were the happiest. That was true whether they lived in rich countries or impoverished ones. When we care, we get a boost to our happiness levels that is equivalent to someone doubling our income overnight.[10] Being of service to others can even extend life expectancy and boost health! Caring for others can be more important than having self-esteem when it comes to our own success.[11] Being self-centered also costs us a lot of energy as we have to keep fighting our natural desire to contribute, which kicks us out of flow.[12]

However, we must find a balance between giving to others and nourishing ourselves. Purpose needs to be grounded in our wellbeing as well as that of others. We have to keep rooted and resourced. The Connector wants to give but if we become sick, we are no use to anyone. If you find yourself becoming addicted to giving in some way, it's probably a pattern (for example, one that tries to have people like you because you are 'nice'). Drop it and come back to your purpose. The last thing you want to do is be so committed to others that you neglect your own health and happiness, and that of your loved ones. The world wants us vibrant and vital. Giving must flow from the power and energy of the Great We, as opposed to the limited Tiny Me, which soon runs out of puff.

Compassion, service, and generosity are only authentically of service to the world when they come from the **HEART** and not the **HEAD**. Don't be of service because you think it is 'right.' Don't do it to make people like you. Don't do it because someone has told you you 'should.' The moment you flip back into doing it to get something out of it, you blow it. The Tiny Me, driven by the Protector, will always try and hijack our good works to make up for what it thinks it lacks. Only the Connector can give freely without needing something back, because it already has everything it needs within.

Be of service because it comes gushing out of you, because it is inevitable. Do it because it is who you truly are. Do it because, if you aren't of service, you can't be your truth.

Then it will be serving you as much as others, even if it is not done with that intent. This resonates with the African philosophy of *Ubuntu*, which means 'I am what I am because of who we all are.' I was struck powerfully by this life philosophy when I worked as a science teacher in rural Zimbabwe, aged 18. All of us live in a complex network of people and places, whether we can see it or not. We are all interdependent. *Ubuntu* says that our joy is inescapably dependent on the joy of others. When we serve others and collaborate authentically, from love not strategy, we thrive collectively. Purpose is how we connect with the world most effortlessly in love, truth, and creativity; with **HEART**, **HEAD**, and **HANDS** all opened up to what is possible.

Discovering purpose

PURPOSE ISN'T A CAREER choice, brand vision, or goal. It is how you care and share at any time, with anyone. It may involve winning a Pulitzer Prize, yet it's just as likely to involve looking out for the people we love, expressing ourselves freely when we feel stuck, or discovering how to be better friends and parents. Yes, you may have big dreams. You might have a vision for a business empire or want to make a great movie. You might be desperate to start a family or fired up to end world poverty. Yet none of these are your purpose. These are big, hairy, audacious goals and we'll be looking at how to find and bring them to life next. Purpose may inspire them, help define and refine them . . . yet it is not them.

Purpose can fuel an enterprise or a project, but it is just as much at home in the line for the restroom at a nightclub; in the middle of a dull meeting; getting the kids ready for school; or on a first date. The more practiced you are at allowing purpose to flow, when the sh!t hits the fan, you will be ready to serve others as opposed to play out strategies and patterns.

When you let go of all the 'shoulds,' you will almost certainly discover that your purpose amplifies one of: Playing, experimenting, creating, learning, sharing, loving, caring, teaching, transforming, adventuring, or healing. These are all ways to contribute to the flourishing of others while blossoming yourself.

Free from doubts and fears, cynicism and self-criticism, your purpose is the sum total of every bit of love and wisdom you have gleaned from your life experiences, mixed with the skills and talents that you have honed through engaging with them **wholeheartedly**. All of it is then distilled down to a tiny drop of pure essence, which you express as the moment sees fit. Your most intense life experiences leave an imprint in your body.mind, like a garment stained and stretched from being worn. Rather than attempting to scrub out the marks, you can harness them. Your scars become beauty spots, your greatest assets.

This essence percolates through your entire body.mind, bubbling up into every experience.

Your purpose is who you are when you feel most alive, most of use, most awake. This is not necessarily the same as when you feel most approved of. If you think your purpose is to make lots of cash, be famous or win something, it just means the Protector is doing the talking. Thank it for its contribution and help secure it by appreciating it for trying to protect you. Then ask your Connector for the real answers. It knows your purpose inside out. In fact, it has always known. Purpose, love-in-action, is the energy that animates it. It's the part of you that has led you to heal, gain insight, and take risks to get you to where you are.

Your purpose is unique to you. It cannot be right or wrong and it certainly cannot be better or worse than anyone else's. Purpose is your creative spirit, free from blockages and limitations, as it engages with life and helps you and others thrive. It is exultant, powerful, and inexhaustible. The only person who can stop you from letting it out is you.

Don't worry if you can't define your purpose in words. Having the exact words to describe your purpose is not nearly as important as feeling it burn like a flame within. As long as you feel your purpose inside, you'll know whether you're 'on purpose' or 'off purpose.' When you feel on purpose, it radiates out through your feelings (**HEART**), thoughts (**HEAD**), and actions (**HANDS**). Just as when a baseball connects with a ball, every time you make a choice how to be or behave, you either feel a

Meh

This is off purpose. Or you feel a

sch**weet!**

If you can feel that sweet spot, you are on purpose. You can find your sweet spot no matter what curve balls come at you.

Think about your day today. What did you do when were you on purpose? What about when you were off purpose?

What will you do with your purpose?

No MATTER WHAT YOUR actual career or trade, whether you are unemployed or a hotshot executive, stay-at-home parent or a traveler, your purpose will help you create meaning out of every moment.

You don't get to choose your purpose. It is the result of the unfathomably complex interplay between genes, experiences, up-bringing, and environment. But you do get to choose what you do with it.

If your purpose is to do with play, you could start to introduce a cheeky 'get to know you' game at the office and bring things to life a little. If your purpose is to do with family, you could work to create more trust and community within your team. If your purpose is about healing the world, you could help your room-mates understand why recycling is important (without judgment of course). Anything at all can become fundamentally meaningful and purposeful if you choose it to be.

If you (or rather your Tiny Me) ever think that your circumstances are just too awful for your purpose to engage with them, then the Oscar-winning movie *Life is Beautiful* is an awesome inspiration. The hero, played by Roberto Benigni, is a man whose imagination and playfulness radiates from him. His purpose is to make people laugh, smile, and see beauty in life. Facing imminent death, he focuses on making his son laugh, even as their Nazi captors are preparing to kill them both. Now that's living purposefully.

Living purposefully doesn't mean that life will suddenly be 'easy' though. Your purpose may compel you to change how you act inside your home or in your workplace. It may influence the projects you invest in; even how you like to spend your vacations. Our purpose is rarely convenient. Often it is not even socially acceptable.

You don't have to share your purpose with anyone. But, if you do, it's not unusual to share it with passion and conviction, only to find the people around you responding to your beaming face with looks of disbelief or downright fear. Our loved ones may not get it at first. In reality, they may never get it. People who haven't found their purpose, and who don't feel deeply connected to themselves, are often challenged by those who live purposefully. It can freak them out. Change can be extremely threatening, so it's important to empathize with your loved ones and allow them time to adjust to your higher frequency lifestyle. It may take a while.

Whether people around you get it or not, they are not you and you cannot live your life for them (and they can't live theirs through you). This doesn't mean being selfish or ignoring your duties. It means finding how to join up all the competing needs in your life within a purpose story that comes from your truth, from your connection to the Big U, and *nothing* else.

Whatever you do, don't bend to others' opinions when it comes to your life's purpose. Of course, feedback from other people is always useful and coaching can help you to find your blind spots, pesky assumptions, or resistance. But ignoring your purpose brings with it the most excruciating suffering a human being can know. To choose *not* to express your unique essence, your role in service of the Great We, guarantees that you will suffer. A searing definition of hell is coming to the end of your life and meeting the person you could have been, if you'd followed your purpose.

Please don't sell yourself out because other people aren't able to get or appreciate your vibrancy. Trust yourself. Trust the Connector. As long as you live your purpose each day, you'll stay fitted, awake and thriving.

Now, with all this mojo rising, what do you want to create?

SWITCH ON TO PURPOSE

Switched Off: Purpose is a myth because life is inherently meaningless. The right thing to do is to be rich/famous/professional/ educated/ethical/hedonistic/world-changing (delete as appropriate).

Switched On: Purpose is revealed when we release our patterns and express our essence. Purpose allows us to make meaning out of even the harshest experiences. By contributing to the wellbeing of others, we enact an empowering narrative of growth, learning, and thriving.

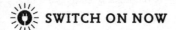 **SWITCH ON NOW**

So, right now, get your Connector into the mix. Breathe. Relax. Maybe close your eyes. Choose to switch on. Trust and surrender as much as you can.

HEART: Feel into your emotions, all the way through your body.mind. Breathe away any fears or upsets, shoulds or musts.

Over the last seven days, what moments have given you feelings of great love, deep satisfaction, or purpose?

Over the last month, when have you felt most switched on? What were you doing? Who were you being?

Over the last six months, when have you felt most alive and electrified? What were you doing? Who were you being?

HEAD: What are the greatest problems you have encountered in your life? In overcoming them, what talents, gifts, and ideas have you developed?

What do you want your epitaph to be?

What do you want your grandkids to say about you?

HANDS: Letting go of any shoulds or musts, thinking across an average day, what activities most inspire you?

What about when you were a kid, before any seriousness or ambition snuck in?

Which memories most electrify your body.mind when you think of them?

BREAKTHROUGH QUESTIONS

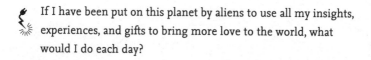 If I have been put on this planet by aliens to use all my insights, experiences, and gifts to bring more love to the world, what would I do each day?

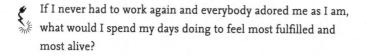 If I never had to work again and everybody adored me as I am, what would I spend my days doing to feel most fulfilled and most alive?

Session 07

Possibility

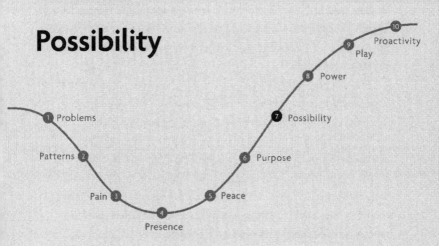

WHEN WE SWITCH ON, possibilities begin to fly like sparks across our minds and burn like embers within our hearts. If we nurture them, tending, pruning, and feeding them, before long a creative breakthrough will burst forth. We exchange our old assumptions for new insights, insights that emerge from the future we are moving into. Listen to the whispers and dreams that swirl inside. Pay attention to the half-thoughts that flutter just out of reach of consciousness. These are the signs that an Ah Ha! is getting ready to break through.

The celebrated South American novelist Isabel Allende has sold over 50 million books. This incredibly productive and much-loved artist says this of her creativity: 'I'm not the one who invents the stories; I'm like a radio that picks up the waves. Somehow, if I move the dial very carefully, I'll pick up the wave and get the story. But the story doesn't belong to me; it's somewhere out there floating.'[1] She's not alone. Writer after writer, artist after artist, scientist after scientist has claimed that are not the source of their creativity. The composer J S Bach said, 'I play the notes as they are written, but it is God who makes the music.'

Outpourings of creativity are interrupted when we allow our judgments, opinions, criticism, and comparisons to get in the way. Assumptions are the enemy of insight; and they will always lead to a fail eventually. Even if old patterns have kept us safe, successful, and rich, if we insist on clinging on to them, eventually the world will move on and we will be redundant (or made redundant). When we let go of our assumptions, there's no limit to the possibilities on offer: Awesome travel experiences, stellar lovemaking, transformational community projects, expressive art, or impactful businesses.

The moment an insight comes to mind, we can feel the opening; and the outpouring begins. Every time we switch on to a problem, and have a breakthrough insight within, we open up fields of possibilities that we can harvest for years. Our purpose will guide us to crack open problems that matter.

With a truly open **HEART**, free from fear, an open **HEAD**, free from assumptions, and our **HANDS**, we can change the world.

So what possibilities do you want to spend your days and nights striving to bring to life? Given that, on average, you will live for around 40 million minutes, how will you make them count?

The creative spirit

IF SO MANY CREATORS acknowledge that creativity comes through them, not *from* them, where on Earth *does* it come from then? Well, we know that the part of ourselves that we think is in control—the strategizing Tiny Me—is not all we are (see Session 04, page 108). While the Tiny Me puts our ideas onto paper, or shares them in mathematical formulae, I believe that the inspiration comes from the creative spirit, the Great We. It's the part of us that has endless breakthrough insights and ideas as soon as we get into flow.

If you spend time observing where ideas come from when you have them, you will probably find that they just burst through into everyday consciousness. There is no, 'I want/need . . .' There is just, 'Wow, what about . . .?' Great ideas, big breakthroughs, seem to be as surprising to us as they are to others.

Time and time again, the creative spirit has inspired visionaries outside their normal 'I' perspective. Paul McCartney says that the idea for 'Yesterday' came to him in a dream but he ignored the tune for a couple of weeks (the Tiny Me always thinks it knows best eh?). He finally wrote it down. It has now been covered more times than any other song in history. This was a major musical breakthrough. The gifted German scientist Friedrich Kukele struggled for months to understand benzene, vital in the production of plastics, drugs, detergents, pesticides, and explosives. One night, he dreamed of a snake eating its own tail, the ancient symbol of *ouroboros* (which represents rebirth in many cultures). Kukele woke up the next day with the idea that the benzene molecule is shaped as circle, like the snake. It was a major scientific breakthrough.

Breakthroughs emerge from our *entire* body.mind, in all kinds of states of consciousness, not from some mythical location of pure reason in the higher brain. Ideas live within us, in the gut, heart, muscles, and brain, as much as they do on paper. This is why entrepreneurs can be more successful than large corporations at bringing breakthroughs to life, even though they have a fraction of the resources. They give their all to them. It is also why great artists are a rarity; most people aren't prepared to give their whole body.mind over to their art. It takes determination as much as genius to birth new ideas.

> **Breakthrough is a full body.mind thing. It involves our entire system working in harmony, from our emotional brain to the millions of neurons (and possibly bacteria) in our guts.**

 ## TUNING IN FOR A BREAKTHROUGH

In a landmark study, rappers were put into fMRI scanners while performing. First, they sang lyrics they had written in advance. Then they were asked to improvise in the moment, in flow. The difference between their brains in these two states was enormous. With the scripted lyrics, areas of the pre-frontal cortex associated with control, decisions, and judgment lit up. But when the MCs were freestyling, the areas of control, willpower, and attention were all less active. In the moments they gave up being conventionally 'smart,' they were most creative! Similar results have been found with jazz musicians when they improvise too.[2]

People given psychedelics also show muted activity in their brain's control center. The deeper the inhibition of their prefrontal cortex, the more intense the trip.[3] Studies show that distance and space can also really help us break through. By consciously taking a break to play ball, go on a vacation, or have a shower, we force our busy brain to stop focusing on a problem and allow our creative spirit to come up with the goods.[4]

There is a system of brain activity that shows up when the brain is at rest. It fades out whenever we start doing a task. This Default Mode Network (DMN) turns out to be more active at rest in people who have more spontaneous ideas. Resting, letting go, allows our body.mind to wander between ideas and connect up the dots, free from tension and pressure.[5] The DMN seems to activate fully when we then see something creative that we totally love.[6] Early studies show that we can use the more focused, 'smart' parts of our brain to direct our DMN to wander, care-free, in directions which might come up with the ideas we are looking for. In other words, we can consciously promote the chances of serendipity without trying to control it.[7]

Contrary to what we might assume, the upper brain, which we need to make comparisons, judgments, and decisions, has to become *less* active if we want our imaginations to soar. We can't force creativity to come through; we can simply create the right conditions for it. The creative spirit, the Connector in action, cannot be controlled. It can just be unleashed. This is why reconnection practices can inspire us and unlock our creative juices (see Session 04, page 122). They connect us to the Great We, the creative spirit, while loosening the Tiny Me's grip on its prejudices. Picking up the sensations and feelings in our body.mind is crucial, for much of our insight lies deep within.

As soon as we bring our full attention to a problem, we fire up the body.mind to break through. A little bit of intention gets the juices flowing. The Connector comes out to play as the creative spirit. But, for a few hours, days, or even months, we may not come up with an answer. We have to trust that the creative spirit is working on it, throughout our body.mind with its billions of synapses and quantum connections. Henri Poincaré, a mathematician, scientist, and philosopher (and all-round genius) said this of the creative spirit:

> [It] is in no way inferior to the conscious self; it is not purely automatic; it is capable of discernment; it has tact, delicacy; it knows how to choose, to divine. What do I say? It knows better how to divine than the conscious self, since it succeeds where that has failed.[8]

It's working away in the background, outside of everyday awareness, until . . .

Ah **Ha!**

A breakthrough emerges like the sun bursting through the clouds on a foggy day. The creative spirit has been at work—wandering, recombining, contemplating—until finally it has something worth sharing with us. The assumptions disappear and new insights arrive out of nowhere. We can feel this happen throughout our entire body.mind.

Breaking Through at the Edge of Chaos

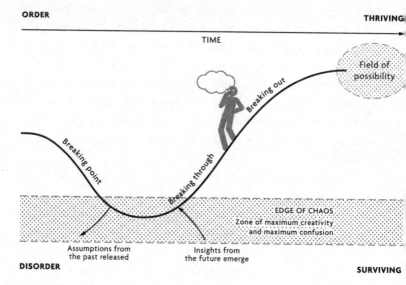

The likelihood is that there will be times when you have broken through the old but you haven't quite worked out what comes next. The LEGO pieces are all around you and you have no idea how they fit together again. Welcome to the edge of chaos. Many people find this place challenging because it is messy, ambiguous, and full of risk. It usually feels scary in the **HEART** and confusing in the **HEAD**. Assumptions and insights are battling for prominence and the mind can get very confused.

Feelings of overwhelm or confusion are signs that you are at breaking point, ready for a breakthrough. As Chuang Tzu, one of the great Taoist philosophers, put it: 'Let go of your assumptions and the world will make perfect sense.'[9] If you can embrace the chaos, sit happily in confusion, and keep reconnecting to the source, the insights and ideas will break through eventually. This is why dreams, meditation, vacations, showers, and other activities where we let go and open up (as opposed to get tight and shut down), all encourage breakthrough.

The Eureka moment

BREAKTHROUGHS COME WHEN YOU are prepared to let go of what you assume is the 'right' or 'winning' solution and instead let your creative spirit find the way forward. You have to let go of the past to be a dynamic part of the future. You cannot keep your old beliefs *and* have breakthroughs. Instead, you have to be willing to trade in assumptions for insights. Like assumptions, insights are also beliefs, but they are informed by possibility. Insights spark ideas. One juicy insight can lead to 10, 20, or 100 different ideas. One Eureka! moment can furnish us with years of transformation. The insight is really the breakthrough. The ideas are simply the many ways we could harness that insight to make a difference. Many of the ideas won't work. But the insight, or breakthrough, will inspire more.

Here are the ultimate assumptions we looked at before (see Session 02, page 66, and Session 03, page 83) and some fresh insights and ideas that could emerge once they have been let go.

The 'Life is tough' story
Ultimate assumptions about human nature/the universe
Life is tough and only the strong make it.

Breakthrough Insight
- Perhaps this is what my parents believed and I don't have to believe it too.
- Perhaps life will flow when I stop resisting things . . .

Breakthrough Ideas
- I have decided to frame my current project as if it were the most simple, fluid, and easy experience, providing me with joy every day.
- I am also going to be vulnerable in my next couple of business meetings and see what happens.

The 'men are untrustworthy' story
Ultimate assumptions about human nature/the universe
All men are untrustworthy.

Breakthrough Insight
- Perhaps I'm protecting myself from disappointment because of my past.
- Perhaps some men are awesome and I have just not been able to see it . . .

Breakthrough Ideas
- I'm going to invite a man out on a date who is nothing at all like my old boyfriends and see what happens.
- I am going to email my dad to forgive him for the past.

The 'eating/drinking/smoking helps me relax' story

Ultimate assumptions about human nature/the universe
The body is like a machine. It can be made to relax with certain substances.

Breakthrough Insight
- Perhaps I am using this to cover up stress so I don't have to own it . . .
- Perhaps it is time to find ways to release stress that nourish me . . .

Breakthrough Ideas
- I'm going to visualize feeling relaxed every time I find myself wanting a snack/drink/cigarette for the next 24 hours and see what happens.
- I am going to make myself a smoothie every morning, as a gift to myself, and use it to start my day in an empowering way.

Our friends are changing. Our workplaces are changing. Our cultures are changing. We may no longer fit as well as we used to. Luckily, clues for how things are shifting abound. These signals are weak, but they are there when we switch on and look for them. By focusing on a problem with attention and intention, we start to inquire into where life around and within us is headed, which helps us have breakthroughs. In many ways, the 'Ah Ha!' or 'Eureka!' moment is simply us getting ahead of the curve.

Weak signals are in our environment: Reading blogs, asking people probing questions, surfing our social media feeds looking for clues, spotting new products in stores. They can all give us insight into how to shift our career focus or project direction. Weak signals can be spotted in our relationships: How our friends and family are acting, what they are passionate about, what they aren't saying to us, are all sources of insight that can open up breakthroughs that keep us fitted with them (if we want to be, of course). Weak signals can also be spotted in our own body.mind: What is holding our attention? What have we become less interested in? What warnings of potential breakdown can we pick up?

BREAKBEAT BREAKTHROUGH

It's August in the Bronx, NYC, in the early 1970s. Kool Herc, a teenage DJ, is about to invent something that will change the world. Up to that point, DJs would play a track from start to finish before putting the next one on. The assumption was that vinyl was a stand-in for the band, the best you could get without being at a live gig. However, Kool Herc has a problem he wants to crack. He and his peers aren't going to concerts. They want to party, on the block, for cheap. His job is to get everyone fired up as fast and furiously as possible.

With this kind of intention, he spots a weak signal. The coolest dancers wait for the funkiest bit of a track before they really bust out their moves. These are the 'breaks': The main tune drops out, usually leaving just the drums. When the vocals come back in, they stop dancing. They wait a few minutes for the next break, the next funky bit. Kool Herc has an insight. What would happen if he just played the breaks? An idea forms. He takes a few records that have particularly funky breaks and plays them over and over, skipping the majority of the tune. He breaks all the rules. He turns a constraint (people can't get to gigs every week) into a possibility. A new form of music/dance/experience/culture that was more exciting than live music for many people was created. Hip hop was born. The rest, from the Sugarhill Gang to Lady Gaga, is history.

Weak signals are too faint for us to spot unless we cultivate our ability to. As we switch on and start an inquiry, we instruct our senses to be extra vigilant to sources of insight. We fire up our dopamine-driven body.mind to spot *new* paradigms that are emerging, as opposed to reconfirming those from the past. This process, at the heart of the Breakthrough Curve, drives breakthroughs in our personal lives, in business, and in art. Every time we say, 'Ah Ha! Perhaps, I could think/be/do X . . .' we are living from possibility, not patterns. This is the fundamental moment of creativity.

Pixar creatives sensed, and then amplified, the weak signals that suggested to them that parents and kids wanted more ironic, cheeky, and edgy movies over the saccharine-sweet ones of the past. Mark Zuckerberg (of Facebook) sensed, and then amplified, the weak signals that told him that people wanted to connect and share online. A switched on parent, spotting that their kid is showing signs of being bored at school, will use it as a source of insight to open up ideas that can inspire them. We process the weak signals within our body.mind and within our network, and they eventually become insights that create new futures. Eureka!

 ## THE EXEC WHO WOULDN'T LET GO

My consultancy was invited into a well-known California company to help develop innovative solutions to really tough social and business challenges. The president of the business unit was a good guy, near retirement. His younger team of ambitious SVPs and VPs worked with me to identify the big, hairy (and a little bit scary) problems that the company could break through. Big ideas can impact millions of lives (as well as the bottom line) in these arenas. I repeatedly told them the requirements of breakthrough, particularly that they would have to surface and challenge some of their most cherished assumptions if they wanted to find 'disruptive' innovations.

Assuming the president was on board for breakthrough, I foolishly neglected to interview him before the key workshop. As soon as he walked through the door, I knew we were in trouble. His top business leaders—many of whom had multiple degrees from Ivy League institutions and ran departments with hundreds of people—changed how they were behaving. They seemed to stop challenging, stop questioning, stop being up for breakthrough. It appeared, to me at least, that the president wanted to be right about all his beliefs and yet still have breakthroughs. And we know that is impossible. The project was shut down soon after.

The Eureka! or Ah Ha! moment brings with it a shift, deep inside the body.mind, from assumption to insight, past to future. Physically, emotionally, and mentally, we have to give up our old assumptions to allow the insights in. Accompanying each revelation is usually a spark of energy that flies through us. The sensation is often electrifying. We are Joystruck. Simply inventing a creative response to an everyday problem, say inventing a game to play with my son to channel his energy away from being upset, helps me feel that rush of creativity. My neural signatures are being rewired, away from reaction and toward imagination.

Breakthrough = Insight + Ideas

Your capacity for breakthrough insights is not determined by how many new ideas you have but how many old assumptions you are willing to relinquish. This is why tiny start-ups can topple giant businesses and small groups of committed citizens bring down dictators. They have far less political power, money, resources, and manpower. But they are more willing to give up the old to embrace the new. They let go of the 'noble lies.' They give their whole body.mind over to possibility.

You can either be right about your assumptions. Or you can be consistently creative. Never both.

Getting out of the way of yourself

You, ME, AND EVERYONE around us has creativity written into their DNA. It is what makes us human. Creativity is a unique characteristic of living things. No matter how powerful a computer, it cannot be creative. It can look as if it's being creative yet every outcome is predictable, driven by a set of algorithms (equations that generate solutions based on a predetermined set of mathematical relationships). No breakthroughs can emerge from linear mechanisms. However, even the youngest child and the simplest cellular organism can create non-linear breakthroughs that simply didn't exist before.

Living organisms are the creative products of our own creativity. We are **autopoetic**. Powered by biological brilliance, life is continuously creating more life from a bunch of seemingly inert chemical building blocks. As we evolve, both biologically and culturally, we open up more and more fields of possibility that were not there before. The result has been everything from opposable thumbs to Shakespeare's plays. Along the way, nations, political systems, technologies, and enterprises have all been created by our imaginations.

Each field of possibility we open up provides us with new choices. Through making use of those new choices, we open up new fields of possibility. This virtuous cycle, driving breakthrough after breakthrough, is how we have reached the pinnacle of evolution, both through genetic mutation and cultural imagination. You are a direct descendant of this process and you have the right to enjoy your inheritance as a breakthrough artist-at-life.

Pause for a moment and feel, right now, the hundreds of trillions of cells that make up your body.mind. Each one is alive and autopoetic. Each is pulsating with creativity because it can self-create. Which means *you are creative in your essence*, no matter what your old art teacher, uncle, or boss said to you. Every chromosome, cell membrane, organ, and neuron within you is fundamentally creative. You can break through anything,

IF

(and it's a big if) you are prepared to get out of the way of yourself by jettisoning each and every assumption that is holding you back.

Creativity is at its peak when we get out of the way of ourselves. We have to get the Tiny Me out of the way of the Great We so an Ah Ha! can burst through us. In Taoism, this concept is called *wei wu wei*, which can roughly be translated as 'doing not doing.' Action is occurring. Things are being created. Yet it is not the 'I,' in the sense of the Tiny Me, that is doing all the work. We are totally attuned and attentive, yet have let go of control. This same concept is present in Indian wisdom as 'actionless action.' It is similar to the experiences people describe as flow.states. We need our Tiny Me to get stuff done. It is the part of us that practices chords and arpeggios and learns harmonies. It puts in the 10 or 20,000 hours we need to master a skill. However, when it is time to perform, we let the Great We take over because this is how our creative spirit is at its best.

So get out of the way of yourself. Instead, get into
***wei wu wei* with yourself.**

Anything stuck in the pipes from the past will block the flow. A fearful, judgmental, critical body.mind literally tightens up. The muscles prepare to fight, flight, or freeze. The eyes narrow into tunnel vision. We cannot be open to newness if we are controlling. We can't explore new avenues when we are triggered. So we have to keep on letting go, keep on releasing, keep on giving up control. This is what some wisdom traditions call 'purification.' We constantly vacuum away old patterns, allowing the creative spirit to shine through undisturbed.

All of us can practice *wei wu wei* by allowing what is seeking to emerge to do so, without second-guessing, criticizing, or holding it back. Virtually a activity can be an opportunity to practice actionless action. Cooking, p with kids, being on a date, flower arranging, sculpting, writing, exploring a city, and lovemaking can all become moments where we allow the creative spirit to have its way with us.

LETTING THE UNCONSCIOUS DO THE WORK

Getting out the way of ourselves is easier said than done. Hilary Mantel has won the Man Booker Prize (one of the top literary prizes on the planet) twice. She always felt called to write historical fiction, even when it was unpopular with publishers, agents, and the public. She stuck at it and has (clearly) done pretty well by it, even though it took years to get any recognition. She said this about the creative process, 'You have to say to yourself, I take my hands off, I let my unconscious work for me.'[10] According to interviews, she doesn't find giving up control easy but knows that effort alone doesn't create great literature (though it can help in completing a manuscript on time of course).

When we do things in a way that doesn't feel like there is an 'I' doing them—an I that is a small, fearful Tiny Me—we are allowing breakthroughs to come through us. We become 'entangled' with the thing we are creating. We are the subject, object, and verb all at once. We are not merely the dancer; we are the dance and the dancing too. We are not just the scientist; we are the science as well. We are not just the lover; we are the loving and the lovemaking too. Possibilities are not simply 'ours.' They come through us. The more we work at clearing out the old assumptions and letting go of control, the more fitted and brilliant the ideas 'we' will have (and be rewarded for).

Birthing a vision

WHEN WE MAKE A problem the focus of our attention, insights and ideas will eventually form into a cohesive and coherent vision of how we think the world could be. We join the dots between all the ideas that have popped into our body.mind over a few weeks (or years) and give birth to a vision. The vision then grows, breathes, and expands as we give more of ourselves to it. This might be a vision of how your career might look, how your relationships might look, or how your workplace might look. You might even have a vision of how an entire social space or industry could look.

Visions are not escape fantasies. Nor are they wishful thinking. They are deeply rooted in reality, the result of wholeheartedly engaging with a problem and fearlessly allowing our creative spirit to paint a picture of how things could be. Vision is the natural result of lots of little ideas coalescing into a major breakthrough, one that will probably take quite some time to bring to fruition. If you can't hold a possibility within you as a compelling vision for that kind of time period, it is likely that it will never come to life.

Vision like this is so powerful that the world's best-known businesses are happy to pay consultancies hundreds of thousands of dollars to come up with them. I have created visions with companies such as Smirnoff, Microsoft, and Unilever, as well as many bright start-ups, non-profits, and social enterprises. They make a difference to everyone and help everyone work toward a common purpose, filled with inspiration. A vision is so important in the act of creation that without it we are almost certainly doomed to failure. An old Chinese proverb tells us: 'Vision without action is a daydream. Action without vision is a nightmare.'

All the ideas that have changed the world have emerged from people who have used their intentionality to resolve a hazy unknown into a vision of what can, and will, be.

A vision can be a couple of pages of text, a few words and images, or ever simply a full-body feeling. Whether we turn it into a sexy statemer' simply embody it as a leader, a vision is a compelling yet achievable story of how things could be. The story inspires us, and others, to leave behind old paradigms and patterns and embrace a new way. Vision is a tangible yet inspiring alternative to the current reality. As soon as people grasp it, it gives them permission to think, act, and relate in fresh ways. It opens up a space for people to change, grow, and become more.

There is a profoundly lyrical connection between the problems we choose to crack open and the possibilities that emerge from them. Every breakthrough has a logic to it that, to me at least, appears divine. This is where we reap the rewards of response-ability. By owning our problems fully, we get the joy of the revelation of vision. In hindsight, after the breakthrough, we can see that each problem had the seeds of its own resolution hidden within. A vision is waiting for us within a problem, but we cannot see it until we let go of our assumptions.

Here are some examples of visions emerging from common problems. See if you can spot what the initial problem might have looked like, the usual patterns used to deal with it, and what the breakthrough night have been . . .

The vision is:

- To organize a vacation where everyone doesn't just get along, but grows together.
- To build a freelance career that allows us to spend more time on our passion project for kids.
- To use our gap year or redundancy to travel the world and discover how we can make a difference to it.
- To treat every argument we have with our partners as an opportunity to help us learn more about how they (and perhaps the opposite sex in general) think and feel, so we can become more intimate.
- To lose weight or stop smoking/drinking so that we can play sport or active games with our kids (and teach them how to stay fit and healthy too).
- To stop buying stuff and, with the extra time and money we have from not shopping, volunteer at the local care center.

As you can see, vision is never limited to things we want to see happen just for our own benefit. Vision is always about something bigger than the Tiny Me. It is more expressive and expansive than a goal or mission. Goals live in the **HEAD**. Visions live in the **HEART**, **HEAD**, and **HANDS**. It's easy to give in and eat another cookie during a time when your goal is to lose weight and look good. But if you link your goal of losing weight to a vision that includes being healthy and vibrant for those you love, there is an added inspirational boost which helps you break out of the past for good. Love for others can trump any lack of love for yourself.

You'll know when your emerging story, your vision, is becoming ripe and ready because it won't just appear right to your **HEAD**. It will *feel* right in your **HEART** and get your **HANDS** itching to make something happen. You can always use your purpose to winnow through the chaff and make sense of any competing ideas and insights. Purpose will allow you to feel a

DING! when an idea is worth pursuing. Or a

PFFF with ideas that don't fit (or don't fit right now).

You may not get to choose your purpose or your problems, but you do get to choose which ideas, which visions, you invest in and which you don't. Inevitably, along the way, some ideas will have to be sacrificed if you want to focus on the ones that are most thrivadelic for you and your people. Some ideas are right for somebody to do, just not you!

The bolder you are with your vision, the more difference you can make (and the more you will be challenged to grow). If you're going to have a vision, you might as well have one that really pushes you out of your comfort zone. Here are some insane, crazy, lusty visions that might get your juices flowing:

- To bring up your kids so they are equipped to thrive in a changing world.
- To start a music festival that brings new bands and their fans together without corporate rip-offs.

- To write a novel or make a movie that inspires millions to laugh and cry with what is possible when we love fully.
- To build a social enterprise that transforms your community for good.
- To develop a global dance craze that makes the world fit through fun.
- To create a media company that can enlighten, empower, and engage the digital generations to thrive through connection, creativity, and contribution. (This one is mine.)

Of course, not all visions have to be grand. Nor do they have to be the focus of your life's work. However, the more we create in service of something bigger than ourselves, the more we will feel fulfilled. Remember, who cares wins (see page 161). Rabindranath Tagore, an Indian writer (and the first non-Western author to win the Nobel Prize in Literature), said this: 'I slept and dreamt that life was joy. I awoke and saw that life was service. I acted and behold, service was joy.'

The beauty of breakthrough

BREAKTHROUGHS CAN HAPPEN EVERY time we engage with a problem. No matter how tight a space we find ourselves in—ill, broke, broken-hearted—we can create possibility where others simply see problems. It just means giving up your assumptions and habits long enough to allow a new possibility to emerge. This is life as art: To break through the old instead of reacting, retreating, and repeating redundant patterns. You can innovate yourself out of any predicament by switching on and allowing a vision to form within.

Having a vision does not guarantee that our crazy ideas bear fruit though. We will almost certainly fail at turning visions into realities *many times* on our journey. This is most true if we take on big problems. Failure is evidence that something does not fit. That is all. Although failure can feel like a huge OUCH! you cannot really fail at life as long as you are living from your

purpose. So there need not be any pain. Which means there is nothing
to hold you back from dreaming up the boldest of visions and the most
crackpot of schemes. There is no longer any jeopardy for your self-esteem.

PHEW!

What a relief. So, relaxing into your purpose, what is your audacious moon-shot
going to be for the next few weeks, months, or years? What is your unreasonable
idea for your family/home/place of work/community/world? What do you want
to be working on at 7 a.m. or 9 p.m. when everyone else, everyone 'normal,' is
watching TV? How do you want to remix your world, today? Right now?

The bigger the vision, the more it will pull out the best version of you. The
more it challenges you, the more fun you can have lifting your game to make
it happen.

The more insanely huge your idea, the more problems you'll encounter
on the path, and so the more you'll be asked to switch on and expand
because of them.

Breakthrough is not just a source of creativity. It is also a source of happiness,
wellbeing, and thriving. When we use our HANDS to create things, we reduce
tension in the nervous system. We experience less stress because we see
possibilities instead of problems in our HEAD. We tend to feel more positive
in our HEART when we create, which inspires us to keep creating. In this
virtuous circle, the more we engage with problems, the more possibility we
unleash. Studies show that the more creative we are, the higher self-esteem
we have and the longer we live![11] The more confident we feel, the more
risks we are prepared to take inventing new things. The more open we are,
the more we want to collaborate and take on bigger problems. This is the
Thrive Drive in action, where the Connector helps us to flourish:

The Thrive Drive

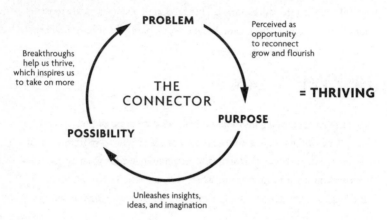

We must unleash our creative spirit with discernment though. We may have many ideas that, although bold, could just bring more suffering and injustice to the world. The Tiny Me can easily distort the creative spirit to build disempowering nightmares instead of empowering dreams. When we tap into it, we can create armies as well as antibiotics. That is why it is essential to find our purpose before we start forming a vision. We want to promote thriving and not suffering with our ideas. The world is already chock-full of projects created by people whose vision was clouded by lack. The business leader who tries to heal the wound of a disinterested father by building a rapacious business empire. The entrepreneur who grew up in poverty who is driven to make, and hold on to, billions so as never to be poor again. The politician who is driven to grab power at any cost because they had so little as a kid.

So make sure your vision—whether it's about how you want your marriage to look, how you want your project to go, or how you want to solve a problem in your community—comes from love not lack. It is the duty of every single one of us to ensure that our ideas come from a healed **HEART**, not a hurt one, that they come from being wholehearted not half-hearted.

Will the vision you have heal, unify, rejuvenate, nurture, and inspire?

Together, human beings can resolve any problem creatively in a way that leaves more people feeling inspired and empowered. We can break through any constraint as long as we are prepared to give up our assumptions (and status) and seek a **win–win–win**.

> **This is part of the beauty of breakthrough. We can always spread love instead of fear, empowerment instead of disempowerment, and freedom instead of control.**

SWITCH ON TO POSSIBILITY

Switched Off: Possibility is produced through blood, sweat, and tears and a lot of luck. Only creative people are good at ideas.

Switched On: Possibility emerges naturally whenever we embrace a problem, bring it inside us, and let go of all the assumptions that lock us in place. Ideas are not really ours. They come through us when we are attentive, intentional, and able to give up control.

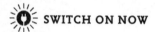 SWITCH ON NOW

So, right now, get your Connector into the mix. Breathe. Relax. Maybe close your eyes. Choose to switch on.

Sensing your purpose, think of one problem in your life that is calling you to break through it.

HEART: Bring it inside your body.mind by owning it. Imagine you have access to the creative potential of every human being on the planet.

How does that feel in your body.mind? Can you sense the creative spirit firing up within? Do any ideas or forms emerge?

HEAD: What did you believe about the problem in the past? What does everyone else believe? What insights appear once you let go of all these assumptions?

What could you believe about human nature or the way the world works that could be more empowering for you and others?

Can you allow a vision to form within your mind's eye of how things could be around this problem once you have broken through it?

Would this vision benefit yourself and others? Can you add in a benefit for the world too?

Does this win–win–win feel like a powerful vision, doable but challenging? Do you want to take it on?

HANDS: Standing one year from now, how do you want this vision to have played out? What about three years from now? Five? Ten?

What do you want your role to be in making this happen?

If you are going to bring this vision to life, what needs to change within you?

What one, simple thing can you do by midnight tonight that would start the ball rolling and move you toward your vision? What could you research or discover? Can you reach out to someone who might be able to support you? Go!

BREAKTHROUGH QUESTIONS

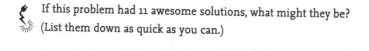 If this problem had 11 awesome solutions, what might they be? (List them down as quick as you can.)

If I had totally nailed this problem before, what would I do about it now?

Power

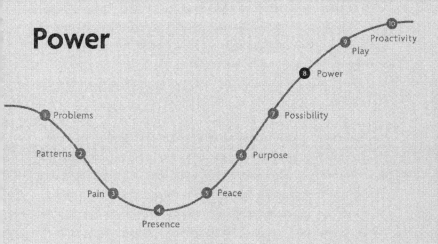

To BIRTH AN IDEA into a system that will usually resist it, we must be at the top of our game. Old habits that sabotage our potential are not going to help. It is time to rewire ourselves with new powers that inspire and enable us. This draws toward us people who can help us bring our ideas to live. As more people get involved, our ideas fly free, ascending to ever-greater heights and taking us with them. The more we commit to our ideas, the more power we find we have in the world. Communities follow conviction.

I've always been fascinated by how martial artists achieve the most amazing feats of strength and agility, even when so many of them seem so slight and diminutive. How do karate kids punch through blocks of solid wood? Where do they get their power? The answer is counterintuitive. It has very little to do with the size of their pectorals or biceps. Research has shown that the power of a black belt comes from their mind and not their muscle, as their brains show massive changes in areas associated with coordination and speed.[1] What manifests as muscle power is determined by mind power (or as we would have it, body.mind power). This is why 83 percent of sports coaches rate mind power as the most important factor in the success of elite athletes.[2]

The more you train your body.mind to think and act powerfully, the faster you can bring your vision to life. Need to be more confident to achieve your vision? No problem, you can rewire your brain to build that skill. Want to be more patient, compassionate, and creative to remix your life? Not a drama. By hacking into the conditioning and consolidation processes (see pages 59 and 88), we can rewire anything. This is because your nervous system, from the brain to the belly, is 'plastic.' It is not fixed, but instead can be changed by how we think (and feel).[3]

Your hardwired reactions, stored in the basal ganglia, will keep on firing even after the original pain that drove them has been dissolved away in love. We can't expect to keep all our old patterns and maintain breakthroughs. We need new powers (a pattern we choose consciously) wired in to prevent the old ones from coming back. Without this, we may find that we creep back toward the familiar. So let's encourage our plastic neurons to form new pathways that encode these new powers and lock in our insights. This will help us sustain our breakthroughs, over days and months, so we can break out of the Survival Trip for good. Then we can build with our HANDS, the things our HEART and HEAD have dreamed up.

Rewiring the brain

EXTERNAL POWER, THE KIND people get from being respected or rich, only lasts as long as people are willing to give it to us. As soon as we lose our position or fall out of favor, our power falls away. There is no telling when this kind of power might be taken from us, as many deposed dictators and fired execs have discovered. However, *inner* power, the kind we stoke up for ourselves, can never be taken away for us *unless* we give it away. The fastest way to relinquish our power is to lose confidence and return to **self-sabotage**.

Imagine, as you read this, that the idea or vision you are holding has come into being. Feel it having happened. Imagine you are the person who made it happen. Notice if there is any part of you, no matter how small or surreptitious, that finds it hard to believe it could be real. Is there any negative self-talk like . . .

- 'It can't really happen, can it?'
- 'Somebody could, but not me!'
- 'In your dreams!'
- 'Never going to happen.'
- 'It's too hard.'

If any part of your body.mind gets tense, worried, or critical, it simply means that you have old patterns still in residence. The Protector will pop up with a pattern as soon as you have an idea that might require you to change and take risks. The thing is, new ideas demand some kind of change. We need to be the shift we want to see. So every breakthrough will incur risk. The evolutionary logic of the stress response is to worry much more about what we can lose than what we can gain. The Protector can easily get fixated on the downside.

> **Although the creative spirit loves to weave imaginative possibilities into big ideas and bold visions, fear and cynicism can destroy this fragile process in its tracks. Ideas can disappear just as quickly as they arose.**

You give away power with every story of cynicism, criticism, blame, and shame. You give it away with every out-of-date habit that undermines your performance. You give it away with every moment of anger or resentment. Power leaks from you like the fluid from a rusty battery with every pattern still operating. If you find yourself being consistently late, disorganized, feeling put upon, moody, doubtful, flaky, disheveled, and so on, then you are sabotaging yourself. It is a sign that the Protector is working overtime, drawing energy away from what you really want. It is time to rewire.

For many years, scientific dogma had it that once the brain reached adolescence, it didn't change that much. However, that belief has now been discarded. The brain can not only trim and prune existing pathways; it can also create new pathways. For example, studies show that just ten minutes a day strumming a guitar, for a few weeks, can change the shape of your cerebral cortex. Cab drivers who have to learn the best routes around a city show changes in their cerebellum, an area associated with space and movement. Even a single workout at the gym can change how your DNA is expressed.[4] As soon as you stop the new activity, the brain and body returns to how it was before. This means that your body.mind can heal from trauma, and develop new skills from scratch. Most of the time, though, we use our insanely flexible brain plasticity to reinforce our old patterns instead of crafting new powers.

We can power up in any area we choose. Using techniques modeled on how the brain actually works, you can create new powers that make being committed, courageous, or confident effortless. The creation of fresh, inspiring, and liberating powers doesn't happen overnight but, by repeatedly burnishing them into the body.mind, you can transform yourself beyond recognition in months, not years. Nothing is too big for us to shift. Selfish to generous. Arrogant to humble. Defensive to open. We can, consciously and intentionally, change how our body.mind is wired, one thought, one image, one emotion at a time. This is huge.

You can transform anything about your personality by rewiring your brain.

We rewire our brains using the same processes that creates patterns: Conditioning and consolidation. We make up our own reality, to some extent, all the time. So we might as well use our imagination to invent stories and feelings that help us create, break through, and thrive. We will swap all those *limiting* beliefs for *breakthrough* beliefs . . . and then sear them into our body.mind with our emotions. Rather than use pain to lock them in, we will use passion. Love seals the deal, making our new powers second nature.

THE GREATEST GUINNESS WORLD RECORD HOLDER

Ashrita Furman (formerly known as Keith) has been the record-holder for 400 Guinness World Records. He clearly knows a thing or two about breakthroughs. One of his first wild challenges was a 24-hour bike race in Central Park, NYC—the winner was the person who clocked up the most miles. Seasoned riders were planning around 350 miles. Inspired by his wisdom teacher, Keith believed he could get to 400 miles, even though he was a complete novice. He bought his first bike ten days before the race. After three hours of cycling, he was exhausted. Instead of giving up, he decided to visualize, and feel, a flame in his heart. Then he imagined himself breathing in light and breathing out exhaustion. He told himself that the reason his legs were hurting so much was because God was massaging them. He was fully switched on. After 24 hours (and only one stop to go to the bathroom), he finished third after cycling 405 miles.

He imagined it. He felt it. He became it. He did it.

You may remember that the word for thriving in Greek is *eudaimonia* (see page 6). The literal translation of this word is 'having a spirit or friendly demon within.' To thrive, we must recruit our not-so-friendly-demons, in our darkside, and help them let go of their angst. We can rewire the Big Shot to be vulnerable and open. We can rewire the Control Freak to enjoy chaos and live more spontaneously. We can rewire the Cynic to be re-enchanted with the miracle of life again.

Powering up

YOU CAN'T GO FROM being 'terrified' of public speaking to 'adoring' it just by telling yourself to do so. A mantra won't work if you are beset by fear and pain. The Protector is a lot stronger than wishful thinking. Only once you have used the breakthrough process to let go of the fear, pain, and lack, can you start to build powers within. You already have them to some degree, even if they are at a low level right now. For example, you have some capacity to speak in public (even if just asking for a train ticket). That means this talent can be built on and boosted into a power. You don't need to pretend you love doing keynote speeches, but you can encourage an enjoyment of sharing your ideas for a start. Then, by rewiring powers and releasing patterns, you might one day find yourself a professional speaker. Stranger things have happened.

It's smart to build powers that will increase the chance of bringing your vision to life. If you want to start a new project, it may be helpful to boost powers around trust, commitment, and creativity. If you want to start dating, it may be helpful to amplify your powers of confidence, optimism, and humor. Ask your Connector to help come up with the right powers for you, right now, to accelerate you on the Thrive Drive. Then you want to turn them into a statement that can help you stay switched on. Here are a few **Switch Statements** you can customize to fast-track this process:

- Each and every day, I am more and more . . . healthy, excited, connected, at peace, etc.
- As each moment passes, I feel even more . . . safe, fulfilled, creative, grateful, etc.
- By day and by night, I grow more and more . . . happy, sexy, healthy, risk-taking, etc.

Make sure your Switch Statements are in the present tense, to avoid telling your body.mind it has to wait until the future to be awesome; and in the positive, because the brain doesn't get negatives so you risk building things you don't want that way. If you say to yourself 'I want to be less lazy each day,' all your body.mind hears is 'I want to be lazy each day.' Not ideal. Always focus on the health, not the hurt.

VISUALIZATIONS AT WORK

Research at Harvard University has shown that feeling and seeing a movement internally fires the same brain regions as actually doing it. Repeating it, over and over, reinforces the wiring. It also builds a sense of expectation in ourselves that we will do the same again next time. Rehearsing moves in the body.mind helps elite athletes perform. Some professional basket players believe that visualizations—whether of the movement itself or seeing the ball pop through the hoop—improve their scoring rate in games. Tiger Woods visualizes his golf ball tinkling into the plastic of the hole before he putts.[5] Repeatedly focusing on positive images spurs how quickly people heal after injury.[6]

Visualizing the future in a positive way can effect your entire life. A study that monitored a group of nuns over many years, from when they donned their habits to when they died, found that those who looked positively on their future before they took their vows ended up living much longer than those who were less optimistic. Only 34 percent of those who looked more negatively at the future lived past 85, while 90 percent of the most positive ones did.[7]

Try out different statements. Words that inspire you, will feel true. Keep them. Words that feel somehow inauthentic will ring false. Drop them. Choose Switch Statements that, when you say them, release stress and open you up to joy. Ideally, you want to get a rush or goose bumps. You *want* to feel lifted. Repeat these Switch Statements to yourself and allow your body.mind to be flooded with the feelings associated with the words. We know that, biologically, emotions fire up the whole system. So amplify this process with as much emotional energy as you can. It is where the real imprinting happens. If you were the most compassionate or committed version of you, what would that feel like? Then pull out all the stops in your neural architecture and inundate your body.mind. The stronger the positive emotions, the faster you will rewire your neurons.

It can help to add some imagery to boost the process, particularly visuals of what the end outcomes might be. It is also smart to add in visuals of some of the steps along the way, especially if you might find them challenging. See yourself choosing an apple over a bag of chips. See yourself doing your taxes for your new start-up with a big smile on your face.

You can fire up and rewire whenever you choose: A cheeky couple of minutes at the bus stop or lying in bed in the comfort of your own home. The more often you feel these emotions within, the faster you'll recall them when you need them most under pressure. I suggest doing it when you wake up and go to bed for three weeks and see what happens. You can also power up during meditation, jogging, or swimming. Above all, power up when you feel yourself being triggered into an old pattern. Avoid criticizing yourself when this happens. Research has shown that if we flip into stress, we can't rewire.[8] Acknowledge the old pattern popping up and then focus on the new power. Say your **Switch Statement** and fire up your emotional system. All you are doing is conditioning and consolidating. But you do have to keep on practicing power-ups if you want to hang on to the powers!

> **Powering up is not magic or voodoo. It is simply mastering our own biochemistry.**

Tuning up

THERE IS A COMMON myth out there that if we have money, fame, or power then we will get to do what we want to do. Then, finally, we will be happy.

HAVE MONEY/FAME/CONTROL ➤ DO THE THINGS I WANT ➤ FEEL HAPPY AND POWERFUL

But this logic is all messed up. We know nobody *makes* us feel good (or bad for that matter; see Session 01, page 33). No amount of money or celebrity can make us feel happy either. Only we can, within. So the way it works in life is the opposite: How we feel influences what we do, which determines what we have.

FEEL HAPPY AND POWERFUL ➤ DO THE THINGS I WANT ➤ HAVE MONEY/FAME/POWER (MAYBE)

We always get to control how we feel inside, but we can't always control what we earn or what work is available. By powering up, we may well end up making a few million or marrying the person of our dreams. However, because we master how to *feel* the way we want to feel, we become a lot less worried about *having stuff*. People want fame and fortune to feel safe, respected, and happy. By creating these feelings inside us, at will, we can short-circuit all that effort and just enjoy the goodness right now. The delicious irony is that, once we stop trying so hard and learn to feel amazing whenever we want to, we are then way more likely to be amazing in the world and be rewarded with the things we (thought) we wanted.

> **We can always feel like we are thriving . . . because we can choose to feel peaceful, purposeful, and powerful at any given moment.**

You can respond to the world around you with love, truth, and creativity no matter what is happening to you. DJs usually have three frequency ranges to adjust when they play a track: Bass, mid, and treble. A good DJ micro-adjusts the levels with every track they play, to create the best experience on the dance floor. This will change depending on their mood, the crowd, the track, the sound system, and the space. Your **HEART**, **HEAD**, and **HANDS** are the frequency ranges you can twiddle within to tune yourself up. Only you can adjust them. Every moment of your life can be optimized with the perfect mix of **HEART**, **HEAD**, and **HANDS**.

You can choose to have the next hour feel any way you want it to. Suffer or thrive? Twist those dials! You can constantly recalibrate your emotions, beliefs, and actions to fit the moment.

You will know when you are fully **tuned up** because the whole of your body.mind will feel coherent and alive: a loving HEART, an inspiring HEAD, and co-creating HANDS. When you are tuned up like this, you have the power to create your own reality within, and deal with any fiascos and disasters without. You are fully tuned up: All channels are open, available, and switched on to life.

Tuning Up

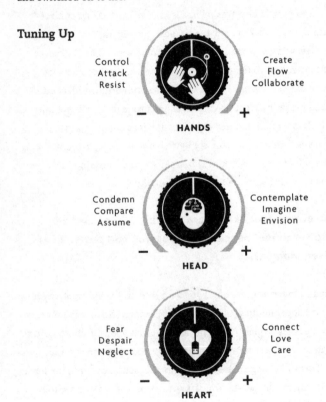

Control
Attack
Resist

Create
Flow
Collaborate

– +

HANDS

Condemn
Compare
Assume

Contemplate
Imagine
Envision

– +

HEAD

Fear
Despair
Neglect

Connect
Love
Care

– +

HEART

If you don't feel this power coursing through your body.mind, or if you notice self-sabotage going on, it means that you are **conflicted** within. No goal-achievement or manifestation process in the world will be worth much if you don't find the conflict and release it. Visualizing yourself having a billion dollars in your HEAD is meaningless if, in your deepest HEART, you don't believe you're worth it. If you want to 'manifest' something and it is not showing up in your life, it is because you are conflicted. Your level of empowerment (and happiness) depends on how often, and how regularly, you are willing to tune up the dials within every time you notice a reaction, charge, or pattern. Scan inside to find where the wonkiness is and adjust the set.

Making regular micro-adjustments in your body.mind helps you move forward, just as a pilot shifts the sail on a boat to catch the wind as it changes. This doesn't mean it is all plain sailing. Life is inherently uncertain and some things are just not meant to be. Anyone who tells us otherwise is either deluded or a charlatan peddling certainty to those who fear the unknown. The ambiguity is what makes life so exciting. We cannot control it! The Big U has its own agenda for our growth and learning. So all we can do is tune up inside and feel as powerful, creative, and content as we can with what is happening right now.

Spreading the love

ONCE YOU ARE POWERED-UP and tuned-up, it is time to engage your people. Your network is much more powerful than you are alone, so it's crucial to invest time and energy into activating it and keeping it healthy. Our network is a two-way street. It stays healthiest when we give *before* we think of getting. That means offering up ideas, inspiration, and support to the people we care about or find inspiring before we look for a return. After our body.mind, our community is our next greatest resource. For anything of lasting value to be created in the world, it will need the collaboration of an entire network. It matters who we keep in our network. If we surround ourselves with people who are switched off, we will be more likely to be switched off. If we hang out with people who are open, alive, and aware, they will pull us into being like they are.

Everything you need to thrive is within you and the people in your network.

Our big, bold vision is often the solution to a problem that no one else can see or wants to see, or a solution that nobody else believes in or can even understand. Your life partner may have given up; your colleagues may have become too jaded. So, to make things happen, we need to bring them along with us. The most powerful way to get people excited and elevated is a new story. If people are not getting our brilliant ideas, there is little value in blaming them for it. What we can do is look at how to adjust our story to capture their hearts and minds more effectively.

Stories move people. They move people to choose risky, new ideas that are emerging from the future, over the safe but limiting beliefs of the past. Steve Jobs, Richard Branson, and Barack Obama are powerful visionaries who have inspired millions with what is possible. Adolf Hitler and Winston Churchill were also brilliant communicators; they just told very different stories of how people, and the world, could be. In culture, different stories compete for prominence until a moment of critical mass occurs and one goes viral. As the American lawyer John Quincy Adams (who became the sixth US president) says in the movie *Amistad*: 'Whomever tells the best story wins.'

However, the story alone is not enough. The people whom we engage with our narrative, need to know that we fully believe it, have embodied it, and won't sabotage it. This is about trust. Self-sabotaging patterns corrode that trust and leave us powerless to get the support and resources we need. We don't want to fritter away our social capital (the influence we have over others) by not returning their emails, missing our appointments, or breaking our promises. So a high level of personal **integrity** is key. We can't control whether others will do what they say they will do, but we can influence whether we do. If we don't follow through, we damage our personal brand. Just like any brand, we can only come back so many times from a failure to live up to our promises. If we do mess up, we have to clear it up fast (by owning it, apologizing, and making good). Otherwise the corrosive acid of disempowerment will start to break down the trust.

Commitment locks the switch on

EVERYONE CAN TALK ABOUT a cool idea they've had: 'Oh I thought of that years before they launched it.' But not everyone makes their ideas happen. Breakthrough of any kind demands a high level of commitment. When you meet people who are committed, you can sense it. They embody their vision inside them. HEART, HEAD, and HANDS are all **congruent**, aligned. Even if they have no external power (like wealth or political clout) you can feel their internal power. They have what I call T.F.R. or 'Total Fucking Resolve.'

The more we embody our ideas, possibilities, and stories, the more people will feel us being congruent. When we are congruent, we bring ideas down from our HEAD, into our HEART and HANDS. Each is saying: 'YES! THIS WILL HAPPEN.' We turn talk into walk. We live the possibilities that we love. We feel them, act them, breathe them, play them. This is T.F.R. When we are congruent, our powers are conditioned into our nervous system as part of who we are. We don't have to *remember* to be on fire. We just *are* on fire. There may well still be moments of doubt and fear. But they are the exception, no longer the rule. As we develop **congruence**, we find that our sense of power—power to influence reality, power to break through—rises exponentially.

With commitment and congruence, we shift a breakthrough from a great idea to a lived reality. Even if it hasn't quite happened in the world yet, *we act like it has already happened inside us.* This is what happens when we break out. It's a done deal within us. It's just a matter of time before it happens in the world. There is no way our vision will not happen, at least in some form or other (how it looks when done is as much to do with the universe as it is us).

People can sense this within you. Would the people in your network buy stocks in you? If you don't think they would . . . then there is more breaking through to do before you can break out.

Break out = Insight + Ideas + Commitment + Congruence

THE POWER OF THE NETWORK

The more open, active, and alive our network, the more power flows from it. This is why having a great network is a predictor of career success.[9] It is not about knowing the right people but about being part of the flow of ideas, metaphors, and insights that counts. Entrepreneurial success—measured by how innovative the start-ups were that came out of Stanford Business School—is also dependent on the openness of our networks. SBS alumni with more diverse networks out-innovate their peers by 300 percent.[10]

Our social connections play a vital role in our wellbeing. In a study of more than 1,000 Vietnam War veterans, those that were connected to the community were much less likely to develop PTSD.[11] When we are happy and compassionate, it can spread through our connections like a virus. It has been estimated that for every happy friend we have, it increases the probability we are happy by 9 percent. An extra $5,000 income increases the probability of being happy by just 2 percent![12] Having good friends can boost feelings of wellbeing and reduce depression and heart disease. Even a tiny social connection—a simple 'Hi!' from a bus driver—can extend an elderly person's life.[13] When we are thriving in relationships, we are thriving in life.

The beliefs and behaviors of people we don't even know—friends of friends of friends, three connections away in our social network—can also inspire (or disempower) us. Scientists at Harvard have (controversially) suggested that people with obese friends, even those they have not met, are more likely to be obese. Happiness is also thought to be 'caught' by people we have never actually met.[14]

Commitment keeps the switch on even when part of you (the scared or exhausted part) might want to switch off. Commitment pulls you back into congruence whenever you get reactive or defensive.

> **When you have commitment—when you have embodied your breakthroughs and are free of inner conflict—people want to believe in you. This is the essence of power.**

Commitment is the only thing that will get you past the inevitable blockages and obstacles along the way. Scan inside you now.

- **Are you thriving . . . or merely thinking about it?**
- **Can you shout across the rooftops, with total resolve, 'I am ready for this!'?**
- **Are you ready, right now . . . or getting ready to be ready?**

If you hear a big YES! to these questions, perhaps with a deep, guttural ooompphh in your core, it means you are committed.

If you hear an 'UMMM . . .' or a 'NOT YET' that is totally OK. There is no morality here, no good or bad. However, it does mean there is something within that will get in the way. You have some incongruence, and it will show up in the way you act, speak, and feel. It may be that it's not the right time; that the vision isn't the right one for you; or that you have some fear within. Better to wait until everything is aligned before you commit fully and publicly, as opposed to commit and then let yourself and others down. Take your time before you make your move. There is no rush. When you leap, leap fully.

Notice how often we use words like 'maybe,' 'might', and 'try' to avoid commitment. Phrases like these pepper our everyday language. They ensure that we have a way out, in case things don't go quite as we'd planned. They keep us uncommitted and so disempowered. When we commit, we remove any back door that might allow us to do a runner. We shut down any wiggle room that can help us avoid response-ability. Nobody can be half-committed. We are either ON or OFF. When the Spanish conquistador Hernán Cortés landed and claimed Mexico in the 16th century, he encountered the rumblings of a mutiny. To give his soldiers no choice but to press on, Cortés ordered all the ships to be scuttled. There was no retreat. All they could do was keep going.

What would it be like to burn the boats that you use to take you back to your comfort zone?

Commitment is incendiary. It smolders away, free from the doubt that quenches flames. There are no question marks. No 'probablies.' No 'one days.' There is just absolute certainty throughout our body.mind. The dials are all tuned up.

Commitment has a catch though. We can get so focused on what we want to create that, if it doesn't happen, we become disappointed and upset. We get attached to the results, not the journey of discovery. One of life's greatest challenges is to remain full of resolve yet totally at peace if things don't go the way we planned. If our Tiny Me starts to worry about whether we will look good or feel happy, we will begin to get 'grippy.' Power leaks. We immediately lose some of our flexibility, our flow, and may well try to control things. We may start to control others too. This undermines our ability to flex with the moment and spot new possibilities. We have flipped from being driven by love (i.e. purpose) to being driven by lack. We're back in the Survival Trip. Eek!

 TESTOSTERONE: THE POWER HORMONE

Testosterone (and other androgens) can promote anger and egocentrism but also feelings of bravery, energy, strength, pride, confidence, and spontaneity in both men and women. It can drive us to seek victory, which is useful when bringing new ideas into a world that often resists them. It helps us find ways to achieve our aims, using whatever way works given the context we are in. In violent places, it drives aggression; in collaborative arenas, co-operation.[15] Stock traders have elevated testosterone when they beat the market, which tends to promote more risk-taking and confidence, a positive feedback loop termed the 'winner effect.'[16]

Assuming a confident posture, like putting feet up on our desk at work, can help us feel more powerful and boosts testosterone levels.[17] But testosterone can also inhibit compassion and connection by preventing oxytocin from binding to receptors in the brain. Fathers, in the weeks after their children are born, can see a 30 percent drop in their testosterone levels, making them more nurturing parents.[18] Men who sleep next to their babies, or have smaller testicles, have a greater chance of being more caring dads because their testosterone levels are lower.[19]

Commitment comes from a connected body.mind. Grippiness comes from a disconnected one. One leads to us thriving; the other leads to stress and suffering. One of the great sources of wisdom, the Indian text the *Bhagavad Gita*, can help us. Gandhi called it his handbook to life. The *Bhagavad Gita* has a passage within it that says something like this: 'When a man has let go of his grippiness, when his body.mind is rooted in wisdom, everything he does is devotion and his actions melt away.'

Instead of focusing on the *fruits* of our labors, focus on the *love* that ripens the fruit. In the place of results, focus on intentions. You can be resolved to make stuff happen, and yet at peace with whatever the outcomes are.

The word **devotion** here is key. When I read Gandhi's notes on the *Bhagavad Gita*, I realized he had devoted his efforts to free India to the Big U. That is how he maintained his power through thick and thin and avoided getting all grippy and frustrated. If you devote your breakthroughs to the Big U, you will relax in seconds. You don't need a result to feel good; you feel good from the start. Your actions and projects are *gifts* of love to the Great We, not attempts to get love. This is a return to actionless action: *Wei wu wei.*

> **Once we accept that we are co-creators of life, with life, we can gracefully take ownership of all our commitments and yet be relaxed if things go awry because, ultimately, we can't control everything.**

We live in a complex, adaptive system, which promotes adaptation and learning. We cannot second-guess why some things don't work out. It may have been to teach us something, or stimulate someone else in the system to expand. All we can do is switch on to any lack of integrity, congruence, or commitment in our body.mind, tune ourselves up, and keep on growing.

The truly powerful are those whose feelings (**HEART**), thoughts (**HEAD**), and actions (**HANDS**) are in alignment with their true purpose, who power up whenever they feel powerless, tune up when they feel out of sorts, and are totally committed to a result yet free of grippiness. We dance like the mighty oak in a storm, without ever losing our ground.

SWITCH ON TO POWER

Switched Off: Power comes from outside. When we get respect and money, we have it. When we have power, we can control people and nature, and so manipulate them to ensure our needs are met.

Switched On: Power comes from within when we are connected to ourselves and the universe. As we align our emotions, beliefs, and actions within, we develop integrity of intention, word, and deed. This congruence empowers us and attracts support. When we commit, we engage the full power of our being into making things happen. We lose power when we self-sabotage.

 **SWITCH ON NOW**

Right now, get your Connector into the mix. Breathe. Relax. Maybe close your eyes for a second while you choose to switch on.

HEART: Remember the last time you felt powerful and masterful. How did it feel? Flood your body with that feeling and amplify it to the max.

Imagine being like this all the time.

Can you offer an idea or project that you are committed to, back to the Big U as a form of devotion?

As you do, can you feel yourself release any needs or expectations . . . leaving a sense of peace with whatever happens?

Enjoy the feeling of raw power it brings.

HEAD: Can you declare to the universe that you are ready to make change happen without hesitation or provisos? Can you exclaim, right now, that you are the person you need to be to have the things you want to have?

If not, can you switch on to be that person?

Develop some Switch Statements that help you build new powers. Say them now, feeling empowering emotions explode inside.

HANDS: Identify a few people in your network (family, friends, colleagues, connections) that you can share your ideas and commitments with.

Are you committed enough to ask for their help? Can you allow yourself to accept support?

If appropriate, make an agreement with them about what you or they are going to do next to keep things happening. Do whatever you can, with compassion, to ensure that the agreement is honored.

BREAKTHROUGH QUESTIONS

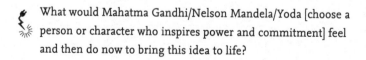 What would Mahatma Gandhi/Nelson Mandela/Yoda [choose a person or character who inspires power and commitment] feel and then do now to bring this idea to life?

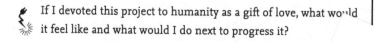 If I devoted this project to humanity as a gift of love, what would it feel like and what would I do next to progress it?

Session 09

Play

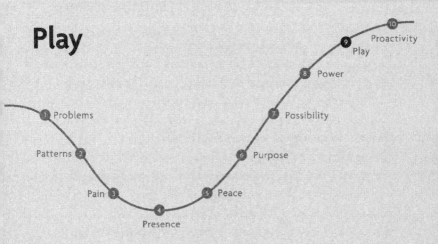

- 1 Problems
- Patterns 2
- Pain 3
- 4 Presence
- 5 Peace
- 6 Purpose
- 7 Possibility
- 8 Power
- 9 Play
- 10 Proactivity

WHEN WE ARE BRINGING possibilities to life we don't want to get too heavy about it, no matter how committed we are. Seriousness breeds stress, which triggers shut-down. We can keep ourselves inspired through periods of fiasco and frustration with playfulness. Play keeps us creative even in the face of seemingly insurmountable problems. Play is nature's way of learning. We can hang out at the edge of chaos, and actually enjoy it. Playfulness gives us a childlike sense of optimism and freedom, which can help us break out from stress and fear into a life of liberty. Every project becomes an opportunity to play in the sandbox. This is committed, wholehearted, focused activity; but play nevertheless!

Having a massive breakthrough is no guarantee of an easy life. We may be so ahead of the curve that we spend our whole lives waiting for people to catch up. For most of his career, Monet was ridiculed. Van Gogh is reputed to have only sold one painting in his lifetime. Nikola Tesla, one of the greatest inventors of his generation, died penniless after helping invent/discover radio, neon lights, wireless communication, X-rays, and electric current.

When it comes to our breakthroughs, it might take months for our life partner to get our new plan to become more intimate. Our kids might resist the breakthrough in parenting we're so juiced up by. Our bank manager many never get the genius of our disruptive business idea and so not want to fund it. Even with the most compelling story about what is possible, sometimes there are still too many obstacles on the way.

So when leading family, friend, or work networks towards a new vision, we must also lead ourselves. We have to master our moods, energy levels, downtime, rhythms, environments, and anything else to ensure we stay at peak performance. If we burn out or get discouraged, we are back in the trap. 'No person can be free until they master themselves,' as the Stoic philosopher (and former slave) Epictetus said.

Play is a powerful lens to achieve this mastery. Being playful keeps us curious and excited as we explore ways to move things forward. Play keeps us in a biodynamic harmony between tension and relaxation, activity and rest, Tiny Me and Great We, as we hang out at the edge of chaos. We keep ourselves open, available, attentive, imaginative, committed; poised for another breakthrough at any moment.

Alexander Fleming, the biologist who discovered penicillin (a breakthrough that has saved millions of lives), was a deeply playful man who loved board games, billiards, golf, and more. He enjoyed doing research purely for the fun of it. 'I play with microbes' he said of his work. 'It is very pleasant to break the rules and to be able to find something that nobody has thought of.' The Nobel Prize-winning scientist Richard Feynman made his most important breakthroughs after he chose to *play* with physics rather than *work* at it, having found himself getting a bit too serious and a bit too tight.[1]

We are natural-born players

BACK IN THE 1930S, a Dutch historian and philosopher, Johan Huizinga, proposed that rather than simply being *homo sapiens*, 'wise man', we are in fact *homo ludens*, 'playing man'. He suggests that at the core of our success as a species, is the fact that we are players not thinkers.[2] Play is nature's way of helping animals learn. Human children play more than any other species. As they play, they develop ideas and skills that move our species forward. Just look at a two-year-old learn how to get what they want on a tablet computer.

Even when living in poverty, kids still prioritize play over almost everything else. They pick up whatever bits and bobs are around and make a game out of it. The education researcher Sugata Mitra has shown that kids given a desktop computer in a box in India (and no other instruction) can, before long, do stuff with it. Even more amazing is that some can also speak rudimentary English.[3] This isn't work to them. This is play!

Your creative activities, whether lovemaking or business building, will reach their zenith when you choose to play at them rather than work at them. As the great German philosopher and poet Friedrich Schiller wrote: 'Man only plays when, in the full meaning of the word, he is a man, *and he is only completely a man* when he plays.'[4]

Yet, sadly, our childlike exuberance to get stuck in and play is progressively chipped away by disapproving parents, teachers, managers, and lovers. Most of all, it is lost through our own disenchantment and self-judgment. We can easily lose the glee a kid has to try something new, and replace it with terror at the thought of what might go wrong. This terror may look like 'stress,' 'being realistic,' or 'worry,' yet these are just fancy words for fear. What we tend to fear most is the thought that we have . . .

FAILED!

Repeat it a couple of times in your mind. What does it feel like in your body as you say it? Can you remember a moment when you failed big? Was there some humiliation, shame, embarrassment?

Breathe it all away, reconnect, and read on.

Chances are, the idea of failure brings with it some negative vibes. Failure is frowned upon in most cultures and we have been conditioned to avoid it. Our society's narrative dictates that it is the winning that counts and we are told this, unsubtly, with every exam we take and competitive job application we submit. People jibing at us for failed relationships, dates, creative projects, and companies just reinforces the pain.pattern crystals within and urges us to avoid even the chance of failure. So we stay in the comfort zone rather than risk a breakthrough. That way lies breakdown, the failure to stay fitted.

 ## WE LIVE TO PLAY AND PLAY TO LIVE

Studies of brain development in children show why play is so important. Play accelerates the development of the brain and helps prune nerves. It stimulates the dopamine pathways of reward and pleasure, boosting our interest in seeking out new things and fresh ideas. We are driven to experiment but without the dangers or stress. Play juices up the prefrontal cortex, increasing our ability to deal with complex situations without reacting.[5] Play helps us prepare for the future and wires nerve pathways for success.

Biologists are discovering that play is an integral part of the entire animal kingdom. In turns out that most animals learn best when playing. Alligators, lizards, fish, birds, and mammals all play. In fact, young animals can use up to 15 percent of their daily calories playing. This means that play is evolutionarily 'expensive' so must be important. Common across the animal kingdom is that play is done for its own sake. It is entered into voluntarily and for enjoyment.[6] Stressed out, insecure, or starving animals do not play.

Freedom to fail

THE TINY ME TENDS to see things as a fail, even when it does not have to. It tends to ignore the small wins, naturally focusing on what might go wrong (danger) over what is possible. However, we can rewire this.

Thomas Edison, of light bulb fame, registered over 2,000 patents. He stated in the *New York Times* in 1847: 'I have not failed 700 times. I have not failed once. I have succeeded in proving that those 700 ways will not work. When I have eliminated the ways that will not work, I will find the way that will work.' Would Edison have invented so many things if he had been constantly worried that if he didn't crack it this time, he would have failed? For him, failure was not possible as long as he was learning, growing, and staying fitted!

We too can reframe what failure means to us. For me, when an idea has 'failed,' it simply means that my expected outcome didn't materialize. This doesn't mean I, or anyone else, is bad or wrong. It's simply an opportunity to learn, adjust my course, and try again. In this way, each failed experiment can be an opportunity for a breakthrough. So if I try a new way of talking to my wife, but it actually makes our fight worse, I learn and try something new next time.

Penicillin was discovered because Fleming *failed* to be a 'good' scientist and keep his equipment sterile. A Petri dish got contaminated and, hey presto, a billion lives saved. Post-It notes, which have made more than a billion dollars, came about because the inventor failed to make glue that was strong enough. Flickr started out life as an online video game, which failed. They found the photo-sharing element was really resonating, so 'pivoted' the business to make the most of it. There is always a way to metabolize failure into triumph if we don't get demoralized or down on ourselves.

You are already more than enough as you are. You don't need external success to prove anything to you. Not any more. You don't need validation from praise and prizes. You are a unique child of the universe, one of billions that are all equally awesome. By expressing your purpose from sun-up to sun-down, you are doing all you need to do to have a 'successful life.' So if you 'fail' with a new idea . . . look at what went wrong, adjust inside anything that was out of alignment, and explore what is possible next.

Feel what it would be like to know that every single one of your goals, visions, plans—no matter how serious—was a game. Feel what it would be like to know that every creative response to life was an experiment. Feel what it would be like to laugh with delight every time you messed up and remember it was . . .

PLAYTIME!

Studies show that people who learn to approach failures like this—powerfully yet playfully—tend to be more healthy *and* more successful whether at school, sports, or sales.[7] As soon as your self-worth is no longer tied up in proving to people that you are a success, you can reclaim your childlike (not childish) ability to play. The lack of scary consequences keeps you lighter and breezier, which keeps you out of the Survival Trip and in the zone of learning. In many ways, my consulting company's work helping organizations innovate is a lot about giving the people within them permission to play. We allow them a safe space to let go of their assumptions and notions, albeit briefly, and entertain radically different ideas, and prototype new activities.

Even if your vision is important, perhaps stopping children being abused, it doesn't mean that getting stressed out is going to help. This 'Activist Complex' is an easy trap to fall into. When I start to think I am 'saving the world' with my projects, I immediately get more tense, righteous, and grippy. This reduces my capacity to create and adapt. Treating goals as games, even if bankruptcy or death are potential downsides, releases you from the neurobiological Survival Trip that stops you thriving.

To borrow a term from software development, life is in continuous ß. We never get a finished product. There is always more to iterate and improve. There is always another game to play. As the founder of IKEA, Ingvar Kamprad, put it: 'Only those who are asleep make no mistakes.'

As long as we are learning, we are thriving!

Thriving at the edge of chaos

WHEN YOU LOOK DOWN at how far you might fall when you take a leap, it's natural to be a little apprehensive. Fear is present when we take a risk and all creativity involves risk. With every new career path, love interest, and passion project, we risk what we have right now for what we could create in the future. Living creatively is full of risk. However, in a world that is changing so quickly, it's just as risky to keep doing things in the same way as it is to try out something new.

If your partner is growing, and you stay the same, you are unlikely to thrive together. Likewise, sticking to a business model that worked in the 1980s may be riskier than building an unproven one. There are no absolutely safe and risk-free choices. Full stop. The emerging fields of complexity science, systems thinking, and quantum theory all point toward the uncomfortable truth that the interconnected world around us cannot be accurately predicted, no matter how much we know about it (which is what many wisdom teachers have been saying for centuries). We can only know probabilities, not certainties. Which means there is always a risk that we won't make it.

At the edge of chaos, where new 'molecules' are forming from 'atoms' of the old system, there are no hard and fast answers. So if we want to thrive in our complex, challenging world, we have to learn how to enjoy hanging out here. Sometimes it takes years for the curve to catch up with us. This can mean years without a huge income, appreciation from our friends, or the support of our partner or parents. As Jeff Bezos, the CEO of Amazon has said, 'To do disruptive innovation, you have to be willing to be misunderstood for a very long time.' So to thrive out here at the edge of chaos, we need to get used to playing in the space between success and failure.

In this space, we want to remain aware, attentive, and focused . . . yet also loose, flexible, and curious. We want to be open to possibility, yet also committed to making an impact. This allows us to pick up, and respond quickly to, weak signals in the world around us. As soon as a breakthrough emerges, whether through 'failure' or 'success,' we are ready to seize it and make something of it. It takes the Great We and the Tiny Me working together in harmony to enjoy, and then sustain, breakthroughs. There is a constant cycling between being super intentional (getting stuff done) and surrendering everything (letting go of the old and receiving new ideas).

It is not just in our behavior that this oscillation occurs. Research has shown that the brain cycles between being active and passive, engaged and released, around 180 times per minute.[8] The brain is itself at the edge of chaos when creating. It oscillates between order and disorder. Without some stability, some foundations, we cannot think in a concrete way about anything. We are in the clouds. Too much stability, too many established patterns that we are not willing to break through, and no possibility can emerge.

When we genuinely feel playful amidst both the triumphs and tragedies, the order and the chaos, we feel fully alive. This is a joy that is totally unaffected by the opinions of others and whether they appreciate us or our work. This joyfulness comes from knowing we are in the middle of the greatest show on Earth, the experience of being at our creative edge. We don't take failure personally, yet we don't take success personally either. They are all a part of the great game, which is a joy to play. We become massively grateful for whatever we have, right now, no matter how tempting the green eyes of jealousy or the red tongue of resentment. As long as we are switched on and engaged in *our* life creatively, we have no logical reason to complain.

It's all in the . . . timing

BREAKING THROUGH IS A marathon and not a sprint. It takes time to bring something awesome into the world. I like to follow the advice of the Taoists: Think like a mountain. While the Ah Ha! moments of elation are epic (see page 175), the quiet plugging away for weeks, months, and years must also be fruitful and fun if we are to stick with it. During the long periods of intentional, committed activity, you need to take care of yourself and manage your energy levels. If you become hectic or exhausted, it can easily trigger a cascade reaction and pull you toward burnout, cynicism, or despair.

Jim Loehr, a psychologist who works with hundreds of top athletes (including Monica Seles) believes that lots of recovery time is the key to staying on top of your game.[9] When we live at the edge of chaos, we need to design in time to relax and recuperate, *and then ensure we take it*. Studies show downtime is key to staying creative.[10] It replenishes limited supplies of attention within our body.mind. We cannot stay focused on something indefinitely.

It's important to pace yourself in a 'rhythmic movement' between lots of activity and lots of rest, balancing the yin and yang of action and inaction. The ideal is to see both hard work and recuperation as play. It's all part of the rhythm we need to break through and break out. There will be shorter periods of rapid idea-creation and excitement, followed by longer periods of effort, mistakes, obstacles, and constant challenges where commitment, rigor, and focus are primary. Both are needed to live, work, and love creatively. Both contribute to the rhythms of a breakthrough life.

Breaking Through Towards a Vision

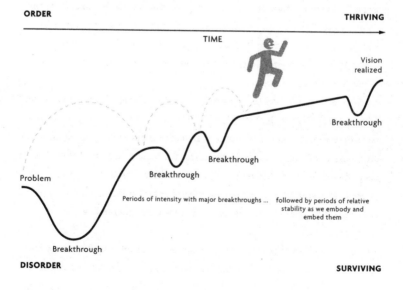

ORDER

THRIVING

TIME

Vision realized

Breakthrough

Breakthrough

Breakthrough

Problem

Periods of intensity with major breakthroughs ...   followed by periods of relative stability as we embody and embed them

Breakthrough

DISORDER

SURVIVING

You want to find ways to maintain your energy and vibrancy for long periods. There is usually a lag phase between initial breakthrough and the results showing up. 'Projects,' of any type, can take days or years to come to fruition. If you have a breakthrough about an addiction, it will still take a while before you have embodied it. If you have one about your parents, it will take time for the shift to be natural when it comes to holiday meals together. Insights and ideas are the relatively easy bit. Keeping ourselves juiced enough to continue despite criticism, lack of resources, or exhaustion is the challenge. Too much pressure and we risk flaking out. Too little pressure and we might wander off to something more fun.

Discovering your own unique rhythm, how you achieve peak performance through blending effort and rest, is crucial. Some kids crawl at six months, others not until they are a year or even older. Your rhythm cannot be judged against anyone else's. One of my ways to recharge is watching high-quality TV drama. After a full day of creating, I love nothing more than to settle back for an hour or two to immerse myself in these alternative worlds. As I do, I can feel myself renew. Some people like to criticize me because I watch a lot of TV. However, they are not me. They don't do the work I do or have the vision I have. So I have to find what works for me. A blast on the running machine, a wander through the woods, a night of reveling, or a living room dance party (all house members are invited) also feature high up on my list of recharge rituals.

The ever-saucy Tiny Me, however, will want to have a breakthrough and then immediately see the benefits of it in the real world. It is impatient for rewards, whether a bonus or round of applause. It likes to put time limits on things, to attempt to create certainty where there is just probability. It is happy to talk about quitting when it doesn't achieve results immediately. Be aware of this kind of self-talk! Thank the Protector for looking out for you, and ask if the Connector is available to help you maintain a flow.state.

There is a right time for everything. Imagine a beautiful rose flourishing in
‌o matter how much you might want it to, it won't flower any quicker
‌r open the buds. All you'll find within is sticky green goo. However,

you can create the best possible conditions for the rose to thrive. You can feed it nutrients. You can move it to a great spot to capture the right amount of sunlight. Above all, you can prune it to ensure all of its passion, all of its possibility, goes into the creation of epic flowers not old stalks. Then, with a little dose of good fortune, you'll enjoy the blossoming petals before too long. Remember, it is the Earth that pushes the flowers up to the sky, not us. We just tend the garden, waiting for the right moment to cut back, plant, and feed.

> **All breakthroughs are alive, a work-in-progress. All our projects are impermanent. Each has its flaws. Each is in a state of *wabi-sabi*, a Japanese term for 'the perfection of imperfection.'**

If you wait, committed and playful, a window of opportunity will open. It is then up to you to

LEAP!

Be careful. The window will close soon enough. The system is in constant flux. Wait too long and the world will have moved on and your breakthrough will no longer fit with it. Delay and you risk your boss/lover/friends/team-mates finding another way forward. Don't procrastinate when your time comes. You have to leap when your intuition tells you it's the right time, or risk losing the moment forever.

The flash of intuition

ALONG THE JOURNEY OF breakthrough, we will be asked to make many decisions about what to do next. Leave our job now or wait a few months and run our project in our spare time? Book a vacation for the family or save for our pension? It's 'normal' to make important decisions like these using a fixed belief (like an ideology), a well-planned strategy, or by asking someone else what to do.

Now, using research or expertise can be a useful guide. It's why I draw on so much scientific study. Getting feedback is brilliant, which is why I have regular coaching chats with many of my most inspiring friends. Yet, if we solely rely on any kind of dogma (a pre-packaged and pre-approved set of beliefs), we miss out on what is emerging here and now. Even discussing what choices we would make in a certain situation, hypothetically, isn't that useful (which is what most moral philosophy, and also the board-game Scruples, is about) because it isn't here, now. There has never been a moment identical to this one, in the entire history of the universe. So how can research from last year, or rules written in a previous century, define accurately what to do next?

This does not stop people using ideology, dogma, and statistics (which always come from the past, of course) all the time to give them the appearance of being right. If we follow the ideological rules or the research evidence, then we have something to fall back on if criticized. The Tiny Me likes dogma because it can always look right, even when we are wrong, because we followed the rules. However, no previous thinking of any kind can remain fitted in a complex world that is constantly evolving. No matter how good the rules are, they cannot stay relevant if they are not able to change as times change.

So you must discover how to sense, with your whole body.mind, what to do next: Logic, emotions, reason, research, insight, gut feel. All of it. Your **HEART** and **HANDS** have as much value as your **HEAD**. As the 17th-century French philosopher Blaise Pascal said in his book *Pensées*, 'The heart has its reasons that reason knows nothing of.' When your **HEART**, **HEAD**, and

HANDS are tuned up, you will discover 'knowledge from within'—the literal definition of intuition.

Inside you are two strong sources of guidance. One is powered by the drive to survive. This is **instinct.** The other is powered by your drive to thrive. This is intuition. Knowing which is guiding you is crucial. Each emanates from a different drive. The Protector's voice, your instincts, will usually get louder, more pressing, more 'shouty.' Instinct is very useful to deal with real threats, but it massively limits creativity, openness, and flexibility. Intuition, the voice of the Connector, will stay clear, certain, and resonant, but it won't get jumpy. It is a 'still small voice of calm.' It emerges when you turn down the chattering and nattering of the Tiny Me to hear it.

THE SLAVE LIBERATOR GUIDED BY INTUITION

The runaway slave Harriet Tubman relied on her intuition to guide her while making her way to freedom in the northern states of the USA, during the time of slavery. She called it the 'voice of God.' She evaded capture for weeks by following it. Once she reached safety, she didn't just enjoy her freedom. She went back to the slave-owning South on at least 19 separate occasions, risking recapture, torture, and re-enslavement, to help hundreds of others slaves make it to freedom too. Using only her intuition to guide her, she hid her people in riverbeds, fields, and woods to avoid the slave-catchers and their dogs that were always hunting them down. Against the unlikeliest of odds, she was never caught, which allowed her to become a leader of the Underground Railroad and a spy and guerrilla agent for the Union Army. She was the first recorded African-American woman to serve in the military.[11]

Intuition, the muse, our inner voice, or whatever you want to call it, feels utterly truthful once we hear it. Often, there is a little flash of energy telling us we have reconnected to it. It is a subtle rush that tells you that there is a match between the world and you, between the Great We and the Tiny Me. Living intuitively, waiting to sense the flash, is an art form. You discern a gut feel from a gut fear. A hunch from a nervous twitch.

There is no need to feel under any pressure to act immediately if you are unsure which it is. It is worth waiting until you are positive before you act. You may be so used to relying on exam grades, diplomas, media stories, cultural norms, and dogma of all kinds to justify your decisions that trusting intuition can be awkward, even alien. Yet intuition is vital for responsive, biodynamic, fitted decision. It is so important that even the US Navy is researching it to help soldiers make better decisions on the battlefield.[12]

However, far from being a vague hunch, intuitions can be tested. They stand up well to feedback from others. People can tell by looking at us and hearing us if we are tuned up, congruent, and intuitive. You're not asking for their advice, just asking them to tell you whether they feel you are in alignment, and whether your proposed way forward resonates with them. Intuitions tend not to waver under scrutiny from our friends. If anything, they just become stronger. On the other hand, instincts tend to shift, depending on who we are talking to and whether they trigger any fears within us.

> **The more we let the Great We provide intuition to our Tiny Me, the more original, poetic, and truthful our lives become.**

We are both/and

ACROSS OUR JOURNEY DOWN and up the Breakthrough Curve, we have come across a number of paradoxes. How can we be response-able for our actions yet surrender to the universe for guidance? How can creativity come from letting go? Why does playfulness help us achieve world-changing goals? How can we own our problems but not the ideas that break through them? How can we be a Tiny Me and a Great We at the same time?

Reconciling such opposites has given philosophers a headache for eons. One of the earliest recorded thinkers in the West, Heraclitus, gave us a hint about how to overcome the paradoxical, polar nature of life: 'They do not understand how, while differing from itself, it is in agreement with itself: Stretched back and forth in harmony like that of the bow and lyre.'

A lyre is an ancient instrument. A guitar would be a modern-day equivalent. Imagine the tension, fertile with potential, that exists across the strings of a guitar between the two poles, the two opposites.

pLUCk!

That's me. And it's you. Our lives are the vibrations of the string of life as it stretches from surviving to thriving, destroying to creating, breakthrough to breakdown. We humans are the harmonic tension between the separate and the connected, the Tiny Me and Great We. Every second of our lives, we get to strike the chord and sing, dance, and groove in harmony with all the extremes of human experience. Through practice, through inner work, we get to play with this creative tension. We can learn how to tune the string as we become one within the kaleidoscopic flow of co-creativity.

Life in Creative Tension

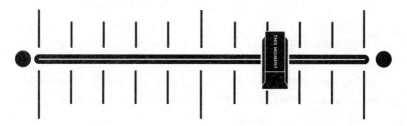

THE PROTECTOR	THE CONNECTOR
The Tiny Me	The Great We
Diversity	Unity
Commitment	Surrender
Having insight / ideas	Releasing assumptions
Doing	Not Doing
Mastery	Flow

It seems that the entire universe exists in polarity. Light, the energy source of life on Earth, moves between two extremes as a wave. Nerves inside us oscillate between two poles of electrical charge. Our emotions flow between love and hate, pleasure and pain. During times of threat and danger, hiding away inside ourselves helps us survive. During times of safety, being highly productive, confident, and imaginative helps us thrive.[13] In a study of 91 eminent creatives, it emerged that creative people were very energetic but often at rest; smart yet also open-minded, even naive; disciplined yet playful; imagine the impossible but realistic about what is doable.[14]

It is not about *either* hard work *or* chilling out. It is about *both* hard work *and* chilling out. We can be both hippy and hipster; both relentless and relaxed; both entrepreneur and enlightened; both mystic and master. We get to access the limitless creativity of the Great We at the same time as delivering projects into the world with the tangible power of the Tiny Me. Our cross-fader is set in the middle, blending both tracks as we live fully in the mix. The binary opposition of dualities so common in the West (see page 114), centered on EITHER/OR, melts into the unity of Big U. It's all about BOTH/AND.

We are *both* Tiny Me and Great We. We have *both* absolute free will *and* yet no control at all. We play in the spaces between.

Our rational mind can get a bit frazzled by this idea. The Tiny Me can't grasp the enormity of the Great We very easily. But how does the idea that you are BOTH/AND feel to your whole body.mind? Does it feel expansive? Intuitively accurate?

The Zen puzzles called *koans* can help us let go of analytical reason and embrace wholeness of thought and feeling. A Zen master will give a student a specific koan to meditate on. A famous one is 'What is the sound of one hand clapping.' Koans cannot be solved through thinking alone. They can only be dissolved through being connected to the Big U. As soon as the student gets it, with their whole body.mind, they have a moment of realization, of enlightenment.

Mu!

The puzzle is resolved. Living a switched on life, committed to change yet continuously surrendering control, is a powerful life-long koan for all of us who want to help our world to thrive. We balance hubris ('I am big enough to change things!') with humility ('Who am I to change anything?'). We do this while we play all-out to make a difference, and enjoying ourselves while doing it.

As the philosopher Sri Nisargadatta Maharaj said, 'Love tells me I am everything. Wisdom tells me I am nothing. Between the two, my life flows.'

SWITCH ON TO PLAY

Switched Off: Play is for children. Making a difference is hard work. We have to fight people to get what we want. Failure is embarrassing and devastating, and must be avoided at all costs. We should make decisions on how to move forward based on rational information.

Switched On: Play is how we stay excited, energized, and imaginative as we make a difference. We can approach any challenge playfully and we will be better at finding solutions. Failure is what happens when bold people experiment. We make decisions as we play, based upon our intuition as well as insight from the world around us.

 **SWITCH ON NOW**

Invite your Connector into the mix. Breathe. Relax. Choose to switch on. Feel your intuition glowing.

HEART: What emotions inspire you to get most playful and curious? Do you need to let go of anything to return to that feeling right now?

Can you hear what your intuition is telling you to do next? Go through your task list and allow your intuition to tell you what it is right to do.

Sense the difference within between intuition and instinct as you go through the list. Feel how different they feel in your body.mind.

HEAD: What is your definition of failure? Define it now for yourself.

Now define what success looks like. Keep redefining it until it feels both uplifting and motivating.

What dogma have you lived your life by that you can let go of to be truly present in this unique moment here? What assumptions might you have made about how to make good decisions in the world?

Could you give up the approval of others and trust your intuition?

HANDS: Do you sense there are some changes you could make to your environment that would trigger more creativity, peace, and playfulness? Do you have any daily rituals that help you feel juiced up that you could amplify? What recovery time have you blocked in your diary for this week?

Is your rhythm matching that of the world around you? Can you adjust it?

Now, sensing your entire body.mind, what window is open right now for all the ideas and visions you have? Are you ready to leap?

What can you do today, or at least this week, that ensures you have made the leap?

BREAKTHROUGH QUESTIONS

 How can I enjoy this experience even more?

 If I were a child, how would I approach this problem in order to have the most fun possible?

Session 10

Proactivity

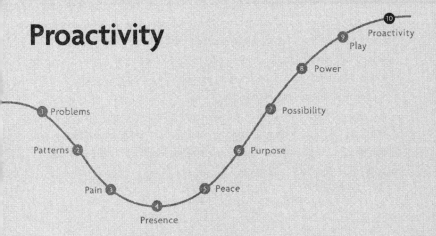

THE MORE PROBLEMS WE break through, the more energy and creativity we free up to take on bigger challenges. By engaging wholeheartedly with the world as it is, unafraid to challenge the status quo with love not judgment, we can come together to co-create a brilliant world. We can be part of a society in which all can thrive, not just the 1 percent or 0.1 percent. With digital technologies and peer-powered networks to help us, this is totally achievable in our lifetime. All for one and one for all!

While I was a teenager teaching in rural Africa, I met a backgammon champion from Harvard University. Over many candlelit nights, he taught me the secret of the game. Although it is ostensibly a game of luck, with a proactive attitude you can always win more than you lose. His insight was this: Whichever way the dice fall, use each turn to maximize your possible options for your next turn, even if that puts you at risk now. The same is true of life. Always make choices that open up new fields of possibility. Keep your options open by becoming proactively engaged in challenges. Then there is always space to flex and move.

If we don't proactively engage in our problems, we risk being overwhelmed by them. They have a cunning way of sneaking up on us without us realizing. Breakdown is never far off unless we proactively scan within, for signs of unrest and unease; and without, for signs that our patterns are not fitting the world. We always have a choice whether to step up for a breakthrough or let ourselves slide toward breakdown.

On the flipside, each problem we metabolize pulls more of our potential out of us. Breakthrough becomes the most exciting game around. As Ludwig van Beethoven put it: 'It seemed impossible to leave the world until I had brought forth all that was in me.'

Time to ride!

Riding on the edge

WHEN SURFERS ARE OUT in the ocean, and a massive wave is approaching, they have two, but only two, options. Ride the wave or risk being sunk by it. Although getting up on the wave is challenging, being pulled under it could mean disaster. If you want to ride the wave of a fresh, exciting breakthrough, you need to master how to stay on the edge of your game. Lean out onto the edge of your surfboard or skateboard and you will go faster. Lean back from the edge and you'll slow down. Are you taking on too many challenges? Not enough? Only you know where your edge is. Only can you tell when you are overloaded and when you are coasting along.

Riding the Breakthrough Curve

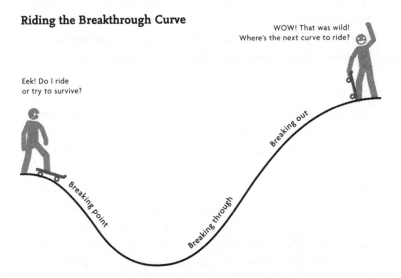

WOW! That was wild!
Where's the next curve to ride?

Eek! Do I ride
or try to survive?

Breaking point

Breaking through

Breaking out

Once you find your edge, you can ride one Breakthrough Curve after another without getting overwhelmed or bored. If things move too fast, you can slow it all down through reconnecting, perhaps through meditation, a long nature walk, or heading out to a rave. If things become boring, all you need do is choose a problem you may have been avoiding or ignoring and bring it inside to metabolize. You can precipitate a breaking point at any moment by taking on another problem. There is usually no shortage of problems on offer:

- Do you feel totally in love with your mind and body? Do you have any regrets (regrets are stories you are not yet at peace with)?
- Are your relationships all thriving? Do you have any former friendships or relationships that ended badly and could be healed?
- Are you fully expressed in your cooking, creating, and lovemaking? Is your life buzzing with collaboration and creativity?
- Are there any areas of work or play where you feel stuck? Any failures as a kid that you haven't yet let go of that are holding you back? Are you ignoring any challenges that have been calling you?
- Are you completely in the zone at work? Are you playing to your full potential in an organization that is making a real difference to the world? Have you taken ownership of any of the negative impacts of your work or organization?
- Do you feel you spend your days aligned with your purpose? Are you working on projects that connect with your noblest aspirations?

Just like surfing and skateboarding, the thrill of taking on bigger problems and metabolizing them within us into incredible possibilities is addictive. A huge research study involving 100,000 people has shown that engaging with problems is part of having a deeply meaningful life.[1] We may not be happy all the time when they hit us, but we can always make them meaningful and so grow with them. We cannot control when they might hit, but we can always keep the edges of the board—our body.mind—sharp and ready to ride.

It may feel a bit like a rollercoaster, up and down, yet this is simply the reality of living life fully. Waves and hills go up and must come down. Ideas inspire us with elation. Obstacles can trigger frustration. This is the creative tension of thriving. We feel intensely the agony and the ecstasy of human experience. This may be unusual when so many people are on lock-down. But do we want to let that stop us sucking everything out of this one life?

We can thrive not despite our problems but actually because of them! When we do, life feels rich and full. As we intentionally allow our patterns to break apart, raw potential glints through ready to be unleashed. Knowing we are right on the edge of our creative capacities is a wonderfully intense experience. Nothing, not even the rush of powerful drug, can match it.

The more we engage, the more creative we become and the more mastery we have of life. We learn how to live.

Standing atop the crest of a Breakthrough Curve you have just cracked, you are bound to notice how many of the people you love and care about are not quite so skilled at surfing the problems of life as you are. Without thinking, you may offer to lift up those who have fallen around you. This is the inalienable logic of switching on. We become leaders without even knowing it.

Those of us who have switched on are the most powerful agents of change and transformation on the planet. We have the inner power to have and sustain breakthroughs for years ahead in any sphere or domain. Rather than simply focusing our activities on trying to change others, we know that we have to be the change we want to see first. We have to switch on and have our own breakthroughs before we can ask others to follow suit. Then we can catalyze and amplify breakthroughs in the various systems we touch.

Switch On: Catalyzing Breakthroughs in All Areas

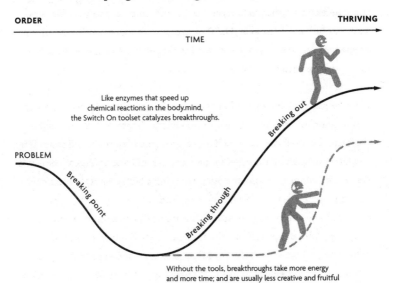

ORDER   THRIVING

TIME

Like enzymes that speed up chemical reactions in the body.mind, the Switch On toolset catalyzes breakthroughs.

PROBLEM

Breaking point

Breaking through

Breaking out

Without the tools, breakthroughs take more energy and more time; and are usually less creative and fruitful

DISORDER   SURVIVING

Switch on to relationships

RELATIONSHIPS ARE ONE OF the richest sources of breakthroughs. This is particularly the case with intimate relationships, but all relationships are rife with problems that we can metabolize into possibility. Relationships are deeply complex experiences. Your patterns and their patterns are in constant interplay. Triggers and reactions ricochet off each other. It can get so confusing, that we can easily lose ourselves within them and no longer know what is our sh!t and what is theirs. It is easy to go about our life gaily projecting our stuff onto them, blaming them for their stuff, complaining about them rather than doing the inner work ourselves. Escape fantasies are common in relationships!

As we deepen intimacy with people, we begin to trust them. There cannot be intimacy without trust. But each time they let us down, or simply trigger the pain of let-down, it will feel worse than when we didn't trust them at all. If we react defensively to something they may not even be aware of doing, they can easily react too. The Protector in both (or all) of you starts to fight the other, defending against perceived threats, rehashing old pain. There is no winning this power struggle. The Protector can only ever deflect; it cannot attract the love, peace, and joy we want to feel with them. There are only three ways forward with this wrestling match:

1 We keep on fighting each other. Each Tiny Me is locked in a death embrace, until someone decides to give up and leave, or chooses to give up and be beaten. If the relationship is still on, one becomes dominant and controlling (while disrespecting the other for being weak), and one becomes submissive and weak (while resenting the other for being a bully). Fights may flare up as each gets tired of their role from time to time.

2 We withdraw from the intensity of intimacy (to some degree), unconsciously agreeing with our partner the limits of closeness. A bunch of tacit rules are drawn up between each Tiny Me, ensuring no one's boundaries (i.e. front) are transgressed too much. Everyone agrees to be OK with the lack of aliveness, zest, and joy that inevitably results. We may well become glorified room-mates instead of passionate lovers.

3 We become dissatisfied with the stuckness, the blockages, the conflicts, and the lack of space to grow. So we choose to switch on and grow purposefully with, and because of, each other. We use each breakdown in communication, collaboration, or lovemaking to explore our patterns, release our pain, and co-create a possibility for how it could be in future. If anyone stops doing the inner work then the relationship will stop expanding, so it is both partners' duty to keep on riding Breakthrough Curves.

Clearly, option three—switched on loving— sounds more thrivadelic, but it is equally clear that is, in some ways, the least 'easy' option. It takes a lot of time and high levels of both intentionality and integrity to take this path. Turning conflict into creativity, with compassion and curiosity, demands perseverance and ultimate personal response-ability. However, the rewards are staggering. The number of breakthroughs and the amount of joy, love, and freshness available is unprecedented.

To grow with, and for, another is true love. This is not about using someone else to make up for the things we lack within. It is about healing our pain within the crucible of intimacy.

Your friend, parent, or partner becomes the only guru you'll ever really need. They will, uniquely, be able to show you, in not always pretty ways, where you are being held back and where your habits and stories no longer fit your reality. Thankfully, there are some powerful tools and techniques, rooted in how our neurobiologies interact with each other, that can help us dance together as elegantly as we can.

Switch on to parenting

IF WE THINK A switched on love life is a trip, becoming a parent might be able to trump it for the scale of challenges (and therefore opportunities) involved. Parenting is the best transformational experience money can't buy. It is an epic rollercoaster ride of breakthrough and breakdown. Every time we think we have it nailed, those cheeky little people—AKA kids—will push another button, trigger another old pattern we picked up from our parents, or do something that terrifies us because we have no idea how to handle it. We teach our children how to be in the world with every story we spin and every habit we act out. So we imprint our patterns on their brains with each passing day. Important stuff.

The flipside is that a child's brain is young and very flexible. Change our parenting style and their brains will rewire quickly because of it. Drop an old blame, shame, or complain story and they will forget it far faster than we will! Switched on parenting gives us amazing opportunities to look at every pattern we have ever used to protect us and see how much it hurts both us and our kids. We can then own those patterns and break through them for good. Without our kids to trigger us, we might never have known we still had them!

We can use these opportunities to delve inside and discover pain that we might have repressed for years. We can heal everything in our past, forgive our parents and ourselves, and get ourselves right with the universe. We can honor the roles our parents and carers played, finding gratitude for the support we did get. Above all, we can choose not to pass on parenting styles handed down from generation to generation in our family, perhaps for centuries, and *design* more appropriate principles, techniques, and ways of being that can have everyone in the family thrive.

This doesn't mean everyone is always happy or peace reigns supreme. It means that everyone is on the path toward increased thriving because, as parents, we are actively seeking new and imaginative ways to connect with our kids, collaborate with them, and co-create.

While no parent is perfect (and trying to be is a total waste of effort because it is downright impossible), we can commit to learning from every mistake we make so that we thrive ourselves and find ways to help our children learn how to thrive too.

Switch on to work

STEPPING OUT THE FRONT door, we can easily get caught up in the whirlwind of work, whether we are studying, working in an office, or employed in a craft or trade. There are plenty of problems to get proactive with: Difficult colleagues, uncreative cultures, unethical business practices, disempowering managers, uninspiring leaders, unfulfilling tasks.

There is often not a lot of ownership, trust, and response-ability in the workplace, which can make innovation and transformation tough. The result is that the majority of employees don't feel engaged in their organizations and don't trust their bosses. A Gallup poll in 2013 said that 70 percent of employees in the USA are either 'not engaged' or 'actively disengaged.'[2] According to one survey, if given the chance, 60 percent of European workers would choose a different career.[3] Work can become a grind full of escape fantasies.

However, if we switch on to work, we can set about breaking through any, and all, of these problems, not just for the sake of our firm or colleagues but for our own mastery of leadership. Change how our businesses work and the world will change fast.

After switching on, you may want to find ways to use the digital revolution to do new things, which were impossible before. You may want to encourage your colleagues to collaborate on more ambitious projects. You might want to bring more mindful thinking and wellbeing into your workplace. You may want to work in an environment that is free from bullying or bravado and rewards creativity and risk-taking. You may want to help the people you work with develop a fresh and future-focused version of how things could be. You may want to ensure that the organizations you are part of are doing their bit to make the world work, not just taking and exploiting. You may even want to start your own organization, engaging in the wild ride of entrepreneurship (ethical, sustainable or social please!); and the world-change that comes with it.

However, as work is not a family or intimate setting, we have to engage people around us in our ideas with a light touch. There are ways to bring more authenticity and creativity into teams and projects without freaking people out. There are languages, codes, and techniques that can help others engage, be empowered and be inspired that are inclusive, sound 'normal,' and everyone can get behind.

Switch on yourself and before long you can get your team switched on too. Your team will be so uplifted and inspired that you can create a viral grassroots 'infection' of open, ethical, and creative people, which transforms work from a productivity treadmill into a canvas for self-expression and making a difference.

Switch on to the planet

RIGHT NOW, AS YOU read this, 18,000 children will die today simply from malnutrition. They are not just in developing countries either. One in 100 kids in New York City, one of the richest places on the planet, is homeless and hungry. There is more than enough food in the world to feed every one of those kids, and every mouth on the planet, many times over. It is sitting in storerooms and warehouses and being thrown out of restaurants and homes without much thought. We have all the logistics, intelligence, and cash to ensure that food gets to every hungry belly on the planet right now. What is missing is the *will*. As Gandhi said: 'There is enough in the world for everyone's need. There is not enough for everyone's greed.'

The truth is, we are not facing a crisis of poverty. We are not facing a climate-change crisis. We are not facing a credit crisis. We are simply facing a painful and lasting crisis of our collective patterns and the stories we use to justify them. Scratch the surface of pretty much any social or environmental problem and you will find, at its core, the hallmark of the Protector (and the Tiny Me, which is driven to compete, control, exploit, and accumulate). So we consume, waste, or eat too much; and share, contribute, and empathize too little all because of a mistaken sense of separation.

> **We cannot heal our ravaged world with strategies developed by the fearful Tiny Me that is responsible for the problems in the first place.**

If separation is at the root of our problems, then it cannot be at the root of our solutions. Instead, reconnection has to be the guiding force behind every welfare innovation, carbon-reduction plan, and aid program. We must become inner revolutionaries before we can become outer ones. We don't need more violent revolutions, political demagogues, or judgmental activism. What we need is more compassion, connection, trust, and, dare I say it, love. We need more switched on people. Leo Tolstoy, who ended up being much more famous in his native Russia for being a spiritual revolutionary than a writer, warned us a century ago in his essay 'On Anarchy': 'There can be only one permanent revolution, a moral one: The regeneration of the inner man.'

If you switch on, and become an inner revolutionary and switched on leader, you can choose any of the problems that are affecting your community and ride the Breakthrough Curve with them. You can do this in partnership with the people in your dorm or the people who live on your street. Or you can connect with people all over the world through digital and real-world networks that bring people with similar passion and conviction to work together. What is key is that *connection* has to be the starting point, and our own patterns the first order of business. If we are not switched on ourselves, we are likely to think up solutions that are based on a distorted, separate, fearful view of reality. As the Buddha said, 'There is no peace outside until there is peace inside.'

Personal development is world development. World transformation demands personal transformation!

Toward a switched on world

WE LIVE IN AN incredible era. Yes, we are facing the most complex set of problems imaginable but we are also being empowered by technologies to collaborate and co-create solutions to them together. Within our networks lie all the ideas, intelligence, money, and meaning we need to create breakthrough solutions to our most pressing challenges. The Internet, born from mechanistic science, is helping us connect with each other organically. It helps us pool our creativity and resources toward projects that are focused on the connected good because we create and deliver them together.

Like the dock leaf that grows near the nettle, ready with an antidote to the pain when we need it, digital technology is helping us heal the social wounds inflicted by the cotton gins and workhouses of the Industrial Age. The web is slowly but surely rewiring the world, inviting us to stay in step with it and become more collaborative, networked, and co-creative. New platforms and apps are helping us to weave together a new global society based on true equality and real democracy. With organizations like AirBnB, SumofUs.org, Ushahidi, and Kiva, we are being enabled by technology to become better, together. Right now, new forms of organization, like holocracies, B Corps, and social enterprises are springing up all over the world, 'inoculating' society against the 'viruses' of opportunistic capitalism and abusive power.

Now, within our grasp—perhaps realistically for the first time in human history—is the tangible possibility of a just and equal society for all.

Most of the technologies and resources needed to solve the majority of the world's thorniest problems are available now. All we have to do is dig within ourselves to find the courage and latent talents we need to put them to work. As we—lovers, parents, employees, consumers, citizens, and pension fund holders—switch on, we begin to transform things. We begin to treat others, and the things around us, as if they are part of us, part of our body. We work with our lover on a project for our local community, and take vacations that give as much to the local environment as we take out. We bring up our children to engage with nature and never put greed above need. We implore our bosses to build new businesses that are sustainable from the get-go, and have as much of a focus on social impact as profit. We build our own enterprises that are more about contribution than they are achievement.

The more we switch on and break through patterns that keep us self-centered, the more we start to feel the planet's pain as our own. We feel overwhelming sadness when we see plastic bags spinning around in the street, here for an eternity. The plight of 'foreigners' affects us, as if it were the plight of our own children. The extinction of another language or species fills us with heartache. Our **HEART** breaks open with the suffering of our many depressed brothers and suicidal sisters. We are moved to our core by the vanishing bees and industrial deforestation. We look for the brands we buy to have a purpose beyond profit and to treat their workers with respect.

We no longer need laws, incentives, and social norms to get us to act sustainably and respectfully. We do it because we *want* to. Because it is who we really are once we fall in love with ourselves and the universe with which we are one. When we have a clear and open **HEART, HEAD,** and **HANDS,** we don't need politicians to tell us what to do. We trust ourselves and our peers, and collaborate for the common good. We no longer see people as competitors, or oppressors. Instead, we see them as part of ourselves. We develop a hunger to knit together the frayed edges of society, in what the Jewish tradition calls *tikkun olam.* We cannot deny the call to heal the world when we switch on because it is our natural state when we feel safe and connected. This hankering for positive change is simply an outpouring of love that is unstoppable as long as we remain switched on.

By switching on, right now and then again and again on a daily, even hourly, basis, you can boost your collaborative creativity and get cracking on building a switched on world, be it with your friends, kids, partner, or colleagues. The key that unlocks the door is the lasting sense of connection; and that we are all in it together. When we remember that we are all a loved and loving part of the Big U, we can shift each meeting, discussion, or debate toward more trust, compassion, and creativity. This fellow feeling, this fellowship, is Brotherhood and Buddhahood for the digital age.

Remember, there is no need to get attached to the outcomes. That's just your Tiny Me getting freaky as it tries to control, predict, and get rewards. You can do as Gandhi suggested, giving your efforts freely as an offering of love back to the Big U that supports all life and *is* all life.

This is enlightenment in *action*.

We turn enlightenment from a lovely personal experience into a force for good. Enlightenment, the indescribable awakening to our true nature as one with the universe, is the start of our journey, not the end-point. We become enlightened *in* the world, *for* the world, *as* the world: Not removed from it in a monastery, yoga studio, or temple.

Many of the great wisdom traditions that promote the idea of enlightenment came into being during times of political stasis. There was little opportunity for an individual to have any power over the shape of society, so the wise turned inward to find freedom. Monks and yogis withdrew from the outer world to focus on inner enlightenment. Today, this is anything but true.

With one mouse click, one career move, and one purchase decision, we can, when we work together, rock the world. We all have limitless opportunities to contribute to the future of our planet once we switch on.

If not now, when?

Listen . . .

THHHH . . . . . . WONK

That's the sound of one of life's curve balls hitting you with a problem that impacts you, your loved ones, or the world. It's your choice whether you ride it toward breakthrough or shrink away from it into your comfort zone. Paranoid or pronoid? Problem or possibility? Survive or thrive? Switch off or on? The choice is yours (see diagram below). Neither being switched off nor switched

The Choice: Switch On or Off

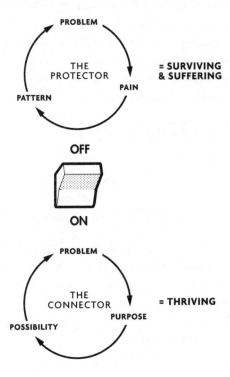

on is in any way right or wrong. They simply lead to very different experiences of this one precious life we each have; and very different societies crystallize around them.

> **The bottom line is this: If you don't like what is happening in your life or in the world, you now know how to change it.**

If you do accept the invitation and ride up along the Breakthrough Curve, your breakthroughs may not be convenient. You will almost certainly have to give up something. Old ideas, familiar rules, comforting ideas, cherished notions of what is right and good. Something. Yet, as you let it go, you will gain something precious and priceless. Ideas. Inspiration. Insight. Intuition. These are the perquisites of thriving in uncertain and unpredictable times.

As soon as you realize a problem has triggered you . . . you get back up on the Curve and ride it again toward freedom. If you want to retreat, or react with blame, shame, or complain, you simply go back inside to find the truth. It's as easy as ABC. Attention. Breathe and Bounce. Get Curious.

HELLOOO . . . !?!

Listen . . .

Listen deeper . . .

Right now the Connector, the Great We, the creative spirit, the Big U is calling you. It usually does so by drawing your attention to an area of your life (or world) that is ripe for a breakthrough. This is what a problem is. It's a signal that some part of you wants to break through.

This is *your* time. Right here.

Nothing is more important than liberating yourself from unnecessary suffering and, in doing so, unleashing your creativity so it can transform every area of your life. Through reconnecting your **HEART** and rewiring your **HEAD**, you can remix anything you don't love about it with your **HANDS**.

This is also *our* time. Right now. Our people are suffering. Our animals are being mistreated. Our planet is hurting.

What is your contribution going to be?

How are you going to bring some of the magic and majesty of breakthrough into your corner of the world, leaving it better off than when you joined it?

By coming together, in trust and truth, we can co-create projects that solve even our toughest challenges so that all humanity can flourish. No matter what our contribution is, we can all shine a little of our light into the darkside of the world of which we are an intrinsic part.

We no longer need to ask what life will do for us. Instead, we celebrate what we will do with life, in all its unpredictable, paradoxical, and often painful glory. Once we realize we are not our patterns, not our habits, and not our pain, then we can co-create anything as a team. Together, as one, everything is possible.

> How wonderful it is that nobody need wait a single moment before starting to improve the world.
>
> Anne Frank, *The Diary of a Young Girl*

SWITCH ON TO PROACTIVITY

Switched Off: Proactivity means we try and avoid as many problems as we can by spotting them in advance. We deal with those we have to and blame the problems around us on anyone else.

Switched On: Proactivity is the source of long-term thriving. The more problems we take on, the more accomplished we become. We can then take on the problems of those around us and help everyone else to thrive too.

 **SWITCH ON NOW**

Invite your Connector into the mix. Breathe. Relax. Maybe close your eyes. Choose to switch on.

HEART: Feeling your purpose burning inside, what problems move you in the world around you?

Sense your friends and family, your wider network, your community, the whole world, the planet.

What suffering is there that calls you to attention?

Safely connected to Presence, can you allow your **HEART** to feel the pain and suffering of others, without this swamping you?

Can you allow your **HEART** to break asunder without losing hope?

Breathe deep. Imagine, as you breathe, that you are breathing in all the suffering, transforming it into love in the cauldron within. Now breathe out that love and send it to everyone you care about and perhaps the world too.

HEAD: What do you want your love life to look like? Your friendships? Your life as a parent (now or in the future)? Your work life? Your community? The planet? The global system?

Remind yourself of your purpose. Feel it in your body.mind. Which of these areas do you want to focus on?

HANDS: Who do you need to connect with to initiate a process of renewal or rejuvenation in one of the systems you touch?

How can you inspire them with a new story about what is possible?

Can you connect with them now and set up a time to talk?

BREAKTHROUGH QUESTIONS

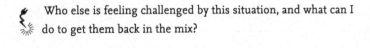 Who else is feeling challenged by this situation, and what can I do to get them back in the mix?

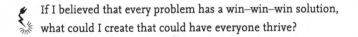 If I believed that every problem has a win–win–win solution, what could I create that could have everyone thrive?

Coda

Riffing on the Breakthrough Curve

THE SMALL, UNASSUMING J-SHAPE that forms the Breakthrough Curve seems to hold some profound secrets within it—about ourselves, creativity as a whole, and the nature of the universe. I am still coaxing those secrets out. However, as I have wondered at the power and elegance of the Breakthrough Curve, I have found it popping up all over the place. I have clocked it in the structure of most movies; the musical form of the sonata; how molecules react to give off energy (which provides all the energy for life in our galaxy); how people learn; how cultures transform; how babies develop; and even in how nations transition from dictatorship to democracy (and many more besides).

Breakthrough Biodynamics and the Thrive Differential

The universe in constant flux, becoming ever more complex = Fit or Fail

TIME

ORDER

THRIVING
More fitted
B

the myth of linear creativity

Breaking out

Less fitted
A

∂T = Thrive Differential

Breaking point

Eruption of insights, ideas, intuitions

Breaking through

C

EDGE OF CHAOS
Zone of maximum creativity and maximum confusion

THE CREATIVE SPIRIT

DISORDER

SURVIVING

It seems that whenever there is a juicy chemical, biological, psychological, or cultural problem to break through, the J-Curve appears (see diagram above). In a universe that is defined by the reality that something has been created from nothing, is it possible that the J-Curve is the essential blueprint of creativity?

I explore this idea, and explain the diagram on the left fully, in a companion ebook, *Switch On: The Wonder of Breakthrough*. In it, I trace many different Breakthrough Curves. I explore the connections between *Breakthrough Biodynamics* and the revolutionary ideas of chaos theory and complexity science. I explore the necessity for problems and constraints to fuel breakthroughs in any system, from the birth of jazz to high-tech entrepreneurship. The book draws parallels between Breakthrough Biodynamics and the deepest insights of the Stoics and Taoists; and Carl Jung and Friedrich Nietzsche among others.

If you've enjoyed this book, please do leave an honest review online for future readers.

Find more Switch On tools and experiences (including free stuff) at www.ripeandready.com

Get advanced copies of books and help shape future ideas by joining our exclusive Thrive Hive at www.ripeandready.com/thrivehive

Nick welcomes comments and ideas. Get in touch:

Via email nick@ripeandready.com
Via Twitter @nickjankel
On the web www.nickjankel.com
Via Facebook facebook.com/nicksenecajankel

Endnotes

A Note from the Author

1   Nachemson A L, Waddell G, Norlund A I 'Epidemiology of neck and low back pain,' in Nachemson A L & Jonsson E (eds) *Neck and back pain: The scientific evidence of causes, diagnosis and treatment*, Lippencott Williams & Wilkins, 2000.

2   Stravinsky, I *Igor Stravinsky: An Autobiography*, Project Gutenberg, 2011.

3   Sagan, C *The Demon-Haunted World: Science as a Candle in the Dark*, Ballantine Books, 1997.

Prelude: Wired for Breakthrough

1   'Stress in America Survey,' American Psychological Association, 2013.

2   Zoladz, P et al. 'Pre-learning Stress that is Temporarily Removed from Acquisition Exerts Sex-specific Effects on Long-term Memory,' *Neurobiology of Learning and Memory*, Dec 2012: 100, 77–87.

3   Hansell, A et al. 'Aircraft Noise and Cardiovascular Disease near Heathrow Airport in London: Small Area Study,' *BMJ*, Oct 2013: 347 (7928): f5432.

4   Nyberg, A et al. 'Managerial leadership and ischaemic heart disease among employees: The Swedish WOLF study,' *Journal of Occupational and Environmental Medicine*, August 2008: 0, 1–5. doi: 10.1136/oem.2008.039362.

5   Conrad, C (ed.) *The Handbook of Stress: Neuropsychological Effects on the Brain*, Wiley-Blackwell, 2011.

6   'Work Stress and Health: The Whitehall II Study,' British Cabinet Office, 2004.

7   Baumeister, R et al. 'Some Key Differences Between a Happy Life and a Meaningful Life,' *Journal of Positive Psychology*, Oct 2013.

8   McCaig, R et al. 'Improved Modulation of Rostrolateral Prefrontal Cortex Using Real-time fMRI Training and Meta-cognitive Awareness,' *NeuroImage*, 2011: 55 (3), 1298–1305.

9   Forstmann, M et al. 'The Mind Is Willing, But the Flesh is Weak: The Effects of Mind–Body Dualism on Health Behavior,' *Psychological Science*, Oct 2012: 23 (10), 1239–45.

10   Langer, E et al. 'Believing is Seeing: Using Mindlessness (Mindfully) to Improve Visual Acuity,' *Psychological Science*, Oct 2010: 21 (5), 661–6.

11   Crum, A and Langer, E 'Mind-set Matters: Exercise and the Placebo Effect,' *Psychological Science*, Feb 2007: 18 (2), 165–71.

12   Benson, H et al. 'Body Temperature Changes During the Practice of G-tummo Yoga,' *Nature*, Jan 1982: 295, 234–6.

13   Kox, M et al. 'Voluntary Activation of the Sympathetic Nervous System and Attenuation of the Innate Immune Response in Humans,' *PNAS*, May 2014: DOI: 10.1073/pnas.1322174111.

14   Kong, J et al. 'Are All Placebo Effects Equal? Placebo Pills, Sham Acupuncture, Cue Conditioning and Their Association,' *PLoS ONE*, Jul 2013: 8 (7).

15   Benedetti, F and Amanzio, M 'The Placebo Response: How Words and Rituals Change the Patient's Brain,' *Patient Education and Counseling*, Sep 2011: 84, 413–9.

16   Kaptchuk, T et al. 'Placebos Without Deception: A Randomized Controlled Trial in Irritable Bowel Syndrome,' *PLoS ONE*, Dec 2010: 5 (12).

17   Joshua, M et al. 'Incidental Haptic Sensations Influence Social Judgments and Decisions,'

Science (RSS), Jun 2010.

18 Bechara, A et al. 'Emotion, Decision Making and the Orbitofrontal Cortex,' *Cereb. Cortex*, 2000: 10 (3), 295–307; DOI: 10.1093/cercor/10.3.295.

19 Siegel, D *Pocket Guide to Interpersonal Neurobiology: An Integrative Handbook of the Mind*, W. W. Norton & Company, 2012.

20 McEwen, B 'The Neurobiology of Stress: From Serendipity to Clinical Relevance,' *Brain Research*, Dec 2000: 886: 172–89.

21 Galvin, J et al. 'The Relaxation Response: Reducing Stress and Improving Cognition in Healthy Aging Adults,' *Complementary Therapies in Clinical Practice*, Jun 2006: 12 (3), 186–91.

22 Kaufman, S 'Opening Up Openness to Experience: A Four-Factor Model and Relations to Creative Achievement in the Arts and Sciences,' *Journal of Creative Behavior*, 2013: 47, 233–55.

23 Bhasin, M et al. 'Relaxation Response Induces Temporal Transcriptome Changes in Energy Metabolism, Insulin Secretion and Inflammatory Pathways,' *PLoS One*, 2013: 8 (5), e62817.

24 Vitalo, A et al. 'Nest Making and Oxytocin Comparably Promote Wound Healing in Isolation Reared Rats,' *PLoS One*, May 2009: 4 (5), e5523.

25 Pavlov, V and Tracey, K 'The Cholinergic Anti-inflammatory Pathway,' *Brain, Behavior and Immunity*, Nov 2005: 19 (6), 493–9.

26 Keltner, D and DiSalvo, D 'Forget Survival of the Fittest: It Is Kindness That Counts,' *Scientific American*, Feb 2009.

27 Bergland, C 'The Neurobiology of Grace Under Pressure,' *Psychology Today*, Feb 2013.

28 Gebhardt, N et al. 'Vagus Nerve Stimulation Ameliorated Deficits in One-way Active Avoidance Learning and Stimulated Hippocampal Neurogenesis in Bulbectomized Rats,' *BRAIN STIMULATION: Basic, Translational, and Clinical Research in Neuromodulation*, Jan 2013: 6 (1), 78–83.

29 Waytze, A 'Psychology Beyond the Brain,' *Scientific American*, Oct 2010.

30 Eisenberg, N et al. 'Emotion-related Self-regulation and its Relation to Children's Maladjustment, *Annual Review Clinical Psychology*, 2010: 6, 495–525.

31 Ongoing research at time of print: http://www.gla.ac.uk/news/headline.

32 Simmons, A et al. 'Altered Insula Activation in Anticipation of Changing Emotional States: Neural Mechanisms Underlying Cognitive Flexibility in Special Operations Forces Personnel,' *Neuroreport*, Mar 2012.

33 Morgan, C et al. 'Relation Between Cardiac Vagal Tone and Performance in Male Military Personnel Exposed to High Stress: Three Prospective Studies,' *Psychophysiology*, Jan 2007: 4 (1), 120.

34 Headley, B et al. 'Long-running German Panel Survey Shows that Personal and Economic Choices, Not Just Genes, Matter for Happiness,' *PNAS*, 2010: 107 (42), 6.

35 Loehr, J *Mental Toughness Training for Sports: Achieving Athletic Excellence*, Plume, 1991.

36 Hadhazy, A 'Think Twice: How the Gut's "Second Brain" Influences Mood and Well-Being,' *Scientific American*, Feb 2010.

37 Liou, A et al. 'Conserved Shifts in the Gut Microbiota Due to Gastric Bypass Reduce Host Weight and Adiposity,' *Science Translational Medicine*, Mar 2013: 5, 178ra41.

38 Schnabel, J 'The Dana Foundation: Does Parkinson's Disease Start Outside the Brain?' Aug 2010: http://www.dana.org/News/Details.aspx?id=43093.

39 Forster, J et al. 'Why Love Has Wings and Sex Has Not: How Reminders of Love and Sex Influence Creative and Analytic Thinking,' *Personality and Social Psychology Bulletin*, 2009: 35 (11), 1479–91; DOI: 10.1177/0146167209342755.

40 Guevara, C 'The Cuban Revolution Today,' *Algiers*, Mar 1965.

Session 01: Problems

1 Calabrese, E et al. 'Hormesis: Its impact on Medicine and health,' *Human & Experimental Toxicology*, 2013: 32.

2 Emmons, R 'Counting Blessings Versus Burdens: An Experimental Investigation of Gratitude and Subjective Well-being in Daily life,' *Journal of Personality and Social Psychology*, Feb 2003: 84 (2), 377–89.

3 Gordon, A et al. 'To have and to Hold: Gratitude Promotes Relationship Maintenance in Intimate Bonds,' *Journal of Personality and Social Psychology*, Aug 2012: 103 (2), 257–74.

4 Seligman, M 'Positive Psychology Progress: Empirical Validation of Interventions,' *American Psychologist*, Jul–Aug 2005: 60(5), 410–21.

5 Emmons, R et al. (eds) *The Psychology of Gratitude*, Oxford University Press, 2004.

6 Algoe, S et al. 'Beyond Reciprocity: Gratitude and Relationships in Everyday Life,' *Psychological Science*, 2008: 17 (4), 319–25.

7 McCullough, M et al. 'Gratitude and Prosocial Behavior: Helping When It Costs You, An Adaptation for Altruism? The Social Causes, Social Effects and Social Evolution,' *Current Directions in Psychological Science*, Aug 2008: 17 (4), 281–5.

8 Subramaniam, K et al. 'A Brain Mechanism for Facilitation of Insight by Positive Affect,' *Journal of Cognitive Neuroscience*, Mar 2009: 21, 415–32.

9 Lau, R and Cheng, S 'Gratitude Lessens Death Anxiety,' *European Journal of Aging*, Apr 2012: 8 (3), 169–75.

10 Lambert, N et al. 'A Boost of Positive Affect: The Perks of Sharing Positive Experiences,' *Journal of Social & Personal Relationship*, Aug 2012.

11 Burg, J and Michalak, J 'The Healthy Quality of Mindful Breathing: Associations With Rumination and Depression,' *Cognitive Therapy and Research*, April 2011: 35 (2), 179–85.

12 Burg, J et al. 'Mindfulness as Self-regulated Attention: Associations with Heart Rate Variability,' *Swiss Journal of Psychology*, Jul 2012: 71 (3), 135–9; DOI: 10.1024/1421-0185/a000080.

13 Michael, W et al. *Exercise for Mood and Anxiety, Proven Strategies for Overcoming Depression and Enhancing Well-Being*, Oxford University Press, 2011.

14 Cohen, S and Walco, G 'Dance/Movement Therapy for Children and Adolescents with Cancer,' *Cancer Practice*, 1999: 7, 34–42.

15 Kushi, L et al. 'Nutrition and Physical Activity Guidelines Advisory Committee. American Cancer Society Guidelines on Nutrition and Physical Activity for Cancer Prevention: Reducing the Risk of Cancer with Healthy Food Choices and Physical Activity,' *CA Cancer Journal for Clinicians*, 2006: 56: 254–81 (Erratum in: *CA Cancer Journal for Clinicians*, 2007: 57, 66).

16 Loewenstein, G 'The Psychology of Curiosity: A Review and Reinterpretation,' *Psychological Bulletin*, 1994: 116 (1), 75–98.

17 Thrash, T et al. 'Mediating Between the Muse and the Masses: Inspiration and the Actualization of Creative Ideas,' *Journal of Personality and Social Psychology*, Mar 2010: 98 (3), 469–87.

18 Batey, M and Furnham, A 'Creativity, Intelligence, and Personality: A Critical Review of the Scattered Literature,' *Genetic Social General Psychology Monographs*, 2006: 132 (4), 355–429.

Session 02: Patterns

1 Castro, J 'Where Does Identity Come From?' *Scientific American*, May 2013.
2 Kahneham, D *Thinking Fast and Slow*, Penguin, 2012.
3 Arzi, A et al. 'Humans Can Learn New Information During Sleep,' *Nature Neuroscience*, Aug 2012: 15, 1460–5.
4 Salimpoor, V. et al. 'Anatomically Distinct Dopamine Release during Anticipation and Experience of Peak Emotion to Music,' *Nature Neuroscience*, 2011: DOI: 10.1038/nn.2726.
5 Di Chiara, G and Imperato, A 'Drugs Abused by Humans Preferentially Increase Synaptic Dopamine Concentrations in the Mesolimbic System of Freely Moving Rats,' *Proceedings of the National Academy of Sciences*, 1988: 85, 5274–8.
6 Mahoney, M and Avener, M 'Psychology of the Elite Athlete: An Exploratory Study,' *Cognitive Therapy and Research*, Jun 1977.
7 Wolford, G et al. 'The Left Hemisphere's Role in Hypothesis Formation,' *Journal of Neuroscience*, March 2000: 20 (6), RC64, 1–4.
8 Feinberg, T *Altered Egos: How the Brain Creates the Self*, Oxford University Press, 2001.
9 Nickerson, R 'Confirmation Bias: A Ubiquitous Phenomenon in Many Guises,' *Review of General Psychology*, 1998: 2 (2), 175–220; key: citeulike: 2634047.
10 For example, see the work of Haidt, J *The Righteous Mind*, Penguin, 2012.
11 For more information, see the work of Kuhn, T *The Structure of Scientific Revolutions*, University of Chicago Press, 1970.
12 Cyrulnik, B 'Ethology and the Biological Correlates of Mood,' Dialogues in Clinical *Neuroscience*, Sep 2005: 7 (3), 217–21.
13 Mahncke, H et al. 'Brain Plasticity and Functional Losses in the Aged: Scientific Bases for a Novel Intervention,' *Progress in Brain Research*, 2006: 157, 81–109.

Session 03: Pain

1 Hazan, C and Shaver, P 'Romantic Love Conceptualized as an Attachment Process,' *Journal of Personality and Social Psychology*, Mar 1987: 52 (3), 511–24.
2 For more on this idea, see the work of Wolinsky, S *The Dark Side of the Inner Child: The Next Step*, Bramble Books, 1993; and *Rescuing the 'Inner Child': Therapy for Adults Sexually Abused as Children*, Souvenir Press, 1994.
3 Daniel, S and Schechter, M 'Forecasting Aggression: Toward a New Interdisciplinary Understanding of What Makes Some Troubled Youth Turn Violent,' *Cerebrum*, Jan–Feb 2011.
4 Oliver, P et al. *Handbook of Personality: Theory and Research*, 3rd edn, Guilford Press, 2001.
5 Vaillant, G *Triumphs of Experience The Men of the Harvard Grant Study*, Belknap Press, 2012.
6 Allen, S and Daly K 'The Effects of Father Involvement: An Updated Research Summary of the Evidence Inventory Centre for Families, Work & Well-Being,' University of Guelph, 2007.
7 Harris, L and Fiske, S 'Social Groups that Elicit Disgust are Differentially Processed in mPFC,' *Social Cognitive and Affective Neuroscience*, Mar 2007: 2, 45–51.
8 Apkarian, A et al. 'Chronic Back Pain is Associated with Decreased Prefrontal and Thalamic Gray Matter Density,' *Journal of Neuroscience*, Nov 2004: 24, 10410–15.
9 Whalley, K 'Childhood Abuse Alters Cortical Fields,' *Nature Reviews Neuroscience*, Jul 2013.
10 Eisenberg, N et al. 'Emotion-related Self-regulation and Its Relation to Children's Maladjustment,' *Annual Review of Clinical Psychology*, April 2010: 6, 495–525; first published online as a 'review' in Advance on Jan 19, 2010; DOI: 10.1146/annurev.clinpsy.121208.131208.

11 Brito, N et al. 'Socioeconomic Status is Associated with Language and Memory Development in the First Two Years,' International Society for Infant Studies, Berlin 2014.

12 McEwen, B. and Morrison, J 'The Brain on Stress: Vulnerability and Plasticity of the Prefrontal Cortex over the Life Course,' Neuron, Jul 2013: 79 (1), 16–29; DOI: 10.1016/j.neuron.2013.06.028.

13 Dias, B and Ressler, K 'Parental Olfactory Experience Influences Behavior and Neural Structure in Subsequent Generations,' Nature Neuroscience, Dec 2013; DOI: 10.1038/nn.3594.

14 Champagne, F and Meaney, M 'Stress During Gestation Alters Postpartum Maternal Care and the Development of the Offspring in a Rodent Model,' Biological Psychiatry, Jun 2006: 59, 1227–35.

15 Mitchell, C et al. 'Social Disadvantage, Genetic Sensitivity, and Children's Telomere Length,' Proceedings National Academy Sciences, Apr 2014.

16 Nili, U. et al. 'Fear Thou Not: Activity of Frontal and Temporal Circuits in Moments of Real-Life Courage,' Neuron, Jun 2010: 66 (6), 949–62; DOI 10.1016/j.neuron.2010.06.009.

17 Diderot, D On Art and Artists: An Anthology of Diderot's Aesthetic Thought, Springer, 2010.

Session 04: Presence

1   Campbell, J The Power of Myth, Bantam Doubleday, 1989.

2   See Iain McGilchrist's The Mastery and His Emissary: The Divided Brain and the Making of the Western World for more on this fascinating topic, Yale University Press, 2nd edn, 2012.

3   Hawkley, L. and Cacioppo, J 'Loneliness Matters: A Theoretical and Empirical Review of Consequences and Mechanism,' Annals of Behavioral Medicine, Oct 2010: 40 (2), 218–27.

4   Holt-Lunstad, J et al. 'Social Relationships and Mortality Risk: A Meta-analytic Review,' PLOS Medicine, Jul 2010: DOI: 10.1371/journal.pmed.1000316.

5   D Umberson and Montez, J K 'Social Relationships and Health: A Flashpoint for Health Policy,' Journal of Health and Social Behavior, 2010: 51 (1), S54–S66 .

6   Libet, B. et al. 'Time of Conscious Intention to Act in Relation to Onset of Cerebral Activity (Readiness-Potential),' Brain, 1983: 106 (3): 623–42; DOI: 10.1093/brain/106.3.623. PMID 6640273.

7   Hussey, A 'If You Can Keep a Cool Head,' Observer Sport Monthly, March 4, 2007.

8   Csikszentmihalyi, M Flow: The Psychology of Optimal Experience, Cambridge University Press, 1988.

9   Chi, R and Snyder, A 'Brain Stimulation Enables the Solution of an Inherently Difficult Problem,' Neuroscience Letters, Mar 2012: 515, 121–4.

10 Newberg A Principles of Neurotheology, Ashgate, 2010.

11 Johnstone, B and Glass, B 'Support for a Neuropsychological model of Spirituality in Persons with Traumatic Brain Injury,' Zygon, Dec 2008: 43 (4), 861–74 (14).

12 Krebs, T and Johansen, P 'Psychedelics and Mental Health: A Population Study,' PLoS ONE, Aug 2013: 8 (8).

13 Duman, R and Aghajanian, G 'Synaptic Dysfunction in Depression: Potential Therapeutic Targets,' Science, Oct 2012; and 'Treatment-Resistant Depression: Glutamate, Stress-Hormones and their Role in the Regeneration of Neurons,' presented at New York Academy of Sciences Mar 2013, are both examples. See MAPS.org for up-to-date research.

14 Alduous Huxley later wrote a book about his experiences of taking the shamanic medicinal plant peyote, titled the Doors of Perception—after a phrase by William Blake in his poem

about the bringing together of opposites, 'The Marriage of Heaven and Hell'—which went on to inspire Jim Morrison and his legendary band, The Doors.

15 Strawson, G et al. *Consciousness and its Place in Nature*, Imprint Academic, 2006.

16 Wilber, K *Quantum Questions: Mystical Writings of the World*, Shambhala Publications, 2001.

17 Henry, R 'The Mental Universe,' *Nature*, Jul 2005: 436, 29.

18 Minkel, J 'Quantum Spookiness Spans the Canary Islands,' *Scientific American*, March 9, 2007.

19 Wei Wu Wei, *Ask the Awakened: The Negative Way*, Non Basic Stock Line: 1st edn, April 2002.

20 Schneider, R et al. 'Stress Reduction in the Secondary Prevention of Cardiovascular Disease: A Randomized Controlled Trial of Transcendental Meditation and Health Education in African Americans,' *Circulation: Cardiovascular Quality and Outcomes*, Nov 2012; DOI: 10.1161/CIRCOUTCOMES.112.967406.

21 Zeidan, F et al. 'Mindfulness Meditation-related Pain Relief: Evidence for Unique Brain Mechanisms in the Regulation of Pain,' *Neuroscience Letters*, Jun 2012: 520 (2), 165–73.

22 Miller, W et al. 'Meditation Increases Compassionate Responses to Suffering,' *Psychological Science*, Aug 2013.

23 Bodhidharma, *The Zen Teachings of Bodhidharma*, Red Pine North Point Press, 1990.

Session 05: Peace

1 Bonta, B 'Cooperation and Competition in Peaceful Societies,' *Psychological Bulletin*, Mar 1997: 121 (2).

2 Feder, A et al. 'Posttraumatic Growth in Former Vietnam Prisoners of War,' *Psychiatry*, Winter 2008: 71 (4), 359–70.

3 Charney, D 'The Psychobiology of Resilience and Vulnerability to Anxiety Disorders: Implications for Prevention and Treatment,' *Dialogues Clinical Neuroscience*, Sep 2003: 5 (3), 207–21.

4 Richardson, G 'The Metatheory of Resilience and Resiliency,' *Journal of Clinical Psychology*, 2002: 58, 307–21.

5 Epes, J *The Sacred Pipe: Black Elk's Account of the Seven Rites of the Oglala Sioux*, University of Oklahoma Press, 1953.

6 Newberg, A *Why God Won't Go Away: Brain Science and the Biology of Belief*, Ballantine Books, 2002.

7 Schiller, D et al. 'Preventing the Return of Fear in Humans Using Reconsolidation Update Mechanisms,' *Nature*, Jan 2010: 463 (7277), 49–53.

8 Barak, S et al. 'Disruption of Alcohol-related Memories by mTORC1 Inhibition Prevents Relapse,' *Nature Neuroscience*, 2013: http://dx.doi.org/10.1038/nn.3439.

9 Armour, J 'Anatomy and Function of the Intrathoracic Neurons Regulating the Mammalian Heart,' in Zucker, I and Gilmore, J eds *Reflex Control of the Circulation*, CRC Press, 1990, 1–37.

10 Fredrickson, B *LOVE 2.0*, Hudson Street Press, 2013.

11 Interview with Nelson Mandela, 'How Nelson Mandela Emerged from Prison a Better Man,' on oprah.com 2000.

12 Nietzsche, F *Ecce Homo: How One Becomes What One Is*, Oxford University Press, 2009.

13 Kierkegaard, S *The Concept of Anxiety*, Princeton University Press, 1981.

Session 06: Purpose

1 Mitchell, M *Complexity: A Guided Tour*, Oxford University Press, 2009.

2 Liu, D et al. 'From Autonomy to Creativity: A Multilevel Investigation of the Mediating Role of Harmonious Passion,' *Journal of Applied Psychology*, Mar 2011: 96 (2), 294–309.

3 Boyle, P et al. 'Effect of Purpose in Life on the Relation Between Alzheimer Disease Pathologic Changes on Cognitive Function in Advanced Age,' *Archives General Psychiatry*, May 2012: 69 (5), 499–505.

4 Fredricksona, B et al. 'A Functional Genomic Perspective on Human Well-being,' *Proceedings of the National Academy of Sciences of the United States of America*, Jul 2013.

5 Moll, J et al. 'Human Fronto-mesolimbic Networks Guide Decisions About Charitable Donation,' *Proceedings of the National Academy of Sciences of the United States of America*, Sep 2006: 103, 15623–28.

6 http://greatergood.berkeley.edu/raising_happiness/post/what_we_get_when_we_give.

7 Spiegel, D et al. 'Effect of Psychosocial Treatment on Survival of Cancer Patients with Metastatic Breast Cancer,' *The Lancet*, Oct 1989: 2, 888–90.

8 Oman, D et al. 'Volunteerism and Mortality among the Community Dwelling Elderly,' *Journal of Health Psychology*, May 1999: 4(3), 301–16.

9 Post, S 'It's Good to Be Good: Science Says It's So,' *Health Progress*, Jul–Aug 2009.

10 Aknin, L. et al. 'Prosocial Spending and Well-being: Cross-cultural Evidence for a Psychological Universal,' *Journal of Personality and Social Psychology*, Apr 2013: 104.

11 Crocker, J et al. 'Interpersonal Goals and Change in Anxiety and Dysphoria: Effects of Compassionate and Self-image Goals,' *Journal of Personality and Social Psychology*, Jun 2010: 98 (6), 1009–24.

12 Rand, D et al. 'Spontaneous Giving and Calculated Greed,' *Nature*, Sep 2012: 489, 427–30 (20).

Session 07: Possibility

1 http://www.writersdigest.com/writing-articles/by-writing-genre/memoir-by-writing-genre/isabel-allende.

2 Liu, S et al. 'Neural Correlates of Lyrical Improvisation: An fMRI Study of Freestyle Rap,' *Scientific Reports*, Nov 2012: 2 (834).

3 Carhart-Harris, R et al. 'Neural Correlates of the Psychedelic State as Determined by fMRI Studies with Psilocybin,' *Proceedings of the National Academy of Sciences USA*, Feb 2012: 109 (6), 2138–43.

4 Jia, L et al. 'Lessons from a Faraway Land: The Effect of Spatial Distance on Creative Cognition,' *Journal of Experimental Social Psychology*, Sep 2009: 45 (5), 1127–31.

5 Beam, E 'Creativity and the default network: Is the Brain at Work while the Mind is Wandering?' *Neurogenesis*, 2012: 2 (1), 11–13.

6 Vessel, E et al. 'Art Reaches Within: Aesthetic Experience, the Self, and the Default Mode Network. Front,' *Neurosci.*, 2013: 7 (258), 1–9; DOI: 10.3389/fnins.2013.00258.

7 Fox, K and Christoff, K 'Metacognitive Facilitation of Spontaneous Thought Processes: When Metacognition Helps the Wandering Mind Find its Way,' in Fleming, S and Frith, C (eds) *The Cognitive Neuroscience of Metacognition*, Springer Publishing, 2014, 293–319.

8 Poincare, H *The Foundations of Science*, Project Gutenberg, 1921.

9 Mitchell, S *The Second Book of the Tao*, Penguin, 2009.

10 Macfarquhar, L 'The Dead are Real,' *New Yorker*, Oct 2012.

11 Turiano, N. et al. 'Openness to Experience and Mortality in Men: Analysis of Trait and Facets,' *Journal of Aging and Health*, Jun 2012: 24 (4), 654–72.

Session 08: Power

1   Roberts, E et al. 'Individual Differences in Expert Motor Coordination Associated with White Matter Microstructure in the Cerebellum,' *Cerebral Cortex*, Oct 2013: 23 (10), 2282–92.

2   Gould, D et al. 'Psychological Foundations of Coaching: Similarities and Differences among Intercollegiate Wrestling Coaches,' *The Sport Psychologist*, Dec 1987: 1 (4), 293–308.

3   Ming, G and Song, H 'Adult Neurogenesis in the Mammalian Brain: Significant Answers and Significant Questions,' *Neuron*, May 2011: 70 (4), 687–702.

4   Barres, R et al. 'Acute Exercise Remodels Promoter Methylation in Human Skeletal Muscle,' *Cell Metabolism*, Mar 2012: 15 (3), 405–11.

5   Ayan, S 'The Will to Win,' *Scientific American*, Apr 2005: 16, 64–9.

6   Driediger, M et al. 'Imagery Used by Injured Athletes: A Qualitative Analysis,' *Journal of Sports Sciences*, Mar 2006.

7   Danner, D et al. 'Positive Emotions in Early Life and Longevity: Findings from the Nun Study,' *Journal of Personality and Social Psychology*, May 2001: 80 (5), 804–13.

8   Gould, E 'Gross C G 'Neurogenesis in Adult Mammals: Some Progress and Problems,' *Neuroscience*, 2002: 22, 619–23.

9   Hans-Georg, W and Moser, K 'Effects of Networking on Career Success: A Longitudinal Study,' *Journal of Applied Psychology*, Jan, 2009: 94 (1), 196–206.

10 Reuf, M 'Strong Ties, Weak Ties and Islands: Structural and Cultural Predictors of Organizational Innovation,' Jun 2002: 11 (3): http://www.cs.princeton.edu/~sjalbert/SOC/Ruef.pdf.

11 King, L et al. 'Resilience/Recovery Factors in Posttraumatic Stress Disorder Among Female and Male Vietnam Veterans,' *Journal of Personality and Social Psychology*, Feb 1998: 74, 420–34.

12 Christakis, N and Fowler, J 'Dynamic Spread of Happiness in a Large Social Network: Longitudinal Analysis over 20 years in the Framingham Heart Study,' *BMJ*, Dec 2008: 337, a2338.

13 Steptoe A et al. 'Social isolation, loneliness, and all-cause mortality in older men and women,' *Proceedings of the Royal Academy of Sciences*, doi/10.1073/pnas.1219686110, 2013.

14 Christakis, N and Fowler, J 'Social Contagion Theory: Examining Dynamic Social Networks and Human Behavior,' *Statistics in Medicine*, Sep 2011: (32), 556–77: 3arXiv: 1109.5235.

15 Honk, J et al. 'New Evidence on Testosterone and Cooperation,' *Nature*, 2012: 485, E4–E5; DOI: 10.1038/nature11136.

16 Coates, J et al. 'From Molecule to Market: Steroid Hormones and Financial Risk-taking.' *Philosophical Transactions Royal Society Biological Sciences*, 2010: 365, 331–43, http://rstb. royalsocietypublishing.org/content/365/1538/331.full.pdf+html.

17 Carney, D et al. 'Power Posing: Brief Nonverbal Displays Cause Changes in Neuroendocrine Levels and Risk Tolerance,' *Psychological Science*, 2010: 21, 1363–8.

18 Storey, A and Walsh, C 'How Fathers Evolve: A Functional Analysis,' in Booth, A, McHale, S and Landale, N. (eds) *Biosocial Foundations of Family to Processes National Symposium on Family Issues*, Springer, 2011, 35–47.

19 Gettler, L et al. 'Does Cosleeping Contribute to Lower Testosterone Levels in Fathers?

Evidence from the Philippines,' *PLoS ONE*, 2012: 7 (9), e41559.

Session 09: Play

1 Bateson, P *Play, Playfulness, Creativity and Innovation*, Cambridge University Press, 2014.
2 Huizinga, J *Homo Ludens*, Routledge, 1980.
3 *The Child-driven Education*, TED Global, 2010 (video).
4 Schiller, J von *Letters upon the Aesthetic Education of Man, Literary and Philosophical Essays*, New York Collier *c.* 1910 (Harvard Classics).
5 Aarnodt, S and Wang, S *Welcome to Your Child's Brain: How the Mind Grows from Conception to College*, Bloomsbury, 2011.
6 Ibid.
7 Snyder, C and Lopez, S Eds *Handbook of Positive Psychology*, Oxford University Press, 2004.
8 Subramaniam, K et al. 'A Brain Mechanism for Facilitation of Insight by Positive Affect,' *Journal of Cognitive Neuroscience*, Mar 2009: 21, 415–32.
9 Loehr, J and Schwartz, T 'The Making of a Corporate Athlete,' *Harvard Business Review*, Jan 2001.
10 Blanchette, D et al. 'Aerobic Exercise and Cognitive Creativity: Immediate and Residual Effects,' *Creativity Research Journal*, 2005: 17 (2&3), 257–64.
11 Clinton, C. *Harriet Tubman: The Road to Freedom*, Little, Brown, 2005.
12 See http://www.wired.com/2012/03/navy-sixth-sense.
13 Preti, A and Miotto, P 'Creativity, Evolution and Mental Illnesses,' *Journal of Memetics–Evolutionary Models of Information Transmission*, Jan 1997.
14 Csikszentmihalyi, M *Creativity: The Psychology of Discovery and Invention*, Harper Perennial, 2013.

Session 10: Proactivity

1 Baumeister, R. et al. 'Some Key Differences Between a Happy Life and a Meaningful Life,' *Journal of Positive Psychology*, Oct 2013: 8 (6), 505–16; DOI: 10.1080/17439760.2013.830764.
2 'State of the American Workplace,' 2013: http://www.gallup.com/strategicconsulting/163007/state-american-workplace.aspx.
3 'Dream Job or Career Nightmare?' OPP, July 2007: www.opp.com/~/media/Files/PDFs/Resources/dream-research.pdf.

Glossary

Assumption: Usually an unconscious belief about how the world works, based on past information as opposed to future possibility.

Attachment: A meaningful bond a person makes to another person, in particular a child to a parent, guardian, or primary caregiver. See the work of John Bowlby and others for more.

Autopoetic: Things that can create themselves without any outside direction or design.

Big U (also **Big Universe**): See **Universe**.

Biodynamic: A holistic approach to creativity and change, which is responsive to the actual lived experience, activity, energy, insight, and intuition of the individual or group, as opposed to having a fixed, predetermined strategy or plan about how things should be that cannot change even when circumstances change.

Body.mind: The highly complex, fully integrated system of mind meshed with body where all human experience occurs.

Break out: The change that occurs when breakthroughs are sustained over a long period of time, becoming embedded in the system and embodied in people.

Breakdown: The experiences of chronic unresolved problems, disempowering stories, self-sabotaging habits, and unhealed pain that make life challenging. Can manifest in spectacular or subtle physical, mental, and/or emotional ways.

Breaking point: The experience of redundant and disempowering patterns that begin to fall apart under pressure due to the internal drive to thrive and/or an inability to fit with the environment. Critical opportunities for transformation. See also **Crisis**.

Breakthrough: A significant creative leap, which positively disrupts the ways things have been and opens up previously unavailable or unseen possibilities that could not have been predicted based on the past. See also **Non-linear**.

Breakthrough Curve: A **biodynamic** process/blueprint/toolkit that enables any problem to be broken through; and transformations sustained over time resulting in a higher degree of fittedness and more thriving. Takes the shape of a J.

Chaos: A state of disorder and unpredictability (in complexity science, chaos appears to be random but has some order due to the end result being sensitive to small changes in the initial conditions, but in a **non-linear** way).

Charge: A felt sensation within that disturbs equanimity, usually pushing us toward or away from something. See also **Instinct** and **Stress response**.

Commitment: A deeply felt sense within that we are totally resolved to make something happen (and we communicate this to ourselves and others).

Conditioned response: Behavioral habits and their associations, usually unconscious, which have been wired deeply into the nervous system having been repeated many times.

Conditioning: The neurobiological process in which behaviors, memories, associations, and states of being are encoded and wired into the nervous system.

Conflicted: A state of inner confusion where two or more conflicting values, habits, emotions, patterns, or stories are held concurrently. The opposite is being in alignment or having **congruence**.

Congruence: A state of inner alignment where our emotions, beliefs, and behaviors all agree, are authentic, and are in harmony.

The Connector: The primary force within every human being that ensures we can connect with others, break through challenges, heal suffering, and thrive.

Consolidation: The neurobiological process in which memories are wired into the nervous system for long-term use.

Creative spirit: A facet of the human experience of the **universe**, available to everyone when switched on, which unleashes creativity, imagination, and possibilities.

Crisis: The turning point in every problem when we decide whether to engage with it, own it, and so transform it; or attempt to ignore it, react to it, or repress it. See also **Breaking point**.

Darkside: Repressed and hidden patterns and pain that we do not always perceive to be part of us (and often project onto others). Contains latent potential, talent, and energy that can be unleashed through breakthrough (when we own it). See also **Personality traits**.

Devotion: Dedicating our ideas and actions to the **universe** and so avoiding being attached.

Disempowering: A story, belief, habit, or emotion that limits growth, expansion, freedom, creativity, joy; and encourages stress, self-sabotage, limitation, anxiety, cynicism, and despair.

Duality: The belief or perception that we are separate from the universe and each other, and/or that the mind and body are separate. See also **Body.mind**, **Non-duality**, and **Universe**.

Edge of chaos: The realm of maximum creativity (and confusion) at the junction between order and disorder where most complex living systems exist.

Embody (also **embodied**): To bring a transformative idea or insight into the body.mind so as to live it in each moment without the need for intentional effort. When this has been achieved, a **breakthrough** has been internalized and the system rewired.

Empowering: A story, belief, habit, or emotion that encourages growth, expansion, freedom, creativity, and joy.

Enlightenment: The realization of our true nature as one interconnected, intrinsic part of a single **universe**. Characterized by an experience of love, truth, and/or creativity. See also **Joystruck**, **Oneness**, and **Universe**.

Equanimity: Remaining calm, curious, and open-minded, avoiding the need to judge or react to a situation.

Escape fantasies: The belief that withdrawing from or completely leaving a situation (person, job, or place) will provide us with the happiness we desire.

Essence: The unlimited potential we are all born with, which is revealed when we released limiting beliefs, personality, and habits. See also **Great We**.

Field of Possibility: The space into which we live, containing all the possibilities available. It is determined by the choices we make and expands as we expand.

Fittedness: A state of being in which we act, think, and feel in an appropriate way within our environment.

Flow.state: A state of heightened awareness, focus, and brilliance, which occurs when we are fully engrossed in a challenging activity in which we also have some mastery. Often causes a sense of time, space, and self to disappear. See also **Enlightenment**.

Frame: The perspective we have on a situation or event; the world-view through which we interpret things.

Front: The collection of defensive behaviors we use to protect us in daily life that have become solidified into our public personality See also **Patterns**, **Personality trait**, and **Story**.

Great We: An idea of who we are that is driven by a sense of **reconnection** to everybody and everything in the **universe**. The alternative is **Tiny Me**. See also **Essence**.

HANDS: A symbol of our behaviors, actions, and physical experiences. How we experience and express our creativity/reaction. Part of the trinity of **HANDS**, **HEAD**, and **HEART** at the core of our humanity. See also **HEAD** and **HEART**.

HEAD: A symbol of our thoughts, stories, and beliefs. How we experience and express our truth/assumptions. Part of the trinity of **HANDS**, **HEAD**, and **HEART** at the core of our humanity. See also **HANDS** and **HEART**.

Healed HEART: See **Wholehearted**.

HEART: A symbol of feelings and emotions. How we experience and express our love/pain. Part of the trinity of **HANDS**, **HEAD**, and **HEART** at the core of our humanity. See also **HANDS** and **HEAD**.

Inner work: Focused attention on inquiring into our experience, healing pain, transforming patterns, and breaking through. See **Inquiry**.

Inquiry: The intention to learn about some part of ourselves or our world through discovery so that we maintain growth and stay fitted to our environment. See also **Fittedness**.

Insight: A new way of seeing the world, which opens up possibilities that were unavailable before due to our previous **assumptions**. Usually based on what the future might hold as opposed to what occurred in the past.

Instinct: Knowledge from within that helps us and others *survive*. See also the **Protector** and **Survival Trip**.

Integrity: Ensuring all our interactions and relationships with ourselves and others are coming from love, truth, and creativity.

Intuition: Knowledge from within that helps us and others *thrive*. See also the **Connector** and **Thrive Drive**.

ISness: The reality of what is happening in any moment that cannot be changed.

Joystruck: A facet of the human experience of the **universe**, available to everyone when switched on, that is accompanied by feelings of bliss, joy, and happiness. Often felt physically as an intense rush of energy.

Lack: A deep feeling within that something important is missing for our safety, wellbeing, and happiness.

Linear: Change that occurs along a sequential, predictable, straight line.

Metabolize: Occurs when we own a problem by taking it inside and turning it into something of value, learning, and growth.

Mindful: Approaching things with as much inner calm, curiosity, and openness in the moment as possible, without fears, assumptions, and worries. See also **Wholehearted**.

Neural signature: The traces of neuronal activity that characterize a specific response or **pattern**.

Noble lies: Beliefs and assumptions we hold that protect us from fear, confusion, and difficulty.

Non-duality: The belief or perception that everything is connected and everyone is part of one thing we call the **universe** or oneness. See also **Oneness**, **Unity** and **Universe**.

Non-linear: Change that occurs in ways that are neither predictable nor straightforward. See also **Breakthrough** and **Linear**.

Oneness: The unified whole of existence where there is no division or duality. See also **Non-duality** and **Universe**.

Order: A consistent and structured state of being.

Own (also **ownership**): The act of fully embracing our problems, patterns, and pain (as well as our purpose, possibility, and power), as opposed to blaming others or attributing them to someone else.

Pain memories: An intense memory associated with a painful or threatening experience that still has an impact on our wellbeing.

Pain.pattern crystal: A metaphor for the entangled fear memories, neural signatures, conditioned responses, and disempowering stories that enmesh together in the body.mind when a human being experiences something threatening, upsetting, or disappointing and it is stored within.

Paranoia: Seeing problems and challenges as evidence that there is something wrong with us, others, or the world; and that something is out to get us.

Patterns: Habits, stories, and ways of being in the world, copied or invented during childhood, designed to protect us from experiencing pain but now tending to limit us. The Sufis call them *nafs*; the Buddhists *skandhas*.

Personality trait: A combination of protective patterns that form a distinctive type of personality. See also **Front**.

Presence: Experiencing the universe as within and around us. Triggers feelings of support, connection, and unity.

Process (also **processing**): Intentionally working through intense or unusual events and experiences, so we can make sense of them, find meaning in them, and learn from them.

Projection: Unconsciously putting our ideas and issues onto other people. See also **Darkside**.

Pronoia: Seeing problems and challenges as an opportunity to realize more of our potential and evidence that the universe is attempting to help us learn, grow, and thrive.

The Protector: The primary force within every human being, which ensures we can defend ourselves, deal with threats, and survive.

Reconnection: Consciously remembering and reigniting our inherent connection to the **universe**.

Reconnection practice: Any practice (e.g. meditation, ecstatic dance, chi gong, mindfulness) that enables us to reconnect to the universe and feel **Presence**. See also **Universe**.

Reconnection response: A conscious response to stress that is characterized by activation of the parasympathetic nervous system, driving stillness, curiosity, and openness.

Reframe: Consciously choosing a different belief or story with which to interpret the world. See also **Frame**.

Resistance: A typically unconscious refusal to own problems, avoid inner work, and minimize breakthrough. Driven by the **Tiny Me**'s fear of change, transformation, and possibility.

Response-able (also **response-ability**): The state of empowerment felt when we fully own problems, patterns, and pain, and so have the potential to create solutions.

Self-sabotage: The tendency for unconscious patterns to undermine our potential to love, create, think clearly, be committed, be **response-able**, have integrity, and generally fulfill our potential.

Self-talk: The words, ideas, beliefs, and **stories** we tell ourselves about who we are, which shape what we believe and what we can or cannot do in each moment.

Sense: To use all our faculties to discern what is seeking to emerge from us, and the world, in any given moment, free from prejudice, assumptions, and desires.

Separation anxiety: A fear that occurs in normal childhood development that arises when we realize we are individuals, separate from our parents, carers, and the universe in which we exist.

Sh!t: A problem or issue (either in the world or within us, or a combination of the two), which is full of potential for personal growth and/or social change.

Still-point: A place within where we feel reconnected, calm, tranquil, in neutral.

Story: The narrative we tell ourselves that attempts to make sense of who we are, what is happening, and what we are doing about it. We enact stories in every moment of life. They **empower** or **disempower** us. See also **Self-talk** and **Vision**.

Stress response: An unconscious reaction to actual or perceived danger, fear, and trauma. It is characterized by activation of the sympathetic nervous system driving the urge to fight, flee or freeze. Also known as the flight-or-fight response. See also **Survival Trip**.

Surface: To bring to light unconscious ideas, feelings, and assumptions.

Surrender: The conscious choice to let go of any resistance to what is happening right now, the ISness.

Survival Trip: Living in a constant state of low-grade, chronic stress—reacting with patterns to life—even when there are no physical threats to our existence.

Switch Statement: A sentence, or series of sentences, consciously designed to empower us. Similar to an affirmation or mantra but crafted to harness our neurobiology.

Switched off: A state of being in the world characterized by inflexibility, righteousness, predictability, resentfulness, control, anxiety, and lack of responsibility. Driven by a sense of disconnection from the universe and the fear, alienation, and stress this brings. This state is usually the unconscious default setting.

Switched on: A state of being in the world characterized by creativity, openness, awareness, **insight**, inspiration, imagination, gratitude, compassion, generosity, spontaneity, responsibility, commitment, **wholeheartedness**, and **mindfulness**. Driven by a sense of connection to the **universe** and the love, truth, and creativity this brings.

Thrivadelic: The capacity to grow vigorously by accelerating contribution, creativity, and connectedness, and so increasing the likelihood of a thriving present and future.

Thrive Drive: Living in a constant state of thriving, feeling connected to ourselves and others, contributing and creating as we take on problems and break through them.

Thriving: The growth, learning, and vitality, and opportunities to contribute, create, and connect—available in every situation, whether challenging or not. Coping with adversity because we can find some meaning within it and some way it can help us be more creative, free, and loving.

Tiny Me: An idea of who we are driven by a sense of disconnection to everybody and everything else in the **universe**. A stable yet limited sense of 'I,' often called the ego, which usually feels small, powerless, and needy in the face of life's challenges.

Trigger: An act or experience that prompts us to react or respond in a specific way. When we are triggered, we play out patterns without awareness having been unconsciously reminded of a past upset, threat, or fear. We react in a pre-determined, uncreative way. It is an influence but not a cause. See also **Own**.

Tune up: To optimize emotions, thoughts, and behaviors so that they fit with our intentions and environment. See also **Conflicted** and **Congruent**.

Universe (also **Big U**): The totality of everything that exists, could exist, and will exist—every particle and source of energy. Both nothing (the void, emptiness) and everything (matter, form). See also **Great We** and **Oneness**.

Wei wu wei: A seemingly paradoxical concept of actionless action, doing but not doing. It arises when we co-create with the universe without getting in the way of it or ourselves. See also **Flow.state**.

Win–win–win: An idea, project, or outcome that has a clear benefit for oneself, others, and the community/world/planet.

Wisdom tradition: A path or philosophy that provides us with wisdom, ideas, insights, experiences, and tools that empower, liberate, and inspire love, compassion, truth, integrity, healing, etc. Usually hundreds, if not thousands, of years old. Not to be confused with a 'religion', which is dogmatic or ideological in nature.

Wholehearted: Approaching things with as much inner peace, love, connection, and abundance as possible, without fears, assumptions, and cravings. See also **Mindful**.